Reading Mistress Elizabeth Bourne

The documents contained in *Reading Mistress Elizabeth Bourne: Marriage, Separation, and Legal Controversies* tell a story of Mistress Bourne's petition for divorce, its resolution, and the ongoing dispute between Mistress Bourne and her husband about their marriage and separation, and subsequently between Mistress Bourne and Sir John Conway both for custody of her daughters and her financial security. The letters capture the contradiction between married women's official legal limitations and the often messy and complicated avenues of redress available to them. Elizabeth's narratives and desire for divorce challenge literary representations of patient endurance where appropriate feminine behavior restores a husband's devotion. The Bourne case offers a unique set of documents heretofore unavailable except through the British Library, National Archives' State Papers, and Hatfield House. *Reading Mistress Elizabeth Bourne* is tremendously important to early modern scholars and our knowledge about and view of women's negotiations for legal autonomy in the sixteenth century.

Cristina León Alfar is Professor of Shakespeare, Early Modern English drama, and Women's and Gender Studies at Hunter College, CUNY. Her first book, *Fantasies of Female Evil: The Dynamics of Gender and Power in Shakespearean Tragedy*, was published in 2003. Her second book, *Women and Shakespeare's Cuckoldry Plays: Shifting Narratives of Marital Betrayal* (Routledge 2017) examines a structure of accusation and defense that unravels the authority of husbands to make and unmake wives. She is co-editor, with Helen Ostovich, of the series "Late Tudor and Stuart Drama: Gender, Performance, and Material Culture." Currently, her research focus is on women parrhesiasts in early modern English drama.

Emily G. Sherwood, Ph.D., is Director of Digital Scholarship at University of Rochester's River Campus Libraries where she helps faculty and students incorporate digital tools and methods in their research and teaching. She is an alum of both the Council on Libraries and Information Resources (CLIR) Postdoctoral Fellowship Program and the EDUCAUSE/CLIR Leading Change Institute. Her research interests include digital pedagogy and scholarship, extended reality, and medieval and early modern marriage law.

The Early Modern Englishwoman, 1500–1750:
Contemporary Editions
Series Editors: Betty S. Travitsky and Anne Lake Prescott

Designed to complement The Early Modern Englishwoman: A Facsimile Library of Essential Works, Contemporary Editions presents both modernized and old-spelling editions of texts not only by women but also for and about women. Contents of a volume can range from a single text to an anthology depending on the subject and the audience. Introductions to the editions are written with the general reader as well as the specialist in mind. They are designed to provide an introduction not only to the edited text itself but also to the larger historical discourses expressed through the text.

Two Early Modern Marriage Sermons
Henry Smith's *A Preparative to Marriage* (1591) and William Whately's *A Bride-Bush* (1623)
Edited by Robert Matz

The Experience of Domestic Service for Women in Early Modern London
Edited by Paula Humfrey

The Correspondence (c. 1626–1659) of Dorothy Percy Sidney, Countess of Leicester
Edited by Michael G. Brennan, Noel J. Kinnamon and Margaret P. Hannay

***Eugenia and Adelaide*, A Novel: Frances Sheridan**
Anna M. Fitzer

Reading Mistress Elizabeth Bourne
Marriage, Separation, and Legal Controversies
Edited by Cristina León Alfar and Emily G. Sherwood

https://www.routledge.com/The-Early-Modern-Englishwoman-1500-1750-Contemporary-Editions/book-series/ASHSER2055

Reading Mistress Elizabeth Bourne
Marriage, Separation, and Legal Controversies

Edited by Cristina León Alfar and
Emily G. Sherwood

NEW YORK AND LONDON

First published 2021
by Routledge
605 Third Avenue, New York, NY 10158

and by Routledge
2 Park Square, Milton Park, Abingdon, Oxon, OX14 4RN

Routledge is an imprint of the Taylor & Francis Group, an informa business

© 2021 Taylor & Francis

The right of Cristina León Alfar and Emily G. Sherwood to be identified as the authors of the editorial material, and of the authors for their individual chapters, has been asserted in accordance with sections 77 and 78 of the Copyright, Designs and Patents Act 1988.

All rights reserved. No part of this book may be reprinted or reproduced or utilised in any form or by any electronic, mechanical, or other means, now known or hereafter invented, including photocopying and recording, or in any information storage or retrieval system, without permission in writing from the publishers.

Trademark notice: Product or corporate names may be trademarks or registered trademarks, and are used only for identification and explanation without intent to infringe.

Library of Congress Cataloging-in-Publication Data
A catalog record for this title has been requested

ISBN: 978-0-367-70036-2 (hbk)
ISBN: 978-0-367-70037-9 (pbk)
ISBN: 978-1-003-14431-1 (ebk)

Typeset in Sabon
by Deanta Global Publishing Services, Chennai, India

To the women in our lives who have provided community, comfort, encouragement, and love.

Contents

Acknowledgments xii
Abbreviations xiv
Editorial Principles and Notes on the Text xv

Introduction: The Marital Dispute of Elizabeth and
Anthony Bourne: *Femme Sole* Status and Its Discontents 1

Letters and Documents 27

1 13 February [1576/7], Master Anthony Bourne to
Mistress Elizabeth Bourne (© British Library Board, BL,
Add. MS 23212, fols. 5–6) 29

2 2 March 1576/7, [Indenture for the Marriage of Amy
Bourne and Edward Conway] (© British Library Board,
BL, Add. MS 23212, fols. 71–72) 31

3 [Undated], Sir John Conway to Master Anthony Bourne
(© British Library Board, BL, Add. MS 23212, fol. 83) 33

4 14 May 1577, Master Anthony Bourne to Master
Thomas Bromley (© British Library Board, BL, Add. MS
23212, fols. 32–33) 35

5 28 January 1577/8, Master Anthony Bourne to William
Cecil, Lord Burghley (HH, CP 160/117, fol. 186) 37

6 6 February [1577/8], Master Anthony Bourne to Sir
John Conway (NA, SP 12/198, fols. 36–37) 42

viii   *Contents*

7   15 January 1579, [Master Anthony Bourne to unknown Lord] (© British Library Board, BL, Add. MS 23212, fols. 28–29)   44

8   18 February 1579, Master Anthony Bourne to Sir John Conway (© British Library Board, BL, Add. MS 23212, fol. 51)   47

9   [Undated], Mistress Elizabeth Bourne to Mistress Morgan (© British Library Board, BL, Add. MS 23212, fol. 187)   48

10 25 June 1580, Master Anthony Bourne to Sir Thomas Bromley (© British Library Board, BL, Add. MS 23212, fol. 66)   50

11 21 July 1580, Sir John Conway to Mistress Elizabeth Bourne (© British Library Board, BL, Add. MS 23212, fols. 125–126)   52

12 [Undated], Mistress Elizabeth Bourne to Sir John Conway (© British Library Board, BL, Add. MS 23212, fol. 127)   54

13 [Undated], Amy, Lady Mervyn to Mistress Elizabeth Bourne (© British Library Board, BL, Add. MS 23212, fol. 195)   55

14 8 December [No Year], Mistress Elizabeth Bourne to Amy, Lady Mervyn (© British Library Board, BL, Add. MS 23212, fol. 180)   56

15 3 July 1582, Amy, Lady Mervyn to Sir Francis Walsingham (NA, SP 12/154, fol. 85)   58

16 [Undated], Mistress Elizabeth Bourne to Sir John Conway (© British Library Board, BL, Add. MS 23212, fols. 86–87)   60

17 1 February [No Year], Mistress Elizabeth Bourne to Sir John Conway (© British Library Board, BL, Add. MS 23212, fols. 106–107)   62

Contents   ix

18 [Undated], Mistress Elizabeth Bourne to Sir John
    Conway (© British Library Board, BL, Add. MS 23212,
    fol. 118)   64

19 [Undated], Mistress Elizabeth Bourne to Sir John
    Conway (© British Library Board, BL, Add. MS 23212,
    fol. 123)   65

20 18 August 1582, Elizabeth Bourne to Master Julius
    Caesar (© British Library Board, BL, Add. MS 12507,
    fols. 204–205)   67

21 [Undated], Wrongs Committed by Anthony Bourne
    (© British Library Board, BL, Add. MS 23212, fols. 7–8)   70

22 6 December 1582, [Mistress Bourne's Petition to the
    Privy Council] (© British Library Board, BL, Add. MS
    38170, fols. 151–158)   73

23 [Undated], Master Julius Caesar's Response to Mistress
    Elizabeth Bourne's Petition (© British Library Board,
    BL, Add. MS 38170, fols. 176–178)   92

24 27 January [No Year], Master Anthony Bourne to
    Mistress Elizabeth Bourne (© British Library Board, BL,
    Add. MS 23212, fols. 9–10)   97

25 20 February [1582/3], Mistress Elizabeth Bourne to
    Master Anthony Bourne (© British Library Board, BL,
    Add. MS 23212, fols. 11–16)   98

26 [Undated], [A written opinion by one Daffarne finding
    that Master Anthony Bourne has no right to "demand
    or make title unto any the manors, lands, hereditary
    goods, or chattels conveyed to the said Sir John
    Conway"] (© British Library Board, BL, Add. MS
    23212, fols. 26–27)   106

27 January [1583/4], [Report of Arbitrators Appointed by
    the Privy Council] (NA, SP 12/158, fols. 140–146)   108

x   Contents

28 18 January 1583[/4], [Arbitrators' Report, Indenture of Award] (NA, SP 13/c, fol. 28) 121

29 28 August 1584, Lucia, Lady Audley to Mistress Elizabeth Bourne (NA, SP 12/172, fol. 174) 128

30 November 1584, Mistress Elizabeth Bourne to Lucia, Lady Audley (NA, SP 12/175, fol. 24) 129

31 1 June [No Year], Mistress Elizabeth Bourne to Eleanor, Lady Conway (© British Library Board, BL, Add. MS 23212, fols. 178–179) 131

32 [1585], Eleanor, Lady Conway to Robert Dudley, Earl of Leicester (NA, SP 46/17, fol. 239) 132

33 [Undated], [Mistress Elizabeth Bourne's Demands of Sir John Conway] (© British Library Board, BL, Add. MS 23212, fol. 68) 134

34 3 February [1586/7], Mistress Elizabeth Bourne to Sir John Conway (© British Library Board, BL, Add. MS 23212, fols. 129–130) 135

35 5 October 1587, Sir John Conway to Mistress Elizabeth Bourne (© British Library Board, BL, Add. MS 23212, fols. 81–82) 138

36 November 1587, Eleanor, Lady Conway to the Lords of her Majesty's Privy Council (NA, SP 12/205, fol. 124) 141

37 27 February [No Year], Mistress Elizabeth Bourne to Sir John Conway (© British Library Board, BL, Add. MS 23212, fols. 133–134) 143

38 7 March [No Year], Mistress Elizabeth Bourne to Sir John Conway (© British Library Board, BL, Add. MS 23212, fols. 131–132) 146

39 [Undated], [Sir John Conway to Mistress Elizabeth Bourne] (© British Library Board, BL, Add. MS 23212, fol. 135) 148

40	[Undated], Mistress Elizabeth Bourne to [Sir John Conway] (© British Library Board, BL, Add. MS 23212, fol. 136)	150
41	[Undated], Mistress Elizabeth Bourne to [Sir John Conway] (© British Library Board, BL, Add. MS 23212, fols. 143–144)	152
42	[Undated], [Sir John Conway to Mistress Elizabeth Bourne] (© British Library Board, BL, Add. MS 23212, fol. 149)	155
43	[Undated], Sir John Conway to the Lords of the Privy Council (© British Library Board, BL, Add. MS 23212, fol. 183)	157
44	[Undated], Mistress Elizabeth Bourne to [Sir John Conway] (© British Library Board, BL, Add. MS 23212, fol. 157)	160
45	[Undated], Mistress Elizabeth Bourne to [Sir John Conway] (© British Library Board, BL, Add. MS 23212, fols. 165–166)	162
46	[Undated], Mistress Elizabeth Bourne to Sir John Conway (© British Library Board, BL, Add. MS 23212, fol. 169)	164
47	[Undated], Mistress Elizabeth Bourne to [Sir John Conway] (© British Library Board, BL, Add. MS 23212, fols. 153–154)	166
48	15 March 1589, At Greenwich, [Acts of the Privy Council] (NA, PC 2/16, fol. 553)	168

Places 169
People 174
Index 186

Acknowledgments

The editors would like to thank a wide community of scholars, including some on Twitter, who have answered our calls for assistance. These include Susan Amussen, Tamara Atkin, Sarah Birt, Matthew Harrison, Tracey Hill, Miriam Jacobson, Hester Lees-Jeffries, Anna McKenzie, Michael W. Pearce, Will Rossiter, and Martine van Elke. A huge debt of gratitude goes to Manya Gaver who wrote Cristina from London to ask if there was anything she needed at the British Library. Over 200 images later, we had much better copies of the Conway Papers than we had in Xerox copy. This project would not have been possible without the archivists and librarians at the British Library, the National Archives, The Folger Shakespeare Library, and Hatfield House who sent us electronic images of the documents we needed. They were extremely helpful and ready to answer our questions. We are also grateful for the time and community of the Churchill and Sarsden Heritage Center. Their work to make public the history of their area helped us identify some key dates and people related to the Bournes. And the same is true of our institutional librarians, especially the Interlibrary Loan and Acquisitions staff at Hunter College, Bucknell University, and University of Rochester, River Campus Libraries. All of these institutions provided critical access to their physical and digital collections and databases that made this work possible. Finally, profound thanks to Sara McDougall who provided Latin translation and a summary of Sir Julius Caesar's comments on Elizabeth Bourne's petition for divorce.

Cristina would like to thank friends and colleagues who have—as they always have—supported and encouraged her work on the manuscripts. Chief among these are Barbara Webb, Trudy Smoke, Helen Ostovich, Annette Kym, Elke Nikolai, Mitch Chan, Angela Reyes, Paul McPherron, Mark Bobrow, and Isabelle Duvernois. Family have put up with a lot, or, more accurately not nearly enough. Love and promises of a different kind of life to Emad Alfar, Celia and Paolo (who kept her company every day of the project), Judy Rose, and Alejandra León. Most especially, thanks go to Emily for taking on partnership in a project she really did not have time for. Having brought Emily on board so early in the project—as early as 2005—it would have felt wrong to complete it without her.

Emily would like to thank family, friends, and colleagues who have provided care, encouragement, and feedback at various stages in this project over many years and iterations. Thanks, in particular, to Anna Siebach Larsen, Maggie Dull, Autumn Haag, Kathryn Phillips, Lindsay Cronk, Lydia Auteritano, Mario DiGangi, Glenn Burger, Richard McCoy, Jeffrey Masten, Gordon McMullan, and Alan Stewart. Ron Sherwood, as always, was there for every moment; his support is unparalleled. Lynn Sherwood would have loved to have seen the completion of this project; it is from her that Emily learned a love libraries and research. Finally, much gratitude and thanks goes to Cristina. This manuscript would not exist without her. She brought Elizabeth Bourne into our lives and carried this project with curiosity, intelligence, resolve, patience, kindness, and humor.

This work has been generously supported by Hunter College through The George N. Shuster Faculty Fellowship, The Graduate Center, CUNY through a Presidential Research Grant, and the Folger Shakespeare Library through Grant-in-Aid for Emily to participate in Jeffrey Masten's course on *Editing and Its Futures*.

All documents from the British Library appear by permission, © British Library Board; National Archives documents are held under a Crown copyright and are Open Government License. The letter from Anthony to William Cecil, Lord Burghley is reproduced with permission of the Marquess of Salisbury, Hatfield House.

Abbreviations

Add.	Additional Manuscripts
BL	British Library
CP	Cecil Papers
HH	Hatfield House
NA	National Archives
SP	State Papers

Editorial Principles and Notes on the Text

General Description of the Letters

BL, Add. MS 23212 is currently listed as "MISCELLANEOUS letters and papers relating principally to disputes between Anthony Bourne [son of Sir John Bourne, Knt.] and his wife, Elizabeth [daughter of Sir John Conway, Knt.].[1] Among them are original letters from: 1. Anthony Bourne to his wife." The correspondence does not follow any particular logical order. They are not bound by date. Many of them have been damaged with tears and smudges. On each letter, there is a stamp, "Conway Papers." The original "Conway Papers" was separated into three parts, the first two pertaining to Edward Conway, his extended family, and other prominent people of the time. These were originally housed in the National Archives and that is where we accessed those cited here. The third part is BL, Add. MS 23212, which was originally sent to the British Museum. Fol. 2 contains the following inscription in a modern hand, "Letters & Papers concerning the Disputes between Anthony Bourne and his wife. Of no importance." BL, Add. MS 12507, which contains Mistress Bourne's letter to Sir Julius Caesar houses, as described in the manuscripts catalogue, "ORIGINAL AUTOGRAPH LETTERS, chiefly of the Nobility, addressed (with few exceptions) to Sir Julius Caesar, between the years 1579 and 1619. Vol. II. Edward Cecil, Viscount Wimbledon: Letter to Sir J. Caesar: 1611.Sir Julius Caesar, judge: Original Lett." This letter, which we have as a digital image, is well preserved. Mistress Bourne's petition to the Privy Council, read and commented on by Sir Julius Caesar, is contained in BL, Add. MS 38170, a "COLLECTION of original papers and letters of Sir Julius Caesar, Master of the Rolls, relating chiefly to Chancery cases submitted to him for his opinion or adjudication; 1582–1619." This document is also well preserved.

---

[1] In fact, Elizabeth is the daughter of Edmund Horne and the stepdaughter of James Mervyn.

Principles of Modernization

In our process of preparing the selected correspondence found in this volume, we have modernized the originals while also retaining original language and styles, word choice, and structure. We removed line and folio breaks and silently expanded contractions. We have retained word forms such as "quoth" rather than "said," "liveth" rather than "lives," and "hath" rather than "has." Other phrases or structures of speech and obsolete word forms have also been retained, such as "repaired from my house" rather than "left my house," "fact" rather than "deed," and "affy" rather than "rely on." All definitions of archaic or obsolete words, legal terms, and concepts are from the *Oxford English Dictionary Online*. We have otherwise regularized spelling and punctuation.

Roman numerals have been replaced with Arabic numerals. In regard to money, because authors inconsistently use "li" and "pounds" (written out) we have followed their inconsistency, retaining "pounds" when it is used and "£" for "li."

Crossed-out text has been silently omitted unless sections include very legible and particularly compelling bits of context or word choice.

Occasionally we bracketed an interpolation when we are reasonably confident of a word. In other cases, we have bracketed either [indecipherable] or {...} as needed, with notes in letters indicating where tears are located.

The format of each letter is standardized with date, the name of writer and addressee, and shelf number. In some cases, no dates or addresses were provided. Sir John Conway's habit of noting writer, receiver, and summary information has been retained, though we note that his handwriting is particularly challenging (something he admits himself). These notes are often how we know who the recipient is. His summation of a letter provides insight into his perspective. His notes are usually on the same side of a folio as the address, and in our collection they appear at the ends of each letter.

We have presented the letters according to date to the best of our knowledge. Because many letters, especially those written by Elizabeth Bourne, are not dated, we have bracketed the date and noted our rational for it. According to the records in the Acts of the Privy Council, letters in the dispute between Lady Conway and Elizabeth, for example, started as early as 1579 and continued through 1587/8. We have placed them in the latter end of this decade. Thus, while the records are extremely useful, we have had to make certain decisions based on the content of letters.

Introduction: The Marital Dispute of Elizabeth and Anthony Bourne
Femme Sole Status and Its Discontents

In 2003 Cristina Alfar visited the British Library in search of men's stories of marital betrayal for work she was doing on a book. What she found was Mistress Elizabeth Bourne who not only accused her husband, Anthony, of adultery, but of economic distress, a wish to infect her with syphilis, and plans to murder her. Many of her letters and her petition to the Privy Council raise the existence of the "bastards" he fathered with Mistress Pagnam, the often-named "other woman." Her repetition of "bastards" is loaded, not only as a particular kind of accusation, but as a personal afront to herself and to her own two legitimate children, Amy and Mary. Her voice, its many moods from loneliness and despair to rage and accusation, is striking. She is rhetorically skilled—as James Daybell has argued about her and other female letter writers of the period. But along with utilizing appropriate and familiar forms of rhetoric a woman might deploy, her emotion and sense of wrong, the sense that choices are too limited for her (and other women of the time), must arrest readers and force them into reckoning with a person.[1] If we were taught that "women were chaste, silent, and obedient," Mistress Bourne was none of those things. In a time when virtually no one could get a divorce, she demanded one of Queen Elizabeth's Privy Council. Alfar's project, designed initially around male bonds and accusations of cuckoldry, shifted over the years to a book on female bonds and counter narratives of marital betrayal. This was in no small part due to Elizabeth Bourne and the other women of the Tudor and early Stuart periods who spoke out about the wrongs done them by authoritarian and brazen husbands.

Elizabeth and Anthony Bourne were both children of court officials under King Henry VIII, King Edward VI, and Queens Mary and Elizabeth. Anthony Bourne's father, Sir John Bourne, was Queen Mary's Secretary of State.[2] Loyal Catholics, Sir John and his son were known for harassing Protestants, with words and swords, and were jailed as a result.[3] At the

---

1 See Daybell, "Elizabeth Bourne," 178. For work on the kinds of rhetorical strategies women employed, especially in modes of supplication and complaint, see Jennifer Richards and Alison Thorne, "Introduction," 14–16.
2 Much of what we know about the Bournes comes from Charles Angell Bradford's analysis of "The Conway Papers."
3 In 1563, the Bishop of Worcester offered a detailed account of Anthony Bourne's violence against a group of Protestants: "Sir John Bourne's eldest Son blaspheming and swearing,

coronation of Elizabeth I, Bourne left London for his estate at Battenhall, in Worcester. Anthony's connections at court were mostly, then, in the past. The Mervyn family (after his marriage to Elizabeth) and Sir James Crofte, who was Queen Elizabeth's Controller of the Royal Household and guardian of his sisters, were all he could claim to nobility. He never inherited a title. Though he was admitted to the Inner Temple in 1560, there is no evidence that he took the bar.[4] Anthony never distinguished himself for anything other than fighting, leaving the country without a warrant, adultery, the fathering of bastards, and debt. Elizabeth's father, Edmund Horne, died in 1553 having served under Henry VIII as a "Gentleman Pensioner and in 1537–8, he, as 'Esquire for the Body,' received the office of Steward of the Lordships of Hook Norton, Kelyngton, Throppe and Carsington in the County of Oxford." He accompanied officials to Flanders and Boulogne, and to "France with the king's majesty in his Grace's Battle, accompanied by six archers on foot and five horsemen. For these services he receive[d] royal grants of land besides the office Steward of Fairford in Gloucestershire."[5] Amy Clarke, Elizabeth's mother, married James Mervyn after Edmund Horne's death. Mervyn was knighted by Queen Elizabeth, "who visited him and his wife at Fonthill in 1574." Under Queen Elizabeth, Amy Mervyn became a "Gentlewoman Extraordinary of the Privy Chamber" in 1559. Queen Elizabeth stood Godmother to Elizabeth's half-sister, Lucia Mervyn.[6] Elizabeth was a ward of Henry Jerningham, Master of the Horse and a member of Queen Mary's Privy Council.

"I may live in quiet and be free from his violence."[7]

There were two types of legal pronouncements regarding marital separation in early modern England: divorce *a vinculo matrimonii*, a release from the bond of marriage where the marriage is declared invalid and annulled; and divorce *a mensa et thoro*, a legal separation from bed and board where neither spouse is allowed to remarry. Annulments were granted on the grounds of bigamy, pre-contract, non-consummation, enforced marriage, and when either party was underage. Separations were granted primarily on the basis

---

said *Now you are among Papists. As for you Mrs. Avyce, you are a Shrew. And, Mrs. Wilson, your Husband is a good Fellow. You can want no Help; if you do, send for me.* It is no marvel if Sir John Bourne's Son use such Talk; for he himself calleth Ministers' Wives Whores" (John Strype, *Annals of the Reformation* 390). In *Fasciculus Mervinensus*, Anthony Bourne is described as "an extravagant worthless man, who deserted his wife and children and went with a paramour to live abroad" (Drake, *Fasciculus Mervinensis* 20).
4 Bradford 39–40.
5 *Ibid* 16–17.
6 *Ibid* 24–25.
7 BL, Add. MS 12507, fols. 204–205.

of adultery and cruelty. As Susan Dwyer Amussen observes, "[b]oth women and men sued for separation, but more women did so than men."[8] Despite a theoretical equality in access to legal redress, "a sexual double standard usually applied so that husbands could separate on the grounds of adultery alone, while wives had to prove cruelty."[9] Julius Caesar notes in his response to Elizabeth Bourne's petition against her husband, Anthony Bourne, that legally a woman could petition for a divorce *a mensa et thoro* based on adultery.[10]

> The canon laws of this Realm do at this day admit a divorce between a man and his wife. And in the case doth as well lie on the woman's side to challenge and have a separation from her husband being an open adulterer, as on the man's side to have a separation from his wife being an adulteress.[11]

While Caesar states that both men and women could seek divorce based on adultery alone, the word "open," preceding "adulterer" and missing before "adulteress," serves as a reminder of the discrepancy in this apparently equal law: a man could separate from his wife if he could prove she had committed adultery; a woman had to prove that her husband was a known adulterer.[12] This difference appears slight, but while a man only needed to prove one instance, a woman needed to prove that her husband had frequently and openly sinned, which usually became part of a larger complaint against his moral, economic, and spiritual threat to her and their household.[13] Because of this double standard, in practice men sued for separation in instances of adultery while women based their petitions on accusation of cruelty. Regardless of the reasons for such petitions, ecclesiastical courts favored a "come to charity" model for disputes; they emphasized living in harmony over granting separations. Consequently, as Laura Gowing has shown, a divorce *a mensa et thoro* was granted on a limited basis with men suing successfully based on adultery 42% of the time, while women's claims of cruelty were successful in 26% of the surviving cases. Most divorce cases

---

8 Amussen 127.
9 Stretton, *Marital Litigation* 4.
10 Tim Stretton calls Sir Julius Caesar "[Request's] most influential master" (*Women Waging Law* 8). For Caesar's rise to Master of the Rolls (Court of Chancery), see L. M. Hill, *Bench and Bureaucracy*, esp. 54–87. On the Privy Council's attention to familial disputes (including the Bourne case), see Hill's "The Privy Council and Private Morality" 205–218.
11 BL, Add. MS 38170, fols. 176–178. At the time of Elizabeth's petition in 1582, Julius Caesar was not yet a Master of Requests, but was an up-and-coming lawyer in London with strong connections to court through Francis Walsingham (Hill, *Bench* 7–16). Walsingham is also the likely tie between Elizabeth and Caesar as both Elizabeth and her mother, Lady Amy Mervin, wrote to Walsingham requesting his help with the separation (NA, SP 12/158, fol. 85).
12 Butler, *Divorce* 14.
13 Gowing, "Language" 34–35, and Gowing, *Domestic Dangers* 188–189.

4   Introduction

never made it to judgment; those that did took approximately two to three years to process.[14] Despite the difficulties, there was one benefit to ecclesiastical law: Church courts regularly ignored the doctrine of coverture.[15]

Husbands and wives could not sue each other, except in "ecclesiastical courts, which allowed married women to bring actions in their own right," in instances of defamation and "separation proceedings."[16] Elizabeth took advantage of her right to sue at court, admitting in her initial letter to Caesar that "About four years past, I did retain counsel and did serve [Anthony] with process. And he would not appear and answer it."[17] Within this statement, Elizabeth reveals a problem with the ecclesiastical process for divorce: Anthony stalled Elizabeth's first attempt at a legal separation by refusing to appear in court. According to ecclesiastical law, a wife is able to sue in her own person, but if the other party delays or refuses to comply, the church courts are limited in their recourse. The church could excommunicate a person or demand penance, but arresting or fining a delinquent litigant was only an option for common law courts. Considering the difficulty of proving cruelty, the time to judgment, and the limited success of separation lawsuits, Elizabeth's impulse to circumvent the church court appears sound.[18] While her powerful networks of support and her financial means opened up channels that she would have otherwise lacked, Elizabeth still had to assume the posture of deference, chastity, and desperation in order to obtain the legal status of *femme sole*.

Though ecclesiastical courts granted women the right to bring actions to court without the permission of their husbands, women faced added scrutiny in going to law. Women seeking separations risked slander and accusations of adultery from their husbands in retaliation, while those who sued on the basis of cruelty were obligated publicly to detail the humiliations they suffered at the hands of their husbands.[19] In each instance the possibility of public infamy placed women in jeopardy and exposed them to social and economic vulnerability. The potential monetary losses of dissolving a marriage could prompt a husband to slander his wife. If a woman was found guilty of adultery, she forfeited her portion rights, any inheritance that had

---

14   Gowing, *Domestic Dangers* 181.
15   Stretton, *Women Waging Law* 29–30. For instances of other courts open to married women acting as *femme sole*, see Subha Mukherji, "Women, Law, and Dramatic Realism" 251.
16   Stretton, *Marital Litigation* 3.
17   BL, Add. MS 12507, fols. 204–205.
18   Within the surviving documents, it is unclear if Elizabeth Bourne has Julius Caesar process her suit through the Church court. In his response to her petition, he answers her questions based on the laws of the Ecclesiastical courts; however, there are no records of the Bournes' case within the surviving court records and the Indenture that grants her a portion and recognizes her "sole life" is demanded by and submitted to the Privy Council (NA, SP 13/c, fol. 28.).
19   See Stretton, *Women Waging Law* 222–225; Dolan, *Dangerous Familiars* 80–88 for a discussion of the Earl of Castlehaven and his wife.

been under her husband's control during their marriage, and her husband's obligation to pay for her maintenance. Consequently, allegations of cruelty were often met with countersuits of adultery for financial reasons.[20]

In this way, the courts reiterated that chastity without community confidence in and recognition of that virtue could limit the power of the good wife performance. In fact, it suggests that a woman's actions were less significant in constructing her reputation than the collective interpretation of her actions. A wife might use cultural knowledge in order to produce what Kathryn Schwarz calls "authentic impersonation." In Schwarz's terms, "the performance of feminine roles answers the need for social stability, and privileges the issue of how virtue signifies over the question of whether it refers."[21] In a letter written from Elizabeth Bourne to Anthony Bourne, she attempts to explain to him the reasons that she refuses to live with him. The detailed history of their union that she presents in the letter as evidence of her resolve to deny his "wisheth reconciliation" seems unnecessary because she is writing to her husband, who presumably knows their history. But as the note at the beginning of the letter reveals, Elizabeth sent a draft of the letter to Edward Conway for his review and asks that once he has "perused [her] letter" that he share it with Caesar before returning it her. In sharing the letter with Conway and Caesar and asking them to sign the letter—and in doing so providing public witness to its contents—she hopes to control their interpretation of the events chronicled in the letter and also prevent any attempt Anthony may make after to "misconster [her] meaning."[22] The public dissemination of her letter complicates the notion of private correspondence.[23] Considering the intended wider audience, Elizabeth takes great pains to detail the many problems they faced in their union in contrast to the ideals of marriage purported in religious writings and cultural expectations of marital accord. Adamant in her doubt of his ability to "unfeigned retire from sin to virtue," she claims that without his genuine reformation it would be a "dangerous life for us to live in so near [fel]lowship as man and wife."[24] Her letter explicitly draws on narratives of marital harmony and cultural fears of the chasm between seeming virtuous and being virtuous, though this anxiety usually applied to women's chastity, not that of men. In calling out his lack of ability to leave his adulterous life behind him, Elizabeth suggests that a man's reputation and the community's judgment of his fitness as a spouse may be tainted by the public knowledge of, or belief in, his sexual transgressions.

20 For more on the accusations of cruelty see Gowing, *Domestic Dangers*, chapter six, especially 206–229.
21 Schwarz 11.
22 BL, Add. MS 23212, fols. 11–16.
23 See Daybell, *The Material Letter* 12, 18–19, 111, for a discussion of the false notion that early modern letters were private.
24 BL, Add. MS 23212, fols. 11–16.

Elizabeth Bourne's petition dated 6 December 1582, in which she catalogues charges against Anthony as evidence of her need to obtain a divorce *a mensa et thoro*, combines many of the same rhetorical strategies that appear in her letters: she names Anthony a prodigal husband; acknowledges the cultural stigma of speaking publicly against him; portrays herself as a vulnerable wife in need of protection from his violence (emotional, economic, physical, and spiritual); and includes a litany of honorable witnesses who may attest to both Anthony's malicious behavior and her suffering, thereby referring the judgment of their reputations to a larger community. Over the course of eight double-sided folio manuscript pages, she represents herself as a long-suffering wife while crafting a narrative about Anthony that renders him an unfit husband who embodies the bad spouse trifecta of cruelty, adultery, and abandonment.

Elizabeth expands her critique of Anthony's tendency to feign virtue in order to show how it adversely impacts not only their marital accord, but their property, as well. The concern over the stability of the estate is raised throughout her letters. In doing so, she shows herself to be a shrewd landowner, in contrast to her husband who repeatedly sells his father's property and hers in an attempt to procure more money, which Elizabeth argues he spends on his many mistresses. In her petition, she establishes that Anthony dissembles reconciliation in order to gain access to her inheritance. She claims that shortly after they were married, "he left my company and lived in the liberty of his ranging affections with diverse women."[25] According to Elizabeth, when she confronts him, he pacifies her: he asserts that financial disagreements with his father keep him from home. Elizabeth suggests that they travel with her family; he concedes and "he continued for a time in good usage of me, to my great comfort."[26] The implication of Elizabeth's narration is that a wife merely desires the presence of her husband and his kindness to requite her labors. Elizabeth reports that Anthony assures her that the sale of her property is necessary "for the relief of [them] both, during his father's life," and that when Anthony receives his inheritance upon his father's death, "he would recompense" his wife.[27] In Elizabeth's retelling, she notes that Anthony "win[s her] consent" to the sale and that he provides assurances to her mother and friends. The inclusion of outside witnesses suggests that the economic well-being of the family is a public matter, that others can attest to Elizabeth's claims, and that when Anthony is foresworn, he breaks his oath to his wife and the witnesses. Directly after he receives payment for the sale of Elizabeth's land, "he left [her] alone as before and continued in London by the space of half a year and spent £500 in vain love with a gentlewoman."[28] In naming her husband an open adulterer since

25 BL, Add. MS 38170, fols. 151–158.
26 *Ibid.*
27 *Ibid.*
28 *Ibid.*

the outset of their marriage and crafting a narrative that exposes a pattern of behavior whereby her husband only returns home to gain access to her inheritance, Elizabeth establishes herself as a long-suffering wife with a husband who swears and breaks oaths as it suits his needs.

Elizabeth underlines the threat of Anthony's promises—broken or not—by detailing the litany of ways he has threated physical violence. She is acutely aware of Anthony's intention to kill her:

> That he would never be quiet, nor his conscience satisfied until he had killed me for a whore. [...] All which threatening speeches confirmed with solemn oaths makes me assure myself of death through his means if once, by consenting to live with him, I offer him so convenient a means to exercise on me his purposed malice and bloody cruelty. Neither can I assure myself of safety upon any bond or oath of his whatsoever.[29]

Repeatedly, she draws contrast between Anthony's declarations that he wants her back and will reform and his promises of bodily harm. She knows that both of these cannot be true and that his past actions support continued violence and justify her fear.

The further challenge of Elizabeth's case derives, in part, from the fact that despite her husband's long abandonment where he "refused to live with [her] these six years, in breach of his holy vow of chaste matrimony," Anthony now desires to return home.[30] Her petition, then, becomes a protective strategy—a countersuit to Anthony's request to the Council that they require that she accept him—and an example of Amussen's claim that legal separations "formalized living arrangements most couples had long since made."[31] Though Elizabeth had previously sought a separation from the Ecclesiastical courts during their time apart, Anthony's return acts as a catalyst prompting her to pursue the divorce with a heightened sense of urgency. In defense of her refusal to appear before the Council at Anthony's behest—for fear of her lack of legal recourse should he take her into his possession against her will—she claims that beyond "satisfying of [her] betters and the world," she narrates her history to safeguard against slander and the ruin of her reputation, "to avoid the imputation of an unreasonable creature in myself."[32] In couching her petition against Anthony as a show of deference to satisfy the Council, she thwarts accusations of willful disobedience—in refusing to appear before the Council—and the stigma of shrewish women who complain about and chide their husbands.

---

29 *Ibid.*
30 *Ibid.*
31 Amussen 127.
32 BL, Add. MS 38170, fols. 151–158.

8 *Introduction*

For Elizabeth, the expectation of feminine silence within the good wife trope comes into conflict with the equal expectation of obedience to authority. She exploits this conflict to her advantage as she positions herself as a reluctant petitioner. She bemoans:

> So heavy be these griefs and so unfit a thing it is for a wife publicly to complain against her husband, that, if unwillingly by his own want of God's grace and good consideration I were not compelled, I would rather commit his sins, with my sorrows, to the silence of my grave than to the view and judgement of any living creature.[33]

Her keen understanding of the dangers, the "discursive risk,"[34] of speaking out against her husband in a public sphere primarily inhabited by men suggests a political and legal savvy that is in some ways incongruent to the image of private patience and suffering—her willingness to take his "sins" and her "sorrows" to the grave—she portrays through her petition. Elizabeth's narrative teems with evidence of her knowledge of "acceptable models of female behavior at court," that she appropriates as a performative tactic to achieve her desired goal: a separation from her husband.[35] Throughout the petition she uses a rhetoric of endurance to describe her torment, which allows her to maintain a balance between idealized female passivity while fulfilling her need for legal action. Her account of Anthony's continued adultery, as well as her economic, emotional, and physical duress, underlines her vulnerability and her need of the Council's help.

As discussed previously, while adultery and cruelty are the primary grounds for a legal separation in the early modern period, there existed a gendered division in cases whereby men claimed adultery and women cruelty. The split reflects cultural fears of gendered disorder. The unchaste female threatens to disrupt patrilineal succession, marital and social order.[36] For men, the line between appropriate levels of violence for correction and inappropriate tyranny is often more blurred. Drawing on the work of Martin Ingram, Frances Dolan claims that despite acceptable forms of physical correction, in Ecclesiastical cases where men were accused of cruelty, "the community judged such men's domestic violence as a symptom of uncontrol and abnormality," even to the extent of assuming that such inability to restrain oneself implies "mental disturbance or instability."[37] For men and women, then, the gendered accusations of adultery and cruelty both result in broader implications of social instability that requires community enforcement and containment.[38]

---

33 *Ibid.*
34 Bodden 57.
35 Mukherji 255.
36 Gowing, *Domestic Dangers* 219.
37 Dolan, *Dangerous Familiars* 102–103.
38 For a discussion of community monitoring of abuse, see Butler, *Language of Abuse*, chapter five, 184–225.

Throughout her petition, Elizabeth crafts a narrative of Anthony as unstable and prone to emotional outbursts that endanger their estate, her person and family, and by extension society. Elizabeth claims Anthony ordered her to return to him half of the portion allotted for the maintenance of her and her daughters. In response she offered him "the whole, so he would refuse" Mistress Pagnam (his long-time companion). According to Elizabeth:

> He fell so passionate at this my answer, that he reviled me with all the ill words he could devise. He offered me the terror of his dagger (which my father, Sir James Mervyn, saved me from), with solemn oaths vowed he would tear the skin off my back. If he might not, he would blow up me and my house with gunpowder, but he would be revenged and rid of me.[39]

In offering him her entire portion if he would leave his mistress, Elizabeth begins the narrative by situating herself as the morally superior one in their relationship. She does not deny him his claim to her finances, but she asks that in return for her acquiescence he agree to live a chaste life. Her deference to her husband simultaneously acts as a corrective. Rather than accept her offer, he verbally abuses her, threatens her with a dagger, and when her stepfather refrains Anthony from harming her, he vows bodily harm and revenge. The specificity and severity of the crimes he threatens—skinning her and blowing up her house—function to shock the reader and suggest that Anthony is unhinged. Her use of "passionate" as her descriptor for his behavior implies his volatility and excess of emotions. In this one example, among many, Elizabeth represents herself as the wronged spouse attempting to help her husband reform. She points out Anthony's readiness to forsake his bond in demanding part of her portion. She shows his refusal to leave his incontinent life with Mistress Pagnam. She names him emotionally unstable. And she verifies the immediate and future threat of cruelty beyond the physical: he is capable of verbal, emotional, physical, and economic violence. Finally, in noting that she would have been harmed without the intervention of her stepfather, she situates herself as a defenseless woman in need of protection while providing a credible witness to the entire event.

Elizabeth's broadening of her definition of cruelty to include various types of intimidation follows standard conventions for female litigants. As Gowing has observed,

> Although canon law restricted the definition of cruelty to physical violence, plaintiffs and their witnesses, especially women, attended with as much care to the economic, mental, and verbal cruelty that gave violence its

---

39 BL, Add. MS 38170, fols. 151–158.

10   Introduction

context, revealing the broader popular conception of marital breakdown.[40]

As both Bourne and Gowing's work on domestic violence show, early modern culture defined a range of abuses as violence and considered them all as evidence of instability in a marital union.

Though cruelty is the only offense that Elizabeth needs to prove in order to secure a separation, she spends a substantial amount of time detailing Anthony's alleged adultery. Elizabeth mentions ten specific instances of adultery in the petition. Many of the women she mentions by name, including several wives of gentlemen. In providing names and reiterating stories told of Anthony's exploits, she satisfies the demands for divorce set forth by Caesar: Anthony is an "open adulterer." The descriptions include charges of illegitimate children, excessive spending, and instances of disease. Even when describing "his loose life"—a phrase she uses repeatedly—she takes pains to demonstrate how his excess with women spills over into a lack of restraint in other areas of his life, or as she states, "ill doings breed ill thinking and of corrupted manners spring perverted judgements."[41] She situates his adulteries as a symptom of a broader pattern of corruption. In this pattern she includes spiritual depravity, claiming that his "licentious and wanton life doth make me fear lest he be grown into a kind of atheist, a thing most dangerous to them that shall live with him."[42] The suggestion is that if someone is capable of the depraved behavior exhibited by Anthony, they must have lost faith in God. In naming Anthony an atheist, Elizabeth moves beyond the claim of him as an unfit husband who may physically cause her injury, to a larger argument that his soul is damaged and, therefore, he is untrustworthy and likely to bring about the ruin of others, including their children. She reiterates an early modern cultural link between adultery, religion, and the threat of contamination when she notes that, "punishment of adultery by the laws now in use with us is excommunication" and,

> since he or she worthily incurreth excommunication, who keepeth company with an excommunicate person, especially such a one as Master Bourne, who maketh a jest at the judgement of God and still growth from worse to worse, waltring and wallowing in his filthy lust: I hold it damnable for me to live with him.[43]

Elizabeth employs a rhetoric of religious devotion to justify her desire to live separate from her husband. While she positions her argument as one of declaring her own virtue and commitment to God—in contrast to her

---

40   Gowing, *Domestic Dangers* 210.
41   BL, Add. MS 38170, fols. 151–158.
42   *Ibid.*
43   *Ibid.*

husband—she intimates that if the Council forces her to live with him, they will not only place her body in jeopardy but her soul, as well.

Lady Amy Mervyn, Elizabeth's mother, similarly employs a rhetoric of desperation on behalf of her daughter when writing to Sir Francis Walsingham to follow up Elizabeth's own "supplication to my Lords of the Council."[44] As one of Queen Elizabeth's ladies in waiting and wife to one of the Queen's legal advisors, Lady Mervyn wielded some influence at court, as is evidenced by her correspondence with Walsingham. Mervyn begins her letter with seeming disdain for her daughter's "unwilling mind to be reconciled to her husband." She suggests that if motherly affection did not force her to "tender [Elizabeth's] well [b]eing as [her] own," she would be furious that Elizabeth refuses to follow the advice of her betters who wish her to reconcile with her husband. By chastising her daughter's behavior—in her refusal to live with Anthony, her disregard of advice, and her "living a fugitive in continual fear" rather than submit to the Council—Mervyn acknowledges the proper behavior and obedience required by Elizabeth's status as a wife and a woman subject to patriarchal authorities (her husband and the Council). However, Mervyn also acknowledges her position as a mother who is obligated to defend her daughter; if she did not, she claims she would make a "shipwreck of nature, conscience, and credit." In claiming her status as a mother, Mervyn provides a sort of rhetorical apology for her subsequent defense of Elizabeth and her plea for aid for her daughter. In echoing Elizabeth's own descriptions in her correspondence, Mervyn prays, "Nay, would to God she should live but in fear and not rather in assurance" of Anthony's violence. Further, she points out that as a *femme covert*, Elizabeth lacks legal redress if Anthony forces himself upon her property, person, or goods: "What law can she have against him if he shall either enter upon her lands or can come by either her person or any of her goods." She offers witness to Anthony's supposed habit of disregarding his legal agreements: "what will he care for the breech of his bond," when he has done so before. She closes her plea by asking the Council's assistance in protecting her daughter from Anthony's assured abuses, "I beseech you consider what better dealing than after this rate can be expected for my daughter, unless your honorable compassions and authority prevent him." In locating the Council as Elizabeth's last hope of defense against a man Lady Mervyn claims is prone to violence and breaking his oaths, she argues for their intervention, stresses the necessity of community support for wives in vulnerable positions,[45] and points out the heightened precarity for women

---

44 NA, SP 12/154, fol. 85.
45 Elizabeth Bourne drew much support for her separation from her own family members who were powerfully connected at court. Her mother, Amy, Lady Mervyn, notes that she will "make such friends as I can for the favor of your cause" and that Elizabeth's stepfather, James Mervyn, similarly "solicit[s]" at court for Elizabeth (BL, Add. MS 23212, fol.

who must balance the often conflicting requirements of patriarchal deference and self-preservation. Lady Mervyn's acknowledgement of her daughter's unorthodox actions and her defense of the same affords one example of early modern women's need to preface their appeals, particularly those addressed to men, with a stated understanding of appropriate models of female behavior. Similarly, in asking for assistance that if granted would go against the patriarchal projects of marriage and patrilineal succession, Mervyn situates the request as unconventional, but necessary when men fail to provide suitable conditions for marital accord. In attesting to Anthony's poor credit—as seen in his disregard for his bond—and tendency toward violence and economic ruin, Mervyn affirms cultural expectations of appropriate male conduct while simultaneously maintaining that her son-in-law's conduct fails to meet such expectations.

"Therefore, good Master Bourne, do me right."[46]

The boldness of Elizabeth's petition and the alternating vulnerability and entitlement she displays in it were central to Alfar's first chapter of *Women and Shakespeare's Cuckoldry Plays*. Elizabeth's strength and defiance of most rules of female conduct still stand out today, but "The Conway Papers,"[47] in particular, bears witness to a simultaneous sadness and frustration with the limitations of a legal system that we might argue did right by Mistress Bourne. While the Indenture of Award is one that clears Sir John Conway of any wrong in his handling of Bourne money and property, it also makes clear that Elizabeth was awarded *femme sole* status, given rights over lands and property, and allowed a separation from her husband with whom she was no longer expected to live.[48] The resolve of the Bournes to live separately and Anthony's intent to live with Mistress Pagnam are clearly stated in another document with the same date.[49] Anthony sold his rights to The Manors of Holt and Battenhall in order to extinguish Elizabeth's dower, essentially to buy her out.[50] Their properties and money were separated, and

---

195). Further, Lucia, Lady Audley, Elizabeth's sister, attempts to encourage Elizabeth to stay with her, claiming that "my home shall ever be to you as your own" (NA, SP 12/172, fol. 174).
46 BL, Add. MS 23212, fols.11–16.
47 The correspondence which comprises all of BL, Add. MS 23212 and a number of documents held in the National Archives State Papers.
48 See Alfar's previous work on the agreement, "the *Arbitrators Report, Indenture of Award* protects Elizabeth from any further harassment by her husband and also puts her financial care during 'her sole life or separation from the said Anthony her husband' into the hands of John Conway" (*Women and Shakespeare's Cuckoldry Plays* 61).
49 NA, SP 12/158, fols. 140–148.
50 Butler writes, "*Bracton*, which distinguishes much more carefully between annulments and judicial separations, makes it clear that an annulment extinguishes a wife's right to dower, but a separation from bed and board does not" (Butler, *Divorce* 80). Anthony's attempt to

Anthony once more left the country in the company of the infamous (and yet impossible to find definitive information about) Mistress Pagnam and their "bastards."

The challenge that arose, however, was that all of Mistress Bourne's property and money were conveyed by Anthony to Sir John Conway, as were the educations and marriages of their two daughters. How it was precisely that Conway became involved in the Bourne dispute is unknown to us. Neither Bradford nor Smith indicate knowledge of how it is that Anthony's property gets conveyed to, or his daughters placed under the wardship (effectively) of, John Conway. Lamar Hill writes that "In 1575, Anthony placed all of this family's assets in trust, with several kinsmen and a prominent neighbor, Sir John Conway, as trustees,"[51] which made them responsible for paying the Queen a £1000 fine when Anthony left the realm without a license. According to the Statute of 13 Elizabeth, Ca3, "An act against Fugitives over the Sea,"

> If any born within this realm, or made free denizen, hath departed or shall depart the realm without the Queen's license under the great or privy seal, and shall not return again within six months after warning by proclamation, he shall forfeit to the Queen the profits of all his lands during his life, and also his goods and chattels.[52]

Though restitution is granted upon the offender's submission, the Bournes incur a £1000 fine that places them in an economically precarious state. Similarly, Anthony's actions—breaking the laws of the realm while publicly absconding with another man's wife—cause further damage to the family's reputation, which makes seeking aid more challenging for Elizabeth because his credit is found lacking. Hill writes, "Eventually a new trust was established with Sir John Conway as sole trustee. In addition to their lands, he was given the right to determine the marriages of the Bourne's daughters."[53] As a consequence of these legal maneuverings, all designed to extricate Anthony from debt and the Tower, Elizabeth found herself under the authority of John Conway. Consequently, the freedom she ostensibly won from Anthony came with the price of still having to answer to and depend on a man, whose profit from her lands and money were also in dispute in the later 1580s. Thus any satisfaction we may feel about the legal victory of the separation must be mitigated by the pathos of her later very angry letters to Sir John Conway about her need for money and her inability to see

---

    counter-accuse his wife of adultery, may have been an attempt to keep her from these rights (*Divorce* 81).
51 Hill, "The Privy Council" 206.
52 Great Britain, 13 Elizabeth, Ca3.
53 Hill, "The Privy Council" 207.

14 *Introduction*

her daughters, who were in the keeping of his wife, Eleanor, Lady Conway, while he was in Flanders in the service of Queen Elizabeth. The correspondence we have included between Elizabeth and John is important in its documentation of what could happen to a *femme sole*. Elizabeth's story did not just end when she won the right to live separately from Anthony, and her break from him was not conducted in a manner that gave her financial independence. Understanding her subsequent relationship with John Conway, therefore, becomes integral to her story and the story of this marital dispute.

In about 1587, suffering at the hands of a very angry Lady Conway who wrote to the Privy Council about Mistress Bourne's continual accusations against her for wrongly holding her daughters from her, Elizabeth wrote to Conway, "This were very hard, a very bad order for me that was born to something and must come to nothing."[54] This sad sentence encapsulates both the high expectations of a young woman who was the child of courtiers at the Tudor court and the disappointment of the wife whose marriage to Master Anthony Bourne left her with steadily diminishing resources and no influence over her daughters' lives. "You lay the fault in myself," she wrote in response to Conway's letter reminding her of her need for him only because she lost the support of her own friends and family. "Indeed, it is true. For if I had not committed my living children and goods into your custody, I could not have been so dealt with. I have the wrong and others have the shame."[55] In a characteristically sarcastic and pointed counter-accusation, Elizabeth refuses to accept his depiction of her or his position of moral superiority. Rather, she entrusted her children and her goods, her lands, and her money to him only to have him betray her. What she understands to be Lady Conway's unlawful stealing of her daughters—a theft she sees as both a loss of authority in their lives and of companionship—is at the center of a dispute throughout the later 1580s.

Consequently, we might say that the separation did not release Mistress Bourne from coverture, but only transferred it to another man, in this case, Conway. As Sara Butler observes about the status of the *femme sole*,

> Essentially, the legal fiction levelled the economic playing field for women, diminishing the real power of coverture by erasing its impact on daily life. It offered the potential for women to hold a 'rough equality' with men. Without actual examples of married *femmes soles*, a

---

54 BL, Add. MS 23212, fols. 131–132.
55 BL, Add. MS 23212, fols. 131–132. We believe that this letter is in response to BL, Add. MS 23212, fols. 81–82 from John Conway to Elizabeth Bourne.

positive assessment of women's independence in the medieval marketplace is less credible.[56]

For Mistress Bourne the real power of coverture was not diminished. Elizabeth relied on Conway to treat her fairly and to conduct her business according to the agreements between them. Defiant as always, Elizabeth accused him of theft, of taking money and land that belonged to her and, most of all, of cutting her off from her daughters, from seeing them, but also from determining who their husbands will be. Having been quite satisfied by the plan for her eldest daughter, Amy, to marry Conway's eldest son, Edward, she was dismayed by Amy's final marriage to one of Conway's younger sons, Fulke, a marriage she felt was inferior to her daughter's rank and worth. While she may have been wrong to trust Conway, she admits, it is he who bears the shame of having defrauded her.

The letters, therefore, are indicative of what an early modern woman expected from the men in her life. Mistress Bourne is failed by her husband and Conway, both of whom use their legal authority over her to their advantage. The marriage of Amy Bourne, for example, to Fulke Conway, rather than to his elder brother Edward, allowed the Conway family to benefit from Amy's dowry without giving up Edward's property and title to a young woman whose parents could provide no other advantages than her dowry (which was reduced from £5000 to £1000 when Anthony allowed all his property to be conveyed to John).[57] This move anticipated Edward's final elimination of Amy's inheritance of Fulke's property at his death:

> On Fulke's death, his brother Edward assumed financial responsibility for the Irish estates—and for his widowed sister-in-law Amy (née Bourne; see above). She was awarded £400 a year for life from the Irish estates in 1633, and seems to have acquired lands in Wales worth £3,500. The second Viscount Conway later negotiated his way out of this obligation, according to a document signed by Thomas, Viscount Wentworth, then Lord Deputy of Ireland, which decreed that since Amy had 'receaued allready six thousand five hundreth Pounds, together wth a Jointure of fowre hundreth Powndes Per Annum' her 'Preferrment and Prouision ... hath been very Honorable & Noble'.[58]

Conway men, in this regard, practiced theft of Bourne women's properties, protecting what they felt belonged to the family, a family that did not include Bourne women. While Amy certainly seems to be provided for in Edward's version of her inheritance, he diminishes the assets left to her

---

56 Butler, "Femme Sole Status."
57 NA, SP 12/158, fols. 140–146.
58 Smith 15 of 22.

by her husband. Thus, Conway men go to law in order to deprive Bourne women of what is theirs. In this light, the possibility that Conway broke a marriage contract between Edward and Amy in order to reserve Edward's title and inheritance for a more advantageous match is likely.

"Do me right," Elizabeth Bourne writes John Conway, "I desire it earnestly as you may see by my long forbearance, which works nothing to me but hardy and good to you."[59] "Do me right," she also wrote to her husband.[60] Both letters evidence her anger and the extent to which she felt wronged by the men who controlled so much of her life. Linda A. Pollock's work on anger as a gendered emotion, as one that was a threat to male authority, points out that "Elizabeth Bourne's angry letters reveal ... women were willing to express rage, and to do so without apology, if they thought the circumstances justified it."[61] Pollack sees Bourne's anger as just, as do we, and as motivated by her need to live in hiding, by her husband's threats, and by the continued dependence she had on men like John Conway. As Gwynne Kennedy argues, early modern moralists gendered just anger masculine.

> The result is a presumption of the legitimacy of certain types of anger in men that is not extended to women. Women who claim a right to just anger consequently have a large obstacle to overcome; they have few models or subject positions available to authorize that kind of anger.[62]

Kennedy cites Elizabeth Spellman, who argues that subordinate groups, such as women, are denied anger as a legitimate response by dominant groups. Anger is most likely to be read as "disobedience, hostility, or rebellion by those in positions of superior authority when that anger is directed at them" (13). And in fact, the act of being angry, of claiming anger on the part of a subordinate acts as a claim of equality (13). Despite the negative associations of anger for women, Elizabeth deploys it as a form of power and moral superiority. Readers will find her exquisitely sarcastic and scathing of her opponents, among whom she counts her husband, Conway, and Conway's wife, Eleanor. She is, then, unintimidated by any negative connotations with being an angry woman. It is, instead, an animating force of energy and rhetorical strength. At the same time, Elizabeth Bourne learns, especially through the 1580s, that equality, independence, and justice are elusive. Not even the 1583 Indenture of Award which states her sole status and her separation from Anthony Bourne can give her independent property rights if her husband conveys them out from under her.

---

59 BL, Add. MS 23212, fol. 131.
60 BL, Add. MS 23212, fols. 11–16.
61 Pollock 579.
62 Kennedy, *Just Anger* 12.

Elizabeth's ownership of Sarsden, a manor and parish in the Cotswold's in the county of Oxfordshire, dates from her father's death, and is also at issue in the later letters. As we note in the places index, while the Horne family had held the property since the late 1400s at least, in 1542, Henry VIII granted Sarsden to Edmund, his first wife Elizabeth, and their descendants, along with the advowson of the parish church. It is property Elizabeth Bourne wished to return to (and perhaps does at one point at least), and which she worried about in letters to Conway. The property proved a challenge to manage from a distance, notwithstanding her caretaker, Hawkins, who oversaw much of the work of the land and animals (we have included some of the letters to Conway in which she talks about her tenants, hay, and cattle to show her competence as a landowner). Keeping hold of the land is an important legacy for her daughters, at least as stated in the Indenture. According to documents at the parish church, Sarsden was sold to Sir John Walter at her death and not passed on to Amy and Mary. Given her letters about managing the property, did the land provide some kind of income, despite being conveyed to Conway? Was Elizabeth allowed a living from that land, at least once the affair started (see below)? It is possible since she tells Conway that he can have some corn. But even the presence of Greville as a tenant on the property does not tell us whether she received his rent. According to the Indenture, Conway would receive it. The question is whether this legacy and settlement was enough. Perhaps it is all we can expect, or even more than she might have expected. Yet she remained discontented, with letters that are not only expressions of anger, but also of loneliness. To have spent so many years fighting for independence only to have been handed from one man's authority to that of another is a dissatisfying conclusion.

The financial settlements, however, were complicated. Her anger is notable partly because Elizabeth reiterates, in what appears to be her own words and with her signature as proof of her understanding, the terms under which money, property, and control over her daughters are turned over to Conway:

> I am content and well pleased and do give my free and full consent that Master Bourne assure all things absolutely, without any trust, condition, limitation, or use to be reserved to me or to any person for me, and am further contented and well pleased that according to the plain word and covenants of an Indenture of three parts, bearing date 14th day of October in the 21st year of the Queen's reign, that Sir John Conway shall enjoy all {…} to his own proper use and benefit, according to the express words of the Indenture. In witness of which truth and my willing consent to the same, I have written this note of remembrance with my own hand, faithfully promising Sir John Conway to set my hand and seal to a joint and sufficient warranty with Master Bourne, … that he may and shall quietly enjoy without any trust, use, limitation, or meaning of any part of it to be intended or reserved to my use or behalf. I bind myself by my faith and my truth always to acquit and

18 *Introduction*

> discharge him of all trusts of or for any part of anything that is or shall be conveyed and assured by Master Bourne and intended to me by any meaning, bill, book, agreement, or writing.
>
> E. Bourne[63]

Elizabeth clearly agreed to give Conway the right to "enjoy to his own proper use" everything conveyed to him in the named Indenture. Yet she accuses him later of having claimed ownership wrongfully. It is possible she thought he would be a silent trustee, if you will, allowing her to manage her lands and her daughters.[64] Indeed, there is a clause in the Indenture that suggests Conway will treat her with special care. The arbitrators note two things in separate documents (as noted), first that,

> nothing comprised herein shall extend to, exonerate, or discharge the said Sir John Conway from any trust or confidence reposed in him (if any such be) touching any portion of lands or other substance whatsoever due, limited, or appointed for the maintenance of the said Elizabeth Bourne during her sole life or separation from the said Anthony, her husband,[65] nor after the decrease of the said Anthony from any benefit she may reap by virtue of any trust at any time heretofore committed unto him (if any such trust was so repos[ed]).[66]

And second, that,

> Sir John Conway of a friendly consideration and care of his well doing, and withal to further a quiet state between him and his wife,[67] they being agreed then upon actions to lead their lives separately asunder until by their further assents they should with good liking be fully determined to live in one dear society and company; in the mean that Mistress Bourne

---

63 NA, SP 12/158, fols. 140–148.
64 Butler argues that, "A wife never relinquished ownership of that property to her husband, even though he actually controlled that property during the marriage. Common law deemed that he held title only 'in right of his wife.' Medieval English law and society still considered all real property hers, even if in practice the management of any dowry or inherited lands rested entirely in the hands of her husband. Some separated wives believed that the termination of marital relations should also halt their husbands' marital property rights" (*Divorce* 86). It is likely Elizabeth Bourne believed this right to continue even in the face of lands conveyed to Conway, despite the distinction between "use" and "profit" used in the Indenture and summary document (of the same date).
65 This moment in the Indenture of Award indicates clearly that Elizabeth Bourne was legally named a *femme sole*, *n*. "*Law*. Now *historical*. An unmarried woman; (sometimes) *spec*. one who is divorced or widowed. Also in the English and other common law legal systems: a married woman whose legal status, esp. with regard to her right to own property or to carry on a business, is that of an unmarried woman."
66 NA, SP 13c, fol. 28.
67 Anthony and Elizabeth Bourne.

might live quietly, in person, without violence to be offered by Master Bourne or by any his procurement, and that she might have and use the custody, commodity, and profit of all lands and tenants, revenues, and profits, and also all goods, apparels, and household stuff, or any other benefit or meet thing which by any of her friends and allies should be lent, given, or sold her toward her maintenance without seizure, intermeddling or disturbance of Master Bourne or any other by his means. In this consideration partly and chiefly as it may further appear by an Indenture bearing date of 29th day of June in the 22nd year of her Majesty's reign that Sir John Conway should quietly enjoy all profits, lands, and goods conveyed.[68]

First, we see both that if there were an agreement or trust agreed to by Mistress Bourne, Conway would still be bound by it. Second, any property that should come to Mistress Bourne after the conveyance of all past property should be retained by her and not newly conveyed to him. This is a tidy decision that really did no good for Elizabeth, but allowed Conway to amass quite a bit of wealth from the lands held by Anthony and/or Elizabeth. Consequently, Amy and Mary went to live with Conway's wife; Amy was married to Fulke; and the money remained largely in his control, to the point that Elizabeth begged him, occasionally, for money. In addition, because she lived in hiding, much of the time, from Anthony, whom she feared, she depended on Conway to arrange lodging for her (we have not included letters of this kind). This became inconvenient and even humiliating when her hosts informed her of their need for the space she occupied. Again, the woman who had hoped for so much from her life ends with far less than she feels she was entitled to and even less than she believed she had agreed to. Her anger was a logical and inevitable response to a system that took as much away from her as it awarded, leaving her still in a virtual state of coverture, though no longer under Anthony. Newly reliant on Conway, whose trustworthiness was doubtful, she gained the right to live separately from her husband but not to independence.

Sara Butler's *Divorce in Medieval England* provides illuminating information on cases of separation and to what a wife might be entitled. She writes that in the 14th century a woman married to an abusive husband might be entitled to alimony, which could assume

> a more permanent form. At times, court officials required husbands to provide their separated wives with financial assistance for the duration of their lives. Only occasionally do the rulings in cases of judicial

---

68 NA, SP 12/158, fols. 140–146.

separation include particulars about maintenance agreements, such as the amounts to be paid or the payment schedules.[69]

Both Anthony's letter of 1577 and the above quoted agreement show that Elizabeth Bourne was provided with the use of the lands, goods, and household stuff, while John Conway enjoyed the profit of them. This was to be the case until her death, at which time all properties would be left to Amy and Mary Bourne.[70] Thus, Elizabeth officially retained a home and lands (even if she rarely lived there), but she lost all revenue from those lands. While the Indenture of Award[71] made Conway responsible for the maintenance of Elizabeth Bourne (in the same sentence in which her "sole life and separation" from Anthony is made clear), her complaints to him in the latter part of this decade suggest that Conway failed to honor his agreements. She did not believe that he lived up to these trusts, especially in the contracted marriage between her daughter, Amy, and his son, Edward.

We know that, officially, a married woman owned no property and had no legal rights, yet this case belies that knowledge.[72] Suits in Chancery mentioned in documents, along with the attention of Queen Elizabeth, Sir Francis Walsingham, Sir Thomas Bromley, and others (in the Privy Council hearings) about the Bourne marriage, testify to two things: first, when Anthony Bourne fled the kingdom for Calais in the company of Mistress Pagnam, he caught the attention of the Queen, who confiscated his property and threw him in the Tower. Elizabeth negotiated a yearly payment of £100 for the £1000 fine set by the Queen. Second, this attention opened a door for Elizabeth Bourne's legal arguments against him as a profligate and negligent husband, an outlaw, an adulterer, and a violent man (who threatened to kill her). While it was his attempt to petition the Privy Council to return her to him that prompted her own petition, which she sent to Sir Julius Caesar, we see that Mistress Bourne went to law repeatedly throughout the 1580s. She insisted on her rights to property, money, and children whether she was

---

69 Butler, *Divorce* 83. See also Amy Louise Erickson, chapter six, "The Nature of Marriage Settlements," 106–113, where she observes that, "Marital separation ... was not at all uncommon" and that, "[i]n the event of an unamicable separation, a wife could sue for separate maintenance or alimony in either the ecclesiastical courts or in equity" (112).
70 NA, SP 12/158, fols. 140–148.
71 NA, SP 13c, fol. 28.
72 Erickson argues that the focus on common law in women's legal matters "ignores the other four bodies of law which regulated property ownership in the early modern period ... [as well as] parliamentary statutes, made by common lawyers sitting in parliament, [which] also played a crucial role in regulating property transmission, principally by intervening in Ecclesiastical law" (5). Subha Mukherji discusses an impressive number of cases in which women were active litigants, in "Women, Law and Dramatic Realism" 251–256.

fighting her own husband or Conway.[73] While the purpose of The Indenture of Award[74] was to protect Conway from Anthony, who is held to a number of promises and covenants, including not to molest, vex, implead, or generally be a nuisance to Conway, it also protected Elizabeth from the same kind of harassment. While it did not (nor was is meant to) award her *femme sole* status, it confirmed it and attempted to protect her from Anthony's violence, either in his own person or through any other person. If women had no legal rights, her affairs would not have been addressed nor would she have been legally freed from Anthony.

The importance of this case to legal scholars of the period remains to be examined. The documents we have selected from "The Conway Papers" and National Archives' State Papers tell a story of the petition, its resolution, and the ongoing dispute between Mistress Bourne and her husband about their marriage and separation, and subsequently between Mistress Bourne and the Conways both for custody of her daughters and financial security. The later dispute is well chronicled in the letters from Lady Conway to the Privy Council, asking them to stop Mistress Bourne from further petitions and a draft or copy of a letter from Conway to the Council defending himself from her accusations and also in the Acts of the Privy Council which regularly record complaints by both parties and acts and decisions brought by the council for hearing and redress.[75] In a document we have not included, Lady Conway records all the money her husband spent on the dispute, both in payments to various men owed money by Anthony and in rents of properties.[76] What the Conways have taken from Mistress Bourne, she maintains, is theirs by right, including custody of the Bourne daughters. In a letter to the Privy Council, Conway argues that he is well within his rights to claim properties and authority over Amy and Mary.[77] According to a document written by Anthony and to the Indenture, he is correct. What is interesting, however, is that the Indenture both confirms and questions this agreement. In part, it reads:

> the said Arbitrators, do award that although they do not find any cause in law to enforce the said Sir John Conway there unto, YET NEVERTHELESS in respect of the present estate of the said Anthony Bourne, and in consideration that it is now full and freely granted and condescended unto by the said Anthony Bourne, that the said Sir John Conway, his executors and assigns, shall have by the intent of this, our present award, the marriage, education, bringing up, and free disposition in marriage of Amy Bourne and Mary Bourne, daughters and heir

---

73 BL, Add. MS 12507, fols. 204–205 and BL, Add. MS 38170, fols. 151–158.
74 NA, SP 13c, fol. 28.
75 These records span 1579–1590, at least.
76 BL, Add. MS 23212, fols. 191–192. No date, but likely c. 1587.
77 BL, Add. MS 23212, fol. 183.

22 *Introduction*

> apparent of the said Anthony Bourne and Elizabeth Bourne, his wife, according to the express words, effect, and purport of a pair of indentures tripartite had and made between the said Anthony Bourne of the first part, Sir John Conway of the second part, and Sir James Mervyn, Knight, and others of the third part, bearing the date the fourteenth day of October, in the one and twentieth year of the reign of our sovereign Lady Elizabeth, the Queen's Majesty that now is.[78]

Because a legal Indenture existed in which Conway was given authority over Amy and Mary, the Arbitrators were forced to acknowledge and corroborate it. It is nonetheless important that they also undermined it by making it clear that there was no legal precedent for such an agreement. The need for it, we submit, is Anthony's mounting debts which he wished to escape so that he could be free to live with Mistress Pagnam. He could not, it is clear, honor the dowry promised in the marriage contract between Amy and Edward. As a result, he sold everything, including his children, and somehow managed to get his wife to sign away her rights to her own property. Conway became the benefactor of Anthony's failures as a way to mitigate the reduction in Amy's dowry. In effect, the profit he would enjoy until the deaths of Anthony and Elizabeth, at which time the lands and money are to be inherited by Amy and Mary, make up for that loss.

The claim to her daughters angered Elizabeth profoundly and precipitated a series of letters to Conway that take an unexpected turn. At first, he attempted to remind her of the conveyance of her property to him, reminders that fail to quiet her. In one response to her, he repeats all the conditions of the conveyance:

> You did, upon a good belief that I would never see you nor your children want, free[ly] consent that Master Bourne should convey all your lands, goods, and debts absolutely to me, according to the express words of his several deeds without any trust, confidence, limitation, or use reserved, intended or meant, to himself to you or to any other to either of your uses.[79]

When this kind of reminder fails, we believe, Conway turns to other tactics and strategies. Her angry letters only terminate when she receives a letter in which Conway declares his love for her. "Put sadness away," he writes,

> though the man have broken promise, and he will keep it well the rest of his life. Wot you why he did it? To try your patience and love. You must

---

78 NA, SP 13c, fol. 28.
79 BL, Add. MS 23212, fols. 81–82.

take it a little unkindly. He will be greatly sorry, and, thereof, more love will increase than was before.[80]

His profession of love, she replied, completely overwhelmed her. Indeed, even for readers—no less than Mistress Bourne—his letter is shocking and unexpected. The tone is unprecedented and shifts the trajectory of their correspondence, not to mention their relationship.

Was he telling the truth? Did she reciprocate? What is interesting about subsequent letters is that during their affair, and we are convinced that there was an affair, either or both may have engaged in a strategy to keep the other placated, soothed into a sense of comfort, a belief that good intentions were meant, that all requests were heard. We have more letters from Elizabeth to Conway than from Conway to Elizabeth (this is true in "The Conway Papers" as a whole), but her letters display an astute combination of declaration, promise, and demand that must be calculated. John Conway's letter certainly comes as a surprise, so much so that James Daybell accepts at face value his claim that it is a translation of something he wanted to share with her.[81] But if this letter comes as a shock, then Mistress Bourne's reply (and her subsequent letters) offer the kind of declaration we might expect upon marriage. She promises him that, "Loving, constant, and faithful you shall ever find me. This, as one revived, all joying in my own sweet Knight. I end wishing ~~you~~ us all that our loves deserves and desires."[82] These sentiments continue in the other letters, but mixed in, more and more often, are requests, even demands, that Conway return her daughter to her.

> I pray you as you love me say nothing but devise ways and means to bring us to live together in friendship as we ought to do to our comforts, as I know you can do if you list, and love me as I know you do. You had drawn a book out for my daughter, which had pretty covenants in it. I think you mean not that which you sent me to Warwick shall stand because it is imperfect as I think I do not remember anything in it that was agreed on between you and me, but a release of all living and children to satisfy the council with. Therefore, I think you mean to make another, but what or how I cannot tell. But all to your wisdom and will I leave it assuring myself you love me and care ~~to maintain~~ for me and, therefore, I assure myself you will devise ways and means that we may enjoy one another.[83]

Bourne manages here both to deepen the relationship and to accuse him of having come to an agreement with her which is then not part of the one sent

---

80 BL, Add. MS 23212, fol. 135 and Daybell, "Elizabeth Bourne" 177.
81 BL, Add. MS 23212, fol. 135.
82 BL, Add. MS 23212, fol. 136.
83 BL, Add. MS 23212, fols. 143–144.

to her at Warwick. She believed they agreed to a release of her living (her money) and of her children. And she is sure he must have meant to send her another agreement because she remembers nothing about the conditions in the agreement she received. This allegation is bookended with the same promise of more intimacy, along with her stated belief that he meant "to care for me." Her rhetoric is deliberate, careful not to offend and yet clear in its intent. Like a dance in which participants move forward and back, turnabout, and move forward and back again, she expresses faith, love, accusation, reproach, demand, faith, and love. Conway must understand, she makes clear, that she grasped the details and ramifications of the document he sent her in contrast to those they discussed, and she rejects it.

The conclusion we come to is that neither Elizabeth nor Conway can be sincere in their declarations of love while also fighting each other, and Anthony, for rights to property, money, and daughters. Acts of the Privy Council from 1587–1589 show that the dispute continued. The Council calls it variously the dispute between Sir John Conway and Mistress Elizabeth Bourne and between Conway and Master Anthony Bourne. The continual pursuit of a legal remedy on the part of both parties contradicts the words of love and devotion. Our last document comes from the record releasing Mary Bourne from Lord Norris (the last home she lived in after Lady Conway's death in 1588). Mistress Bourne petitioned the Privy Council for Mary's release because she turned 14, the age set for her maturity.[84] If Elizabeth is forced to petition the Privy Council in 1590, then it seems likely that neither Elizabeth nor Conway were sincere in declarations of love and devotion. Elizabeth is clear in many letters that she wanted her daughter Mary to live with her. Conway, who apparently wrote her lovingly according to her responses to him, did not release Mary until he had to. Thus, we read their affair as a calculated effort to put Mistress Bourne off (on Conway's part) and to receive Conway's favor (on Mistress Bourne's part). Mistress Bourne received satisfaction on this matter only when her daughter turned of age and only from the Privy Council.

Mistress Bourne's correspondence with Sir John Conway is important in many respects, not least of which because it shows the state of her legal position and her life post-separation from her husband. This life is lonely, still filled with conflict, and far short of what we believe she imagined when she pursued the right "to be by the course of the laws divorced from [Anthony]."[85] The majority of this correspondence takes up the last part of our book, which is roughly split between the pursuit of a separation, the agreements made with Anthony (both by Elizabeth and Conway) having to do with lands, money, and daughters; and her angry and, later, longing letters to Conway. Central are three documents: Elizabeth's letter to Sir Julius

---

84 NA, PC 2/16, fol. 553.
85 BL, Add. MS 12507, fols. 204–205.

Caesar, asking him to take her cause; her petition for separation, which he comments on; and the indenture and related documents securing Conway's rights to everything the Bournes owned. Prior to these documents and surrounding them, are letters from Elizabeth's family to her and to officials. Elizabeth's letters to her mother, sister, and Mistress Morgan which state wrongs she endured at the hands of her family, who have not been sympathetic with or active enough in her cause and also ask for assistance. As we have discussed, Anthony's letters also show a man both selling off property and settling debts while begging for assistance and attempting to portray himself as a man who is misunderstood, wronged by others' opinions, and powerless to do differently than he does. While there are many letters we have omitted from this collection, we believe those we have selected tell the story of the Bournes's marital dispute and the limited victory to be had in a separation from bed and board. While we may want to celebrate Elizabeth Bourne's victorious separation from Anthony Bourne, we see that this victory did not allow her the freedom of movement or financial independence she hoped for. We must be satisfied only that it won her safety from a man who threatened and tormented her.

References

Alfar, Cristina León. *Women and Shakespeare's Cuckoldry Plays: Shifting Narratives of Marital Betrayal*. New York: Routledge, 2017.

Amussen, Susan Dwyer. *An Ordered Society: Gender and Class in Early Modern England*. New York: Blackwell, 1988.

Bodden, Mary-Catherine. *Language as the Site of Revolt in Medieval and Early Modern England: Speaking as a Woman*. New York: Palgrave, 2011.

Bradford, Charles Angell. *The Conway Papers*. Original Typescript. Washington, DC: Folger Shakespeare Library, 1936.

Butler, Sara M. *Divorce in Medieval England: From One to Two Persons in Law*. New York: Routledge, 2013.

———. *The Language of Abuse: Marital Violence in Later Medieval England*. Boston: Koninklijke Brill NV, 2007.

———. "Femme Sole Status: A Failed Feminist Dream?" *Legal History Miscellany*, 8 February 2019. https://legalhistorymiscellany.com/2019/02/08/femme-sole-status-a-failed-feminist-dream/.

Daybell, James. "Women's Letters and Letter Writing in England, 1540–1603: An Introduction to the Issues of Authorship and Construction." *Shakespeare Studies*, vol. 27, no. 1999, 1999, pp. 161–186.

———. "Elizabeth Bourne (Fl. 1570s–1580s): A New Elizabethan Woman Poet." *Notes and Queries*, vol. 52, no. 2, June 2005, pp. 176–178. doi:10.1093/notesj/gji211.

———. *The Material Letter in Early Modern England: Manuscript Letters and the Culture and Practices of Letter-Writing, 1512–1635*. Houndmills, Basingstoke, Hampshire: Palgrave, 2012.

Dolan, Frances. *Dangerous Familiars: Representations of Domestic Crime in England 1550–1700*. Ithaca: Cornell UP, 1994.

Drake, Sir William Richard. *Fasciculus Mervinensis, Notes Historical, Genealogical, and Heraldic of the Family of Mervyn*. London: Metchim and Sons, 1873.
Erickson, Amy Louise. *Women and Property in Early Modern England*. New York: Routledge, 1993.
Gowing, Laura. *Domestic Dangers: Women, Words, and Sex in Early Modern London*. New York: Oxford UP, 1998.
Great Britain, Anthony Hammond, and William David Evans. *A Collection of Statutes Connected with the General Administration of the Law: Arranged According to the Order of Subjects*. 3rd ed. London: Saunders and Benning, 1829.
Hill, Lamar M. *Bench and Bureaucracy: The Public Career of Sir Julius Caesar, 1580–1636*. Stanford: Stanford UP, 1988.
———. "The Privy Council and Private Morality in the Reign of Elizabeth I." In *State, Sovereigns and Society: Essays in Honour of AJ Slavin*. Edited by Charles Carlton. New York: St. Martin's, 1988, pp. 205–218.
Kennedy, Gwynne. *Just Anger: Representing Women's Anger in Early Modern England*. Carbondale: Southern Illinois UP, 2000.
Mukherji, Subha. "Women, Law, and Dramatic Realism in Early Modern England." *English Literary Renaissance*, vol. 35, no. 2, March 2005, pp. 248–272. doi:10.1111/j.1475-6757.2005.00059.x.
Pollock, Linda A. "Anger and the Negotiation of Relationships in Early Modern England." *The Historical Journal*, vol. 47, no. 3, September 2004, pp. 567–590. doi:10.1017/S0018246X04003863.
Richards, Jennifer, and Alison Thorne. "Introduction." In *Rhetoric, Women and Politics in Early Modern England*. Edited by Jennifer Richards and Alison Thorne. New York: Routledge, 2007, pp. 1–24.
Schwarz, Kathryn. *What You Will: Gender, Contract, and Shakespearean Social Space*. Philadelphia: U of Pennsylvania P, 2011.
Smith, Daniel Starza. *John Donne and the Conway Papers: Patronage and Manuscript Circulation in the Early Seventeenth Century*. Oxford: Oxford UP, 2014.
Stretton, Tim. *Women Waging Law in Elizabethan England*. Cambridge: Cambridge UP, 1998.
Strype, John, ed. *Annals of the Reformation and Establishment of Religion and Other Various Occurrences in the Church of England; during the First Twelve Years of Queen Elizabeth's Happy Reign. ... Together with an Appendix or Repository, Containing the Most Important of Them*. 2nd ed., vol. 1. London: printed for John Wyat, 1709.

Letters and Documents

1 13 February [1576/7],[1] Master Anthony Bourne to Mistress Elizabeth Bourne

(© British Library Board, BL, Add. MS 23212, fols. 5–6)[2]

This copy of Master Bourne's letter to his wife to persuade her to answereth a fine to the Lord Chancellor therein, Her Majesty's Solicitor General.[3]
Bess,

   I commend me hardily to you, then do I hope that you have spent the time more merrily in Warwickshire and elsewhere than I have done here. Besides that matter whereof I wrote unto you, which will do you no good to know, withal I have taken great pains for my other business and brought the same to wished effect. I have gone through Sandford clearly and made unto you therein an estate for life. I have also bought one annuity of 50 pounds by the year, to discharge that which is paid out of Cutteslowe,[4] in which you have also an estate for term of life. So as I have made you a large recompense for Stowell[5] and your half part of Lyneham for where these two were worth but £180 by the year; these two which I have joined you purchaser in are to be letten[6] at the least for 400 pounds by the year.

   Now to comfort you more, Sir James Mervyn and I are gone through for Lyneham in such sort as that the next term I dare assure you it shall be ours and yet if it fail, I have to make you a further recompense, conveyed unto

---

1 Anthony Bourne sold Battenhall, a manor in the parish of St. Peter, Worcester, to Thomas Bromley in January of 1576/7. His reference to selling Battenhall in this letter suggests that this letter was written shortly after.
2 This letter is a copy, as noted by Sir John Conway on fol. 6 of this letter. There is no address page. What must be the original is contained in BL, Add. MS 23212, fols. 3–4, and is addressed "To Mistress Bourne at Sarsden, these with speed."
3 Contents description is given by Sir John Conway in fol. 6. The letters are usually accompanied by his (often enlightening) notes, such as this one.
4 Because John Chamberleyn sold Cutteslowe to Anthony Bourne on 2 January 1576/7, this provides further evidence for the date this letter. Anthony Bourne sold Cutteslowe to William Lenthall c. 1588.
5 In 1577, Anthony Bourne sold Stowell to Robert Atkinson and his wife Joyce. Because Stowell belonged to Elizabeth Bourne, here he is compensating her for the loss of her property.
6 Let, *v.1.* 8a. To grant the temporary possession and use of (land, buildings, rooms, movable property) to another in consideration of rent or hire.

you £3000 in money, the same to be bestowed upon Lyneham or somewhat else to your use. Your plate is also redeemed and shall be sent home; your jewel I also have but will advise to leave it when I speak with you.

    Now Bess, I have told you what I have done for you. Let me tell you what I have done against you. I have sold both Battenhall and Holt to Master Bromley[7] and broken with Master Owen[8] upon some respects such as Master Chamberleyn and I both will tell you at my return home. You must, therefore, put your hand to the two fines which Sir Gerard Croker will bring you. I pray you, excuse my breach of appointment with Sir John Conway, for I cannot for my life come hence till Saturday night. So as upon Monday I will be home by dinner.

    And so farewell, good Bess. With hardy commendations to yourself and God's blessing to my young mistresses. London, the 13th of February.

Your loving husband,
Anthony Bourne

---

7 Thomas Bromley.
8 Possibly, Richard or William Owen.

2 2 March 1576/7, [Indenture for the Marriage of Amy Bourne and Edward Conway]
(© British Library Board, BL, Add. MS 23212, fols. 71–72)[1]

By indenture hearing date, the second day of March in the nineteenth year of the reign of our Sovereign Lady Queen Elizabeth, her Majesty, made between Sir John Conway Knight of the one part and Anthony Bourne, Esquire, of the other part, among other things it appeareth.

That the said parties have covenanted one to the other to do their best endeavor that Amy, daughter of the said Anthony, and Edward, son of the said Sir John, shall be together married.

And that to the end the same marriage shall the rather take effect, the said Anthony hath granted and assigned to the said Sir John the government, marriage, and custody of the said Amy until her age of fourteen years or marriage aforesaid solemnized without let or disturbance.

And that if the said Anthony shall fortune to decease without issue male, then he shall leave to the said Amy the moiety of all his lands which he shall be seized of at the time of his decease either lawfully to descend or to be assured to the said Amy and her heirs forever; and also the moiety of all his goods, debts, and chattels, whatsoever.

Provided that it shall be lawful for the said Anthony to dispose £1000 at his pleasure out of her part. And that the said Anthony shall pay to the said Sir John £1000 within eight months after the sealing thereof, and £500 for the said Edward at the marriage day.

And that the said Anthony should find and bring up Frances Conway one of the daughters of the said Sir John in like and equal sort as the said Amy shall be brought up by the said Sir John.

And if it fortune Elizabeth, wife of the said Anthony and mother of the said Amy, or any other his wife to survive the said Anthony, that then the wife of the said Anthony, his executors or assigns, shall yearly pay unto the said Edward Conway after marriage solemnized as aforesaid £100 at two terms in the year during her natural life.

---

1 This document, signed by Anthony Bourne, would have been the copy received by Sir John Conway. It is a document referred to in NA, SP 13c, fol. 28 (Indenture of Award reconciling all debts and holding Conway innocent of all accusations made by Anthony).

And that the said Sir John Conway hath covenanted with the said Anthony that upon marriage solemnized as aforesaid, the said Sir John shall assure to the said Edward and Amy all that his manors of Belne with the appurtenances, and to make the same worth £80 a year above all charges and reposes[2] during the life of the same Amy.

And that if the said Edward fortune to decease after the said marriage solemnized, then the said Sir John shall leave and assure to the said Amy after the decease of the said Sir John Conway £100 more out of all other his lands, and after the death of the now or then wife of the said Sir John one other £100 during the natural life of the said Amy.

And that the said Sir John shall immediately after his decease leave assured the said Edward his son all his manor of Kingley in the county of Warwick.

And that (his debts paid and daughters married) the said Sir John shall assure to the said Edward his manor and Lordship of Luddington and all copies[3] woods and underwoods within his manor of Arrow.

And, finally, that the said Sir John Conway shall sufficiently and lawfully assure and convey all his manors of Arrow and Kingley with their appurtenances to the said Edward and Amy, his wife, and to the heirs of their two bodies lawfully begotten, and for lack of such issue the remainder thereof to the right heirs of the said Edward Conway, forever.

4. This indenture proveth the four considerations.

2 March 19 Eliz Covenants concerning the marriage of Edward Conway to Amy Bourne

Master Anth. Bourne[4]

---

2 Repose, *v*1. 6. b. *intransitive*. To lie in the control or management of a person or institution; to be placed in the hands, power, etc., of.
3 Copy, *n.* and *adj.* A. n. †I. Abundance, plenty. a. Plenty, abundance, a copious quantity. *Obsolete*.
4 The last few lines of this document, starting with "4. This indenture proveth," are written in two distinctly different hands on fol. 72v.

3 [Undated],[1] Sir John Conway to Master Anthony Bourne

(© British Library Board, BL, Add. MS 23212, fol. 83)

The copy of my letter sent to Master Bourne in dissuading him from Mistress Pagnam.

Keep a happy life to yourself and leave death to her chase. If she escape not, the peril as well as you shall enjoy the pleasure, let me answer the murder. Women, as I have said, be good poets. They can fain well. Beware lest she can make better and you mar all. The choice is now in your own hand—

I have here showed you some perils which [threaten] your purpose. Compare them with the pleasure you seek, and as your own reason shall persuade you, so I leave God to guide you. If you take this I speak in ill part, you wrong your friend's good will, whose honest heart more desireth your happiness than your own reason can in this time foresee your evil doings.

Affection is blind, and where she fails, wisdom serves. This being so, I were not a friend to conceal that duty in friendship binds me to speak, and discretion wills you to see. I would to God you had passed as much {…}[2] and proof of law and friendship as I have ever. You would hear more than fear to fall into the necessity to seek favor of any. You shall find in so ill a case the favor of law, and friendship so cold and costly, that had, I wist,[3] will come too late. And my words will be remembered.

Be friend to yourself, and you shall have many friends to favor you. Alter your estate to stand upon petition without the compass of your own help. And you shall go helpless or be hardly assisted.[4] I shall then love myself {…} better, and will not leave to love you of pity that ~~you will~~ not lo[ve your]

---

1 There are several possible dates for this letter. Anthony first flees the realm in March 1577. He is once again "a fugitive" according to the Acts of the Privy Council in 1595. It is possible that he was in France in 1583. We know that in official documents of 1582–1583, Anthony clearly asserts his intention to make his life with Mistress Pagnam.
2 This letter, though a copy of one sent to Master Bourne, has several tears at the right margin. We include it because it shows John Conway attempting to dissuade Anthony from leaving his wife and his country.
3 Wist, *v*. To know; *past participle* = caused to know, informed.
4 A section here is omitted not only because John Conway marked it out but because much of it is unreadable. There are also illegible sections in the left margin of the folio.

{...} self. When you shall need a friend, I am ready to prove {...} same man I seem. If you go on to attempt this peril, I shall grieve {...} and so I rest howsoever you take me. Fare well and have care you may long so do. I wish it, I hope it, do you desire me it and God will send it.

Your well assured friend,
J. Conway

[Indistinguishable]

Though she[5] feigned to you the similitudes of death unless you take her from her husband.

---

5 Likely, Mistress Pagnam.

4 14 May 1577, Master Anthony Bourne to Master Thomas Bromley[1]

(© British Library Board, BL, Add. MS 23212, fols. 32–33)

To the worshipful Thomas Bromley, Esquire, her Highness' Solicitor General, these.

Sir,

You offer me much hard dealing, in sort as I may well repent that ever I knew you. I hoped to have bought you a friend and have purchased an undeserved enemy. And where it groweth I well know, for you will seem that I mean to defraud you of two scurvy leases and two copyholds.[2] Sure, Sir, I mean it not. God, I beseech him, deal by me as I in causes of land and money mean [to] all men.

But, Sir, I come not at you, and what is the cause thereof you can yourself say for me. Why, alas, Sir, if I should do it, I were utterly undone. Yea, and to comfort me more if I had come to you the last time I promised, yourself (as your own man hath reported) had provided to betray me in Cholmeley's house, and to have had me there taken, of which, your purpose having missed, you now seek to withhold five hundred pounds from me, which ~~you lent~~ yourself delivered to Master Wenman, of mine. For the delivery whereof I have your letter, and your word before witness to charge you, as also that you had his sufficient bond remaining with you for the same.

Master Solicitor, offer me not these parties. For, sure, I must exclaim upon you if you do. And shall perhaps be heard though my Lord Treasurer be my heavy lord,[3] besides determine of it that if my living be that withholden me, I will sell my life[4] also, and, therefore, advise you not to urge a man that is grown desperate. For by the blood of God, if you seek this

---

1 Thomas Bromley was not knighted until 1579.
2 Copyhold, *n. Law* 1. a. a. A kind of tenure in England of ancient origin: tenure of lands being parcel of a manor, "at the will of the lord according to the custom of the manor," by copy of the manorial court-roll.
3 Heavy, *adj.* 1 and *n*. VI. That weighs or presses hardly or sorely on the senses or feelings. †22. a. Of persons: oppressive; troublesome, annoying; angry; severe, violent. *Obsolete*. 1452 in Paston Lett. I. Introd. 72 "I ... am informed that the King, my sovereign lord, is my heavy lord, greatly displeased with me."
4 To the devil.

way to hinder me, (having dealt with you in so friendly sort as I have done) assure yourself I dare hazard it to make you enjoy your new purchase but awhile.[5]

Wherefore, Sir, I pray you let me not be so much deprived of my hope as instead of my hoped friend, to perform yourself my fraudulent enemy. And as for what I have sold you, you righting me, if ever I or my man for me go about to offer you the wrong of one penny, I refuse God and his works. So bid I you farewell, the 14th of May, 1577.

Your friend, so used
A. Bourne

---

5 Anthony Bourne sold the manor of Battenhall and copyhold on the property to Thomas Bromley in January 1576/7.

5   28 January 1577/8, Master Anthony Bourne to William Cecil, Lord Burghley

(HH, CP 160/117, fol. 186)[1]

To the right honorable, my good Lord, the Lord Burghley, Lord High Treasurer of England, these.
Right Honorable,

Being charged from you by my singular good Lord, the Lord Compton,[2] truly to advertise you, as well what reports I have passed of you, as withal by what reporters I have been thereto stirred, I am accordingly in all humbleness most ready to obey your said commandment. So do I also beseech you both to hold the tediousness of my said discourse excused, and further to pardon me if the same be not set down in so good sort as my willing heart wisheth it.

It may then please your honor to understand that upon the departure of Mistress Pagnam from her husband, (hearing the fact[3] generally determined to be mine), I repaired from my house in the country to this town with full mind rather to have offered myself to the answer of the cause than to stay till such time as a messenger were sent for me, which course howbeit would to God I had followed, yet not daring (in a cause of such weight) to affy[4] me wholly in myself, thought first good, to use the advice of such as I reckoned to be my more sufficient friends, whereupon, (changing my lodging, the second night after my coming to this town) there came unto me (amongst others) Sir James Mervyn, he in the hearing of one Master Thomas Powell, my brother-in-law, of one Master Will Whitney, her Highness's Receiver for Staffordshire, and of one Master Thomas Vaughan, told me that the night before my coming to the town, it fortuned Sir George Peckham and him to sup with your Lordship, who, (quoth he) first asking me when I had either seen or heard of you, said further, that you had committed a very horrible

---

1 Reproduced with permission of the Marquess of Salisbury, Hatfield House.
2 Henry Compton.
3 Fact, *n.*, *int.*, and *adv.* A, *n.* I Senses relating primarily to action. 1. An action, a deed, a course of conduct; formerly also occasionally) †an effect, a result. Also as a mass noun: action, deeds, as opposed to words. Now somewhat *rare*.
4 †Affy, *v.* 1. a. *intransitive*. To trust in someone or something; to rely on (also upon). Also occasionally without construction.

38   *Letters and Documents*

fact and stolen away a gentlewoman, the wife of one Master Pagnam, affirming also that yourself, you were there, at the taking of her away, I (quoth he) or Sir George Peckham (I wot not how well whether[5]) after some reply made in your behalf, took occasion to demand of him to what punishment your said fact was (by the laws of this Realm) liable, he thereto answered, that there was no certainty set down, but that the statute[6] (as well for the bodily punishment as for the fine) left it wholly in the discretion of the Lords of the Star Chamber,[7] and that (quoth he) shall be whipping at a carts tail[8] through London. That my Lord (said he) were very hard to a gentleman of his accompt besides (if your Lordship knew the man) he hath in him many good parts, which would seem to deserve much better. Yea (answered your Lordship) but the same accompanied with many imperfections, besides that he liveth very dissolutely and shall, therefore, be taught to know himself. He told me, further, that (after a little pause) you also said that my father had left me a thousand pounds land, and (as you were informed) I had sold it all.[9] So as (being full of money) it was the wight[10] I meant to get over the sea upon some practice, for you well know I favored not the time. Whereto he answered that he durst assure your Lordship to the contrary, saying that he knew me to have sold my land, partly upon necessity and chiefly upon dislike of the country where it lay, being minded to settled myself in Oxfordshire, where I had a house by my wife's,[11] to the which I was well affected for the better proof whereof (said he) I assured your Lordship, he is presently in talk with me for a Lordship which I have there lying very commodiously for him. Well, quoth your Honor, I know not his mind, but sure I am the fact is odious, both before God and man. And he shall therefore be punished accordingly. It shall cost him £6000 fine to her Highness, and

---

5   Whether, *pron.*, *adj.* (and *n.*), and *conj.* Signification. I. *pron. adj.* Which of the two. *Obsolete*, *archaic*, or *dialect*. Occasionally used loosely of more than two: cf. either pron. The pron. is occasionally found with the gen. inflexion -es, -s. 1. In direct questions. *a.* pron.
6   We have retained the underlining which is in the original and reveals the particular details that bring Anthony to write this letter.
7   "Before it became a separate court of law in its own right the Star Chamber had effectively been the judicial arm of the King's Council. It was named after the star-spangled ceiling of the room where it met in the old Palace of Westminster. The court presided over criminal cases for the most part but did exercise some civil jurisdiction" (The National Archives, September 2019).
8   Cart's-tail, *n.* The hinder part of a cart, to which offenders were tied to be whipped through the streets.
9   This is likely a reference to Battenhall, sold by Anthony Bourne to Thomas Bromley in 1576/7.
10 Wight, *n. archaic.* a. A living being in general; a creature. *Obsolete.* b. Applied to a thing personified. *rare. archaic.* [Anthony writes "wyhte."]
11 Sarsden.

three[12] to the party for amends, and when I have pulled his feathers, let him then fly whither he can.

He having delivered me these speeches, before these three fore-minded gentlemen and (as I remember) a fourth, one Master George Gifford it was (thereupon) by him and the rest thought good that I in no cause offered myself to the answer of the cause, but that keeping myself secret I should yet stay in London, as well, that I might the more readily hear what was further determined towards me, as also to what better effect he, and others my friends, could sort my said cause, which (their advice) I accordingly followed and stayed at the least ten days.[13]

I all which time (though now I forbear to charge any man doubtfully) yet do I assure your lordship (as I am a Christian man), there came not anyone to me (of any great sort) which confirmed not the self-same (or the like speeches) to be generally given out through all the town, in so much as in the end it was advised me, by all my friends, that I should get me gone. Some said get you into Wales, some into the north, others (whoso advice I was best affected to) as my surest shield from shame) bad get me over the sea, which advice (as I have said) how be it I liked best of, yet would I not go before I had first attempted to get a license, whereof when (after some charge) I not only failed, but with all by the means of certain unrequested letters, which (unlooked for) were sent me into Cornwall by Master John Killigrew, and there found upon me, whileth I stayed there in hope of my license, ignorantly increased the opinion of my first fact, as also discovered my being. I thereupon, (thinking myself now assured to be put into your Honor's hands, who tofore[14] was said to have so far forth threatened me) made a hard escape from the Admiral there and fled the Realm. In which my flight, what mind I bare towards my Prince and country, I leave to your honor to judge, when (having in my hands at the same time) above £4000 (which I could easily have exchanged over, as also have ordered a greater sum to my use, which then lay in friendly hands) took (in effect) not one penny with me, by which my regard of loyal love to my Prince and country. I committed such folly towards myself, as that of long, (and so presently) I rest confiscate[15] and at her Highness's mercy (in effect) for all I have in the world.

Wherefore, my good Lord, for the Love of God, by your honorable means, let me find it. For though (by sundry unfortunate accidents), I have

---

12 £3000.
13 These are events and arguments which Anthony Bourne makes to John Conway in NA, SP 12/198, fols. 36–37, which confirm our belief that the letter is written by Anthony and not by Elizabeth Bourne.
14 † Tofore, *prep.*, *adv.*, and *conj. Obsolete.* A. *prep.* a. Of motion: To before, to the front of; of position: In front of; = before *prep.* 1.
15 Confiscate, *adj.* 1. Of property: Appropriated to the use of the sovereign or the public, adjudged forfeited. (Chiefly as *past participle*.)

increased the opinion of my first begun folly in such sort as that the same (being now gathered together in as gross sum) may seem to deserve the opinion of a singular offense, yet (when so ever it shall please your honor to give me hearing) I hope, you shall rather have reason to pity me, as an unfortunate man (who by want of God his grace, having fallen from him) have (like a weak Christian) frailly yielded myself to the surcharge[16] of blind affection than to play me as one who shall appear to your honor rebelliously disposed towards either my Prince or country. Yet may my letters written into Italy move some imagination to the contrary, but my Lord, let them not for (by the faith of a true Christian man) as the same contain, in one manly word, the name of her Majesty by the term of merciless, so do I protest that the said word, had (in my thought) no further relation than towards myself at what time it was left in Calais by an unknown English passenger, (to be told me by the postmaster there) that her Highness (at the only request <u>of you and Master Secretary</u> Walsingham) had given away all my goods and seized also that little land which I had left into her hands. The same report (which would to God I had never heard) being also the cause that at the same time I wrote withal, that other (unbecoming) letter, wherein I discover my small affection (according to that which in very deed, it then was) towards your honor and Master Secretary. So as, whosoever, I further named in the same, may easily pardon my thought, for as God save me, my Lord, I truly do, and to my greater grief may and do confess that the marks my malice shot at was you two, only.[17]

Whereunto, as I was led by the report which tofore I have written, so did I the more easily believe the same. First because my man, who at the same time I had sent over with mine humble letters to your Honor, him and others my Lords was not returned to me, but (staying three weeks above his appointed time of return) was also said to be imprisoned; next (and that chiefly) for that this your deed (if it had been such) did so fully agree with your former reported threats. All which compared, is on the one side, I (like a most unfortunate man) have to bewail myself and repent me for my folly. So on the other side, do I most humbly beseech you, who are both wise and honorable, mercifully to consider first that an absent man is easily abused by report; next what extremities despair worketh in an imperfect mind; lastly (for the love of God) to forgive me, and to obtain that I may be forgiven. Think (for pity's sake) that loss, sorrow, and thus much shame are punishments sufficient for him that never determined to have offended but only in that first point of wicked affection for which offense, if the loss of £4000

---

16 Surcharge, n. 2. 3. An additional or excessive "charge," load, burden, or supply (of something material or immaterial); = overcharge n. 1. 1603 J. Florio tr. M. de Montaigne *Ess.* i. ii. 3 "Being otherwise ful, and over-plunged in sorrowe, the least surcharge brake the bounds and barres of patience."
17 Anthony attempts to defend himself from having called the Queen "merciless."

at the least, already wasted (for the love of her with whom (since I had her) I never enjoyed one merry day) seem not punishment sufficient then do I most humbly beseech, that my further pledge, loss, and punishment whatsoever may (yet be) the clear redemption of her, who only hath offended, in answering an unfortunate liking, which would to God had never had beginning. So do I wish to myself or my cause short ending, but to your honor long life, with heath and happy increase from the Tower, the 28th of January, your honors in all humbleness,

Anthony Bourne
Perused by me, Owen Hopton[18]

"*Endorsed by Burghley:*-'28 Jan. 1577. Anthony Bourne's letter out of the Tower brought by Lord Compton.'"[19]

---

18 Lieutenant of the Tower. This gorgeously written note runs sideways in the left margin.
19 Quoted from the Calendar of State Papers.

6 6 February [1577/8],[1] Master Anthony Bourne to Sir John Conway
(NA, SP 12/198, fols. 36–37)

To my dear good friend, Sir John Conway, Knight, these.
My good Knight,

As brave as I was to perform a voyage to London, yet being here, I dare not show my head. Matters are so vehemently incensed against me, my Lord Treasurer and the Lord Chamberlain are extremely bent, though (if the matter were to be equally determined) they have (in very deed) no such cause, but howsoever the cause be, their authorities being so far above my skill, I am advised by my wise friends to get me home and keep me out of hands till the matter may be some way qualified rather than to be put up to fatting[2] and then to attend the end of their vigorous pleasures. This advice, Sir, I mind to follow, beseeching you that I may be welcome to you, among others my good friends as a wandering guest. I am informed that I have a great friend among the nobility and for my life I cannot learn who it is. I suppose it to be my Lord of Ormond, whose credit is now very good, and as I have heard, he sayeth favorably of me. Neither do I hear that my Lord

---

1 This letter is distinctive for several reasons. The Calendar of State Papers attributes the letter to Elizabeth Bourne and identifies the date as 1587. However, the writer refers to him/herself as, "the happier man I," and also refers to "my brother Powell" who is Anthony's brother-in-law, Thomas. Further, the signature is just initials, which we have determined to be "AB" and not "EB" because the "A" is made as Anthony Bourne signs his name. While Elizabeth often signs her initials to her letters, her "E" is never ambiguous. John Conway's comment at the end of the document notes that the letter is from "Master B." Finally, the handwriting is more like Anthony Bourne's than that of Elizabeth Bourne. The only evidence against attributing the letter to Anthony is the address and sign off ("my good Knight" is typical of Elizabeth's address of John Conway). In addition, we disagree with the date because in HH, CP 160/117, fol. 183, Anthony relates precisely the same decision not to go to London where he has been called to answer for stealing the wife of Master Pagnam. The date of that letter is 1577/8 and is inscribed by Burghley, which calls the date of this letter (as well as its author) into question. We include the letter partly for its ambiguities and because its cast of characters are relevant to many other documents. This letter shows their connections to the Bourne case and to court.

2 Fatting, *n.* 1. The action or process of making (an animal or person) fat. The sense seems to be that Anthony wishes to avoid London so as not to submit himself to slaughter, i.e., to the displeasure of the Lord Treasurer and Lord Chamberlain.

of Leicester meddleth in the matter nor my Lord Admiral and sure one of these three is the man that favoreth me. But as for my other two Lords, they are terrible, whipping, open penance at Paul's pillory,[3] fining by thousands is the least word they speak, but let them speak in God's name, for as for doing I will keep them well enough from, I fear, me. I shall have cause to use you so as I would beseech you to be at my house on Wednesday next at bed. I will send for my brother Clark thither also, and there I will crave your best advices. I am greatly bound to Sir George Peckham, Sir James Mervyn, and Tom Drewry. So doth my brother Powell also perform himself both honest and friendly in this present cause. The plot is laid already, in such sort as I hope all shall do well, which if it do fall out so the happier man I. If otherwise I must crave aid of friendly advice for mine own brains carry not level[4] to sound so great a cause. At our meeting, I will impart you more. Till then farewell my good knight. London, the 6th of this February,

Your own assured,
A.B.

Master B's letter wherein[5] he refereth the said speeches of my Lord Treasurer and my Lord Chamberlain

---

3 Pillory, *n.* 1. A device for punishment, usually consisting of a wooden framework mounted on a post, with holes or rings for trapping the head and hands, in which an offender was confined so as to be subjected to public ridicule, abuse, assault, etc.; punishment of this kind. Now *historical*.
4 Level, *adj.* and *adv.* 3. a. Lying in the same horizontal plane as something else; on a level with. Also *figurative*, on an equality with; readily accessible or intelligible to.
5 John Conway's notes are always revealing. Here we see he refers to "Master B" and "he."

7 15 January 1579, [Master Anthony Bourne to unknown Lord]

(© British Library Board, BL, Add. MS 23212, fols. 28–29)[1]

My good lord,

It is but a heavy {...} man studieth to play the part of a wisem[an]: he purchaseth {...} whilst to discharge the due of an honest man; he incurreth the {...} of [indecipherable]. It is [indecipherable] good Lord, that I did not enter the bond of mine appearance with such expedition as I might have done; it is true that I came not at Master Lieutenant in fourteen days; it is also true that when he sought me with an unnecessary stir as though I had been some notable offender, he might have commanded me by the least child of his house, and did find me (ere I determined to be lost[)] in the company of a most woeful gentlewoman, honestly accompanied at a most lawful hour, and to a most honest intent. With the nature of this first offense (if it be to be accompted one), your Lordship (as I suppose) is not unacquainted. For had I gone to the Tower and entered bond, having sundry other causes necessarily to be dispatched, then had I been no longer her Majesty's prisoner. Then was it also in Master Lieutenant's choice either to have stayed me for the surplus of my diet unsatisfied (as now he hath done) where by the following of my necessary causes had been impeached or else of his courtesy have given me credit and discharge. So as our being out of her Majesty's protection, I might have been catched up by some of my creditors and, thereby, have rested as miserable or in worse case than before I did. Whether it were reasonable for me to prevent this mischief in myself, yea or no, I leave to your honorable consideration, leaving me also to be justified by mine honest, credible friends, who knew my mind.

What disposition I was of both in duty toward my Lords for the [hum]ble performance of the bonds, as also in honesty due to Master Lieutenant

---

1 There is substantial damage to this letter, with tears in three central locations, apparently at the folds. We have indicated where the tears obstruct our ability to decipher words with {...}. In addition, much of the writing has faded. When necessary, we have indicated our doubts about what is written with [indecipherable]. We include it despite its frustrating gaps because Anthony Bourne's sense of the wrongs against him are clear. He also, in a rare moment, addresses the fate of Mistress Pagnam, for whom he feels (at least he says) responsible. There is no address.

for his satisfying as I possibly might. For the second point, I {...} disliked access to the gentlewoman. She is, my Lord, such a charge {...} of I have reason to wish [me] honestly, utterly, or in part, eased. And {...} my charge as I consider of it in honesty and conscience, she ought to be as she whose honest fame hath been overthrown by me. Am I, then, my good Lord, to shake her off with villainy or to settle her with temperance? Am I to salve what hath past with placing her conveniently and sequestering myself from her orderly,[2] or must wickedly and unconscionably to leave her in the world further spoiled? More than the discharge of these dues, I have neither meant nor attempted. At such time as I was with her she was honestly accompanied. I came to her to dinner, being a reasonable hour of the day and after dinner, determined my departure from her, having appointed supper with Sir John Conway and Master Perry, as they both can witness. The cause of my access to her was this: I determined as on Monday last, which should have been the next day after Master Lieutenant thus unkindly molested me, to have settled my causes with him as before I had done with all others that my necessity required. The next day after that, I meant (as lawfully I might) have departed this town. The cause of my determined departure was and is chiefly to provide her some competent state where she may be removed from me and thereby we both from the world's wonder. Hereof, I came to determine with her many leisures. I had not to do it sooner for I call Master Broughton[3] who is towards the law. Sir John Conway and Master James Perry to my witnesses that I have spent most of the day these 15 days with them, and that some time must be used to dissuade a passionate creature of her follies and to sever an affected woman from him whom she hath either extremely (though unorderly) loved or greatly dissimulated. Your honor, I hope, holdeth it reason[.]

Th[ese my] Lord, are my offenses, these my excuses. Condemn me or {...} at your honorable pleasure. How {...} will bear the burden with patience as far as concerneth myself. Only I crave of your Lordship your honorable favor as far forth as my [de]sert (the same being first duly sifted) shall deliver[4] me worthy. By these (as far as is in me and as in truth I may) I thought good to settle your Lordship. That being done, as other ways most ready {...} humbleness of duty. So now in all willingness to attend your honor, on the other side to bear the determination and check of my faults, without cause, why I am rather prepared in state of my misfortune than either in mind or nature. Consider of me accordingly (good [my] Lord), I humbly beseech you. For

---

2 Orderly, *adv.* 1. According to established order or rule; properly; in conformity with good order or discipline; in a well-conducted or well-behaved manner. Now *rare*. †2. a. In order; in the correct order or regular succession; with appropriate arrangement, disposition, or distribution; methodically. *Obsolete*. b. Duly; fittingly; in due course. *Obsolete*.)
3 Likely, Richard Broughton.
4 Deliver, *v.* †2. a. To free, rid, divest, clear (a) of, (b) from.

were I an indifferent person to the state, as my fortune will have me, a person odious, I have neither offended nor meant offense, but have received such extreme wrongs, such disgraces, and so vile words as (in my simple conceit) some should not suffer to be offered me. For I have lived when I was unfit to have born them how my cause is also secretly enforced I know. The sum whereof is none other but I am complained of because I have refused to pay above my power and to suffer my monies to be extorted from me. My good lord, *Multum latet quod non patet.*[5] But I must bear. I only beseech your good Lordship to admit the end of my cause such as it is of mine own making. Though the course will seem strange to your Lordship, {...} it is yet safe [and] the [redress] too {...}. Lord Compton[6] misliketh it and me for it, but I have {...} advice and saw withal into mine own necessity. I am sure of as much as I desire. There resteth no more but that with your favor you will give him leave to be sequestered from the world who would fain be forgotten that ever he was.

Sir John Conway in this [permute][7] broil of mine hath played me honest and gentlemanly parts.[8] It is reason that I do the Devil right. In some other causes I find him not so blame-worthy as I thought him. Sufferance of my harm hath been his greatest fault. Sir James[9] and the woman herself have chiefly [beaten] and spent me. The partners of the spoil will show the fruits of such getting. For God is a just God.

Your Lordship, I am in all humbleness of duty and to his blessed keeping I commit your honor, whom I beseech to bless, preserve, and increase you. This 15th of January 1579.

Your Lordship's faithful and humble,
Anthony Bourne

This letter is signed in Master Bourne's own hand. In his good [indecipherable] he caused this letter to be written and would not give it me that I might how he did, neither [indecipherable] to his best friends.[10]

After I had paid him all his money, he was arrested but in the gate house, I there. If I had [indecipherable] bound sayeth paid [indecipherable] in France he [had] [indecipherable] [Mon]day.

5   "Much is hidden that cannot be seen."
6   Henry Compton.
7   Permute, *v.* 2. a. *transitive.* To alter, change; to vary. Also Pute, *adj.* Now *rare (archaic).* Pure, mere; utter, outright, unqualified. Only in pure pute, pure, and pute. Anthony's meaning is closer to "pute," but there appears to be a contraction, so that permute seems more in line with the penmanship. Perhaps he means that his broil is constantly altering?
8   This is probably sarcasm.
9   Sir James Marvin, stepfather of Elizabeth Bourne. The woman may be Elizabeth, or may be the unnamed woeful woman of this letter, whom we take to be Mistress Pagnam.
10 John Conway's usual summary of a letter's contents.

8   18 February 1579, Master Anthony Bourne to Sir John Conway

(© British Library Board, BL, Add. MS 23212, fol. 51)

To the right worshipful my good friend, Sir John Conway, Knight, give these.
Sir,

If delay might be available to you and not [utterly] harmful to us both, I protest to you I would be most willing to take what time might like you, but, besides that my wants will not suffice me to forbear. Withal I fear that her majesty will within awhile be less apt to yield mercy (in money causes) than presently she is. If these reports from Spain and France be, as I hear, true, her majesty shall have cause to employ money, and then I fear. So as, Sir, I hardily beseech you to take the pains hither in the morning to the end we may better consider of the matter. I will yield you any aid that my power in reason may yield. I pray you consider of it this night. I thank you for what you have sent. I hope to borrow sufferance on them. Safe they shall be, and I as ready yours to my power. I pray you, Sir, fail not in the morning by half hour past eight of the clock. I protest you there came no meat in our bellies today yet. I hope to stall my debt to Sparks and by means thereof to borrow £100 more. For a time, I will use your bond, but if you so please, whatsoever I endanger you for, I will lessen it in your statute wherein you stand bound to me. I hereby pray your coming that we may resolve. My Lord Compton[1] dealeth most hardly with me.

So bid I you most hardily farewell with both our commendations returned.[2] This 18th of February, 1579.

Your poor friend, half out of his wits by want and fear.

A. Bourne

Master B[3]   It seemeth by that [indecipherable] Lord Compton dealeth hardly with Master Bourne and that [h]is want is great as he lacketh meat to eat.

1 Henry Compton.
2 We believe this is a reference to Mistress Pagnam.
3 John Conway's customary summary.

9 [Undated], Mistress Elizabeth Bourne to Mistress Morgan

(© British Library Board, BL, Add. MS 23212, fol. 187)

To the worshipful Mistress Morgan, at Whetstone, give these.
Good Mistress Morgan,

With my hardy thanks for your great courtesy showed me, I commend myself to you most heartily, praying you amongst the rest of your friendship towards me that you will witsafe[1] to deliver me a letter to good Mistress Blanche Parry and that you will entreat her most earnestly to move her Majesty for me in a reasonable suit. That is that that [sic.] her highness will show Master Bourne and me that gracious favor as to accept her 1000 pounds, which we must pay her, by 100 pounds a year, until the whole sum of 1000 pounds be paid. And we will put in such good sureties, therefore, to her Majesty's use as my Lord Treasurer[2] shall allow of. I pray you good Mistress Morgan, be earnest with Mistress Blanche in this, for God he knoweth if I cannot obtain this favor, I, and all mine, shall presently beg and be undone. Our whole state is but 3200 pounds. Her Majesty must have 1000. Master Bourne's debts and his mother's legacies be another 1000, which must be presently compounded, or he shall be imprisoned and I undone. The rest remaineth in the hands of several debtors which will not be recovered but by time and charges. So that it is an impossible thing for us to pay her Majesty the 1000 pounds in any other sort than by an 100 pound a year and live well. Therefore, I pray you be earnest in this case for your poor unfortunate friend. I will requite any good you shall do me to the uttermost of my power. If you can get Mistress Blanche to obtain me the favor to pay it by 100 pounds a year, till the 1000 pounds be paid, I will give you 200 marks. If you cannot obtain that, I will increase her Majesty's 1000 pounds and make it 1200 pounds to pay it by a 100 pounds a year,

---

1 Vouchsafe, *v.* Obscure forms listed include: *witsave, witsaffe, wytsaue*. I. Senses relating to conferring or bestowing, especially graciously. †1. *transitive*. To confer or bestow (something, favor, or benefit) on a person. 2. To give, grant, or bestow in a gracious or condescending manner.
2 William Cecil.

and give you 100 marks. And your money shall be presently paid you upon either of these ends obtained.

And so I commend your health and Master Morgan's to God and the consideration of me and this cause to your friendly remembrance.

Your loving and unfortunately friend,
Elizabeth Bourne

10 25 June 1580, Master Anthony Bourne to Sir Thomas Bromley

(© British Library Board, BL, Add. MS 23212, fol. 66)

To the right Honorable, Sir Thomas Bromely, Knight, Lord Chancellor of England, Be these, with diligence.
My duty, most humbly considered,

Sir John Conway, having satisfied me in all accompts between us, I am now to deliver him in discharge of my covenants the counterpane[1] of the indenture of bargain and sale between your lordship and me,[2] and also the defeasance[3] of the several bonds wherein I stand bound unto your lordship for performance of covenants.

If we could assure ourselves of your Lordship's life, then were the doubt little, or none at all. But feeling the ignorance of the true indemning which may happen in an executor, or the possible severity of every year sequel that may demand that we doubt not in your lordship, maketh me and them this bold to require them, considering the great peril that may grow to me and mine. By this and such like other accidents besides, I am in covenant for the delivery of them and under pain of £5000 statute staple.[4]

I did, by Master Chamberleyn and myself, make your Lordship privy before I entered the covenants and bonds, and delivered your Lordship their reasons of demand. You then thought upon consideration with Master Chamberleyn and me, their motions so reasonable as you pleased to promise I should have them delivered by the hands of your servant, Master Edmund Hardy, in whose keeping they were by me then left in trust. And now I humbly beseech your Lordship in discharge of Master John Chamberleyn his faithful word, and my weighty bond, that they may be accordingly delivered into the hands of Master Richard Broughton in whom I repose my trust for

1 † Counterpane, *n.* 1 *Obsolete*. 1. *Law*. The counterpart of an indenture.
2 Likely, Batthenhall but could also be a reference to Holt.
3 Defeasance, *n.* 2. *Law*. Now *rare*. a. A collateral deed or other document expressing a condition which, if fulfilled, renders a deed or contract null and void; a clause or condition having this function. b. The rendering of a right, condition, contract, etc., null and void; annulment.
4 Statute staple, *n.* A bond of record, acknowledged before the mayor of the staple, by which a creditor has the power of seizing a debtor's lands in case of default.

the receipt of them, and also for such order and delivery of them as shall be best for my quiet and safety.

I did not adventure to wait upon your Lordship myself, and therefore I have [knighted][5] these my friends, Sir James Mervyn, Master Lyttelton, and Master Broughton to attend your Lordship for the receipt of these things. If Master Broughton come not to your Lordship, by his want of health, then my desire is that you deliver them to Master Lyttelton, to be delivered to Master Broughton, to whom I have referred the determination of all causes between Sir John Conway and myself. And for as much as the delay of time is both perilous and chargeable to me, and that Master Broughton hath but today to tarry in town to order all my causes, I most instantly desire your Lordship, the petition (being in me and them very reasonable) concerning the covenants on both parts, which we have entered, they for the payments of a yearly pension unto me, and I for the discharge of my bond, that your Lordship will stand so much, my good Lord, to accomplish this our joint and lawful request.

In so doing, you shall do yourself right and me both, by reason he and my children shall know how and be more abled to keep covenants with your Lordship and your posterities, which I trust shall justly be fulfilled by him and then to you and yours, as knoweth God, to whom I commend your Lordship with daily increase of honor, this 25th of June 1580.

Your Honor's humbly and faithfully,
Anthony Bourne

Master B's letter to the Lord Chancellor.[6]

---

5 Anthony writes "nitided." "Knighted" is our interpolation; it fits both Anthony's tendency toward irreverence and the act which he deputizes his friends to perform in his place. Clearly, he has no desire to come face to face with Thomas Bromley.
6 John Conway's customary note.

11   21 July 1580, Sir John Conway to Mistress Elizabeth Bourne

(© British Library Board, BL, Add. MS 23212, fols. 125–126)

[The] right worshipful owner at Sarsden, give these.
My good Sister,

I hope you have had a good journey and your health, and so withal a safe return.

I have sent you your bill of Sir James Mervyn's hand. Touching the payment of £36 to Duckett and withal a release for Master Duckett[1] to seal and figure for the discharge of James Coke. If Master Duckett will so upon the receipt of £4 and Sir James Mervyn's bill seal this release and figure it and deliver it before witnesses to the use of James Coke, then you may deliver this bill out of your hand to Sir James or Master Duckett. Otherwise, I pray you advisedly, deal that Sir James finger not the writing. Master Duckett neither before he hath sealed and delivered this release to the use of James Coke.

If Master Duckett stand with you upon charges, it is more than reason. Considering his use of your money in his hand. Besides he concluded with me at Sarsden that he would require no more but a note of Sir James's hand that he would pay him. And he would be pleased with the debt of 40 pounds only. Lastly, Sir James hath by his bill of agreement with me undertaken that Duckett shall discharge James Coke of all things and release him quite when any one now shall pay him over and above the £36 the residues of the debt without any penalty or charges, which is £4. And I pray you, if they differ with you upon this point let Curtis and John Reynolds be witnesses that you tender the four pounds to Master Duckett and Sir James's bill withal. And then if Master Duckett will not end, let me deal with him and Sir James, both, so that you keep the bill of Sir James, his hand and note what day of the month you tender him payment. Let your witnesses note it. And there an end.

---

1   Same as Duckett above. We believe this to be Francis Duckett, rector of Sarsden. In NA, SP 15/26, fols. 30–31 14 May 1579, not included here, James Mervyn references a Parson Duckett and settling of rent and other debts that Elizabeth has incurred at Sarsden.

For your linen, I have opened your trunk and find that it was very ill washed. The greatest part of it fouled with earth in the drying and therefore however much at that marked I have caused to be washed again and the rest not marked. I have with my pen drawn such marks as shall appear to you and cannot be altered. And these holes, I do but [sew] them and lay them up again. I take all of it out of the closet by note of my own hand. So that I warrant you of all losses. I cannot send it you before your going into Wiltshire but when your present return back after hay harvest, I will cause it to be brought you to Sarsden. It is far too much for a horse to carry. In your other trunk there was a little shorter white cloak, a white waistcoat and kirtle[2] of satin, and your damask petticoats, a tartar[3] blanket of feathers, your furs, and so these I send. The others I have laid about in the [chamber] and so will within a day or two put them up again in the [indecipherable]. They are under my newer charges.

And so of the causes, I leave to trouble you further. Only I pray you leave me the last court rolls out and the key of the trunk where the rest be. You may bind them up and seal them and the key within them. And take order they be left with Hall, James Coke, or Bear for me because I hope Master Hobby will be out of the way at Milton.

If I can possibly I will see you on Saturday night before you go your journey. This is my determination. If I fail, fail not you to be absent too long from your friends. I will wish you all things to your [heart's] desire. Chastely, take care of your health, and good keep of little Moll.[4]

Farewell, to your own self, a thousand times this Thursday, the 21st of July, 1580.

Your brother and everlasting friend,
J. Conway

---

2 Kirtle, *n.*¹ 1. A man's tunic or coat, originally a garment reaching to the knees or lower, sometimes forming the only body-garment, but more usually worn with a shirt beneath and a cloak or mantle above. 2. (*a*) A woman's gown. (*b*) A skirt or outer petticoat. (See quot. *a*1825 at α.) Apparently in common use down to about 1650, and now, as an archaism, much more frequent than sense 1.

3 † Tartar, *n.3 Obsolete.* a. A rich kind of cloth, probably silk, used in 15th and 16th centuries; the same as tartarin *n.*¹ 2. A rich stuff, apparently of silk, imported from the East, probably from China through Tartary.

4 Mary Bourne, daughter of Elizabeth and Anthony.

12 [Undated], Mistress Elizabeth Bourne to Sir John Conway

(© British Library Board, BL, Add. MS 23212, fol. 127)

To my very good brother, Sir John Conway, these.

I cannot but take it very thankfully your comfortable lines. It is a thing which in grief gives the best comfort and, therefore, my good brother, I give you many thanks for them. I pray you spare me not if my pain may ease your trouble and somewhat [indistinguishable] ease my misery. I thank God I am somewhat better than I was.

I persuade myself and live in hope to be released out of this bondage. But you must be the means thereto, or else I shall have small help. For myself of myself I can do nothing. You put me in comfort. You have devised a way to end this troublesome life I lead and to bring me some quiet in the end of my days, which I fear will not be many if I continue a prisoner. My hope is in you and I refer all to you. My grief is such as I cannot help myself [indistinguishable]. You see all my own kin have forsaken me.

Therefore, if you ever said you would friend me, now is the time to show it. I do not doubt it, but believe to find it. I am sorry and yet glad I have such cause to try my friends. They that stand with me now be sure my firm friends, by which means they bind me in treble bands of friendship to them whilst I live, which of all bondage likes me best to be laden with friends' courtesies of whom I reckon you chief. And, therefore, do most thankfully take your courteous offer and leave myself to your help, praying the Almighty ever to requite that which I am not able and ever to guide and prosper you to your end.

And this with my friendly commendations to my good lady and yourself, I end,

Yours, bound in treble bands of friendship,
E. Bourne

13 [Undated],[1] Amy, Lady Mervyn to Mistress Elizabeth Bourne

(© British Library Board, BL, Add. MS 23212, fol. 195)

To my loving daughter, Elizabeth Bourne.

    I pray God I may have the opportunity to go to London. And then look what I can do with the conditions already alleged, I will do.[2] Master Mervyn goeth to the court out of hand by whom I will wait to make such friends as I can for the favor of your cause. I dare not yet go myself, for that I must needs go to London first and Tomlinson, my man, is dead of the plague in my new house. And lodging in the court, I shall hardly get, and at uncostly use if I had it. But yet I [doubt] not but between Master Mervyn's soliciting and my {…} shall be able to do you some good, though {…} as {…} would or as in right my thinking [100 pounds].

    Master Mervyn [tells] me your husband wrote a very villainous letter to him in which I was partaker, as he sayeth, but would not let me see it. The best is his despite cannot more move me than the vomiting of a drunken man or the raving of a mad man. But the knavery of them that make it their art to keep him in hatred with those that would be his friends moveth me to compassion, seeing how he is wrongst.[3] But that which I cannot amend I mean not to cumber[4] my wits with. Even so, I bid you farewell, wishing you to let one of your men come to Master Mervyn when he cometh to the court to solicit your cause by his direction if need require. He thinketh to be at London by the end of next week. Your man shall hear of him at one Tandy's a shoemaker dwelling hard within the Whitefriars gate. Farewell and God send you your leg well. Your mother,

                                                                     Lady A. Mervyn

---

1 Given Lady Mervyn's reference to the plague in London and her promise to help her daughter find influential friends, we would place this letter sometime in 1582–1583. Mistress Bourne writes to Master Doctor Julius Caesar in 1583. It could be a promise to help with the fines when Anthony is in the Tower, which would place it in the 1578–1579 plague year. We believe that 1582 is more likely.

2 The letter seems to start in the middle, but there is no preceding folio.

3 Wronged.

4 Cumber, *v.* †2. †b. To confound or trouble the mind or senses; to perplex, puzzle. *Obsolete*.

14 8 December [No Year], Mistress Elizabeth Bourne to Amy, Lady Mervyn

(© British Library Board, BL, Add. MS 23212, fol. 180)

To my very good mother, the Lady Mervyn, these, at the[1]
My good mother,

My duty remembered, I am very glad to hear of your good health, which I perceive by my brother Conway's man whom also told me of your motherly good will and willing mind to do me good, but that you said you were not made privy to any of my causes.

Sure, I am that I made you privy to all I know. If it please you to look upon my letters, you may see no less. But if I have by forgetfulness forgotten anything, sure I am you might [have] commanded the knowledge of it if it had pleased you. If I have committed any fault, I crave pardon, and I hope it be pardonable. If it were great, then I am sure it is howsoever it please you to judge of me. Oh, consider my many enemies and few friends and believe not envy which speaks good of nobody. I say this much because I have found you to mislike, but never knew the cause. I desire but your good will. I will never be a burden to you howsoever my evil fortune and want of friends provides for me. I dare not desire you to do anything for me [lest] you should deny me which would be a double grief to me, but if it please you to do anything for me, I know you need no direction but can direct me if it please you, which, if you would do, I were greatly bound to you.

I know not what extremity my Lords of the Council will use to Sir John Conway to make him yield up all to their hands, which if he do, then am I and mine undone. But if you and my father would join with him, I know it would make him stand the better in it.[2] I hear the Queen means to take nothing of Master Bourne, but a fine which Master Vice Chamberlain[3] hath

---

1 Elizabeth Bourne addresses this letter to her mother, on BL, Add. MS 23212, fol. 181v. It is incomplete in its location and written on the back of Lady Mervyn's letter to her daughter (BL, Add. MS 23212, fol. 180v, "To my loving daughter, Elizabeth Bourne").
2 Sir John Conway would benefit in his cause again Anthony Bourne if Sir James Mervyn and Lady Mervyn would join with him.
3 Sir Christopher Hadden was Vice Chamberlain from 1577–1587 and followed by Sir Thomas Heneage, Vice Chancellor from 1587–1595. This letter is very likely written prior to 1583, which would make Hadden the Vice Chamberlain mentioned here.

gotten for him and his liberty, to which shall be shortly. And then I must keep myself close, for he hath threatened me with many deaths, which I hope by God's grace shall never happen to me.

I had seen you before this time if you had not gone so far off and my business such as I could not be long from Sarsden. But by the grace of God, I will see you shortly, till which time, I commit you to the almighty whom I pray long to preserve you.

I pray you thank my Lady Conway for me whom I am greatly bound to and at this time hath written to two of the ladies of the court in my behalf, which is my Lady of Warwick[4] and my Lady Sussex.[5] Pray you do my commendations to my Lady sister,[6] praying God to send her a son and safe deliverance. This praying you for your daily blessings for me and mine. I end from Arrow the 8th of this December your obedient, [indecipherable],

E. Bourne

---

4 Anne Dudley (née Russell), Countess of Warwick.
5 Frances Radcliffe.
6 Lady Lucia Audley.

15 3 July 1582, Amy, Lady Mervyn to Sir Francis Walsingham
(NA, SP 12/154, fol. 85)

To the Right Honorable Sir Francis Walsingham, Principal Secretary to her Majesty, these.
Sir,
 I understand my daughter Bourne hath written unto you with a supplication to my Lords of the Council. Showing, as I suppose, her unwilling mind to be reconciled to her husband, choosing, rather to sequester herself from all her friends, living a fugitive in continual fear, than to commit herself to your honorable protection, or to follow any advice of those that cannot (without making shipwreck of nature, conscience, and credit) but tender her well doing as their own.[1]
 Nay, would to God she should live but in fear and not rather in assurance that at one time or other (her husband finding her unreconcilable hatred) she should taste of his fury, for rejecting so uncharitably his courtesies. What law can she have against him if he shall either enter upon her lands or can come by[2] either her person or any of her goods. And how can she seek for redress by power of those, to whom now she refuseth to commit her cause? And what will he care for the breech of his bond, that hath nothing to lose. Again, who shall call accompt of her good, of such goods as she in the minorities of her wit, and by the majorities of his craft, hath delivered into his hands? The poor woman being (as he hopeth) made by the drift[3] of his coming, destitute of any to complain unto, specially having now brought to pass that she is not to tarry in this land. But for her better security, is resolved to sell or (as her own letter specifieth) hath already sold all that she hath that she may (not having anything to lose) go over at her pleasure. This

---

1 Lady Mervyn complains that Elizabeth Bourne refused to return to her husband, probably at the urging of and under the protection of, the Privy Council.
2 By, *prep.* and *adv.* ** *Of motion into a position beside, or within, reach.* 15. Near to, close up, into the presence of: chiefly in to come by, for the phraseological and figurative uses of which see come *v.* a. To move or travel towards a place, person, or thing; to approach.
3 Drift, 4. b. Meaning, purport, tenor, scope (of a speech or writing). Now the usual sense. [Also] †5. A scheme, plot, design, device. *Obsolete*.

very practice, by this very same person,[4] was made upon her husband, who left behind him at his departure over sea (wholly at the direction of Sir John Conway) 8000 pounds, to the use of himself and my daughter, whereof neither of them at this day (as I am credibly informed) can show the value of one hundred, neither could the poor gentleman get forth of prison, till he had entered bonds to discharge him of all accompt, then I beseech you consider what better dealing than after this rate can be expected for my daughter, unless your honorable compassions and authority prevent him, which beseeching God to move in you and reward [you]. I leave your further trouble. Your Honor's poorest but thankful friend,

[illegible] Mervyn

---

4 Unknown.

16 [Undated], Mistress Elizabeth Bourne to Sir John Conway

(© British Library Board, BL, Add. MS 23212, fols. 86–87)

To my very good brother, Sir John Conway, Knight, these.
My good brother,

Master Bourne hath marked his time 'till everybody was gone, and the same day that you went from house, he came to Gostwick's.

The next morning, he sent Mistress Gostwick with a letter to me which was to desire my accepting of him and to suffer him to come see me and my daughter, and to have speech with me. The answer whereof I delivered to Mistress Gostwick in these words, that he should pardon me for writing for that I wanted wit to set down my mind so plainly as that his friends and he shall not scan it other ways than I mean it. I prayed him to forbear coming to me, for I would not have any speech nor dealing with him, but with the advice of my friends. Withal, I prayed her to deliver him so hard speeches which he had given me heretofore, which I did so well remember as I could not assure myself of any safety nor good will at his hand.

He said that his was enough to wander five years in forty. I told her that his was great reason that I should see five years of his amendment before I accepted of him and whereas had lived an evil life to live. To live in good company and honest, and whereas he had lived to consume all. He should frame himself to live off that he had and pay all his debts and provide for all his bastards, which were six at the least. So as he had lived this five years to slander me and discredit me, he should now pronounce to the world he had wronged me—and defend my credit to anybody that would speak evil of me.[1] Then should I think he loved me. Then would I seek him as he should not need to seek me. All this Mistress Gostwick delivered him from me. Which set him in some heat that he wrote me another letter, which I refused to read, but sent it him again. Yet I did read it, but it is too long to tell you. But some of the chiefest points I will show you, which was he willed me not to refuse his offered good will. He willeth me not to care for my friends advice. Yet he sayeth he will not refuse to deal with any two friends of [mine] save with Sir John Conway for he will not suffer us to come together

---

1 "speak evil of me" replaces "wrong me," which is crossed out.

this year. In the end of his letter, he sayeth[2] that he will have me whether I will or no. He offereth to be put in sufficient bond to use me well and that he will not spoil me nor my children—but Mistress, sayeth he, this is not it that pincheth you—you are afraid lest you shall be spoiled of your wealth or your liberty. This he ends. Now I hear he hath sent his man this day out with a great sort of letters to Sir Edward Unton and my Lord Compton and divers others I know not what he will do. I fear the worst. Therefore, I mean this day to go privately to my Uncle Bustard[3] and lie there 'till I hear from you.

I have sent my Lady Conway[4] my letter to give her warning of Master B. I thank her. She hath sent me word she would do anything for me and I might assure myself of her friendship. I think it needful that Hawkins were here to keep the house for sure he hath some letter or process from my Lord Chancellor to the Justice for the delivery of me and the possession of the house. Therefore, I would [that] here were somebody that could tell what to do. I pray you ask. Advise what were best for me to do and what he can do against me. And send me word. And if there be no other means for me, I will be gone then, as he shall not find me. For sure I will not be compelled to live with him before I see another [way].

Thus, my good brother, I see that he meaneth my utter spoil and he is not worth a grot. Therefore, I will give all that I have to my friends rather than my own goods should be my undoing. This I leave and live in great care of mind 'till I hear from you, for I know not what best to do. This with my hearty commendations to you and my son Conway. I commit you [to] God whom I pray to preserve us all and send you good end of your causes. From Sarsden, this Saturday.

Your unfortunate sister, but everlasting friend
E. Bourne

---

2 "he sayeth" appears twice in succession in the manuscript. One has been omitted for clarity.
3 Anthony Bustard.
4 Eleanor Conway.

17 1 February [No Year], Mistress Elizabeth Bourne to Sir John Conway

(© British Library Board, BL, Add. MS 23212, fols. 106–107)

To the right worshipful my very good brother and friend, Sir John Conway, these.

My good brother,

    I am sorry that you had not the books you need with you and more sorry that I had them not here for you. But am fain to trust my man to fetch them at Luddington. I pray God all be well. I would be loath to be brought to such extremity again. Sure I am if I had thought you should have needed them, I would have brought them hither, but now I must be contented with that it may happen. For Master Chamberleyn's great shows of courtesies, I know you be too wise to believe. You may use him in sort as you best can to serveth our turn. For I have heard of a neighbor of ours here that Master Chamberleyn and Master Clarke do th[ink] they may by all the devises and means that they can against you and me. And tell Master Chamberleyn that I will never thank him for his 100 pound fine, but do desire him to say the worst he can. I would to God I had been by to have answered him. Sure I am he would have looked very blank. But God help me, poor soul, who hath all the devises and inventions in the world against her. I appeal to God whom will confound them in all their devises and try me clear. For I am sure that there was never gold so soundly tried in the fire as I shall be with their wicked devises.

    Commend me to my cousin Hobby and his wife,[1] and tell them that if they make not the better haste home, their possession at Sarsden will be taken from them. For there wast three men of Master Bourne's yesterday to take possession, or to do some other knave[ry].

    I have sent to my cousin Peniston to send precepts[2] for them both to Sarsden and Churchill and Chipping Norton. And to bind them to their good behavior. Also I have sent to Sarsden to the tenants to watch and ward the house. But I would there were some sufficienter body in the house than

---

1   Richard and Elizabeth Hobby.
2   Precept, *n.* 1. a. 1325. A general command or injunction; a rule for action or conduct, *esp.* a rule for moral conduct, a maxim; *spec.* a divine command.

there is. Therefore, I pray you so soon as you may send some of them down to look to the house. For I fear greatly their knavish practices. I have sent you both the books. I pray you make some end, one way or other, that I may be in some quiet of mind. I wish myself with you and your good company every day. This with my hardy commendations to yourself and my cousin Greene[3] and my cousin Bustard,[4] desiring you all to Sarsden thence. Then I am here from Adderbury[5] the 1 of February.

Your sister and friend,
E. Bourne.

I pray you tell my cousin Greene that her little daughter is very well.[6]

---

3 Anne Greene.
4 Likely, William Bustard.
5 The seat of the Bustard family.
6 This last note from Elizabeth is on the address. There is a note on this address folio made by John Conway which is largely indecipherable.

18 [Undated], Mistress Elizabeth Bourne to Sir John Conway

(© British Library Board, BL, Add. MS 23212, fol. 118)

To my very good brother, Sir John Conway, Knight, these.
My good brother,

According to my simple skill, I have set down my petition to her Majesty,[1] which I have sent you to amend. For I can do it no better, and I think it far from that it should be. I therefore pray you to correct it and send it me. And I will write it [new] that it may be sent to London. For I would fain have it delivered in hope that it will do me [indecipherable] to restore the dispersed creatures together. {...} now live in misery, all discontented and made {...} comfort. I would gladly hear how you do, and the two little ones, and of the messenger's return. This with my hardy commendations and daily prayers to send but some liberty to our comfort, I end.

Yours to her utter most,
E. Bourne

I cannot tell who I shall have to deliver my {...}

---

1 It is unclear what document Mistress Bourne references here. It could be her petition to the Privy Council (BL, Add. MS 38170, fols. 151–158) or her attempt to negotiate a payment plan for the debt to the crown from when Anthony left the realm without permission (BL, Add. MS 23212, fol. 187). Either way, this letter is likely written in the early 1580s.

19 [Undated],[1] Mistress Elizabeth Bourne to Sir John Conway

(© British Library Board, BL, Add. MS 23212, fol. 123)

My very good brother Sir John Conway, Knight.

    I joy not a little of your short return home. It something contents me that you find some [sure] friends although I lost all. It cannot but grieve me greatly to see all my friends thus to deal with me that they cannot be contented to refuse me. But they seek my discredit and take my enemy's part against me, wherein I taste of fortune's bitter spite more than anybody ever did.

    But my hope is you will not forsake me, but help me with your good advice and help, for I mean not to come into my enemy's sweet baits, if I may possibly escape them. You know my mind long before. I am ever the same woman I ever was and not to be removed either with flattery or extremities. It is not this course they take that can persuade me of any good will in Master Bourne nor naturalness in them to me. If I should complain all my griefs to you a whole Bible would not hold them, and yet I little eased and you greatly troubled.

    I am so greatly troubled to see my great extremities and misery, that I know not what to say nor how to help myself but fly to you. If you now forsake me, then I am well. I hope better but my evil fortune fears me with her cruel threats to bring upon me all the worst she can.[2] Master Francis tells me I must not see you. Or else I should greatly desire to speak with you. This misery I live in will have no end 'till death finish it.

    Therefore, since I must needs sequestered from my friends and my children and my living, I had rather be farther off then within an inch and want the comfort of them. Therefore, if you will release yourself of trouble and me of continual grief, take order for my living and help me

---

1 Likely c. 1585. The contents of the letter seem to refer to the dispute over Mary Bourne that Elizabeth had with Lady Conway.
2 Likely Eleanor, Lady Conway whose complaints to the Privy Council about Elizabeth Bourne's complaints in regard to the keeping of Mary Bourne brought everyone back to court.

over so that I may live there till I may have more liberty to have comfort of that I have. This leaving myself to your will, I end with my hardy commendations.

Yours ever,
E.B.

20 18 August 1582, Elizabeth Bourne to Master Julius Caesar

(© British Library Board, BL, Add. MS 12507, fols. 204–205)

To the worshipful Master Doctor Caesar[1] at his house in Paternoster Row or at Master Alderman Martin's in Milk Street, give these in diligence. Master Doctor Caesar,

I do hear so well of your sufficient learning, wisdom, and good dealing with all your clients, that I am greatly encouraged to desire your assistance before any man's. My case is this: Master Anthony Bourne, my husband, did about five years past, take away Master Pagnam's wife, refused my company, and ever since he hath lived with her. He hath by her three or four children living and still keepeth her and her bastards in his charge.

Having now wasted all his own substance and living, and 300 pounds a year of my ancient inheritance by his loose life, seeketh to call me before my Lords of her Majesty's Council to enjoin me to accept of him.

Not for any love or of good mind to amend his ill life, but because he would have that little living which I have left to help him to maintain his woman and her bastards. And that being spent, to cast me off again. If he do not shorten my life otherwise.

I can prove that he hath sworn my death and destruction, to blow up my house, me, and my children, with gunpowder. If that should fail, he would seek the world about to get one for 500 crowns to give me a fig of Italy.[2]

In performance of this, he hath sent one of purpose out of France, a person detected of [a] felony that hath been burnt in the hand,[3] armed, and furnished with dags[4] that hath come secret to the next town to my house, lay there a fortnight, hath never been seen in the day out of his chamber. In the night, he hath sent and allured my servants to come and banquet with him. He hath enquired of them how many persons were in my house, how many

---

1 Julius Caesar received his DCL from Oxford in 1584.
2 Fig, *n*. 1 †2. A poisoned fig used as a secret way of destroying an obnoxious person. Often fig of Spain, Spanish fig, Italian fig. *Obsolete*.
3 Burn, *n*. 3. 2. a. A mark made by burning, a brand. Convicted criminals were branded. [See also *The Roaring Girl*, Thomas Middleton and Thomas Dekker, where Sir Alexander asks Trapdoor to "Hold thy hand up? What's this? Is't burnt?" (1.2. 208–2099)].
4 Dag, *n*. 2. *Obsolete*. A kind of heavy pistol or handgun formerly in use.

did lie within my gates and how many without? Who was then present at my house and who used to repair at what times? In what chamber I did lie myself, and whether I did not use sometimes to walk abroad to take the air?

Whatsoever the charge of the banquets ran to, he always paid it. He showed them he had 40 pounds in his purse. And said he had a thing to do before he departed the country, and if that were done, he shall have twice as much more.

These like words following Master Bourne's great oaths, and agreeable with his malice towards me because my life is a great hindrance to his liberty, puts me in such fear as I dare not adventure to live with him.

He did protest and swear before Sir Francis Walsingham, his honor, that he would never leave Mistress Pagnam, that he loved her bastards better at the heal than he did me and his lawful children at the hearts, that he would live only to profit them all he could and to plague me and mine.

He did swear before his honor, likewise, to make his own faults seem the least, that my youngest daughter was none of his.

He still continueth the same speech to everybody. And yet desireth to live with me again.

It cannot be that a man can ill say and believe of a wife and desire to live with her for her comfort and his credit. This point, added to the rest, wrongeth and despaireth me so much as that for my better safety and quiet life, I desire to be by the course of the laws divorced from him.

About four years past, I did retain counsel and did serve him with process. And he would not appear and answer it.

My man is departed from me that followed the cause, so as I cannot tell you who was then retained for me. But as the cause shall seem you good, so if please you to make the search and to make your proceeding upon that beginning or otherwise as shall like you to my best advantage, I shall thank you and will defray all the charges growing there by upon your bills of accompt.[5]

By this bearer, I have sent you five pounds to retain such as you think meet, to assist you and to frame the beginning of the cause so as I may have process to serve him so soon as you can, that no time be lost. I pray you begin and proceed so soundly that he may be without advantage to reverse or stay the cause. The truth of my wrongs and the faults be so apparent to the world as that I hope you shall not find it difficult. And I am made so assured of your good assistance and care that you will take my cause that it strengtheneth me greatly to bear the heavy passions of my unquiet mind. Assure yourself, Sir, that what pains friendship or charge you shall undertake to bring this good effect whereby I may live in quiet and be free from his violence, I will requite whole that you shall justly say you have dealt for

---

5 Account, *n.* II. 2. a. A financial record or statement; accounting. Accompt, from Anglo-Norman and Middle French, *obsolete*.

a thankful woman. You shall from time to time hear from me in such sort as you shall never want money to proceed in the cause.

I pray you, good Master Doctor Caesar, have a care of me and compassion of my wrongs. I will have due consideration of you, both by myself and my friends.

If there be cause for you to have any farther instruction or special notes to grow the cause and the beginning upon, if you send me your will in writing by this messenger, I will satisfy you in all I can.

By search, you shall find Mistress Pagnam's divorce upon Master Bourne's fault with her, and so you shall find who was heretofore retained for me, and out of what court the process came, and what was done or may be done upon the same.

I desire to know by this bearer when I shall have process to serve Master Bourne, that someone may attend you for the same. Withal, my earnest desire is that you will by course of law sequester my body into the safe-keeping of Master Edward Conway, son and heir apparent of Sir John Conway, who is to marry with my eldest daughter, until the action be tried and ended between Master Bourne and me.

Now I am driven to conceal my life and to absent myself from the council's letters through fear of Master Bourne's violence and lest he should take me in to his possession against my will. I pray you send me word by your letters by what time you can and will get this sequestration for my safety. In the meantime, I will relieve myself with hope and send to you for the same when you shall appoint me.

This committing my careful cause to your friendly consideration, I commend your health and happiness, proceeding in all things to God. And I bind myself by this writing of my hand to pray for and to requite you by all the good means I can.

This 18th of August 1582.
Unfortunate and unknown to you,
but she that desireth to be bound to you,
Elizabeth Bourne

21 [Undated],[1] Wrongs Committed by Anthony Bourne

(© British Library Board, BL, Add. MS 23212, fols. 7–8)

Articles of Mistress Bourne's reasons.[2]

The injuries, wrongs, and misdemeanors of
Anthony Bourne since the death of his
father, Sir John Bourne, Knight[3]

Imprimis: immediately after the decease of his said father, his mother (the good Lady Bourne)[4] being very sick and like to die, [Master Bourne] came with 11 or 12 men with weapons drawn (in rage), with great threatening words and abominable oaths (in his mother's chamber, his father long under the ground) to kill his mother and the rest if they would not avoid the house, and afterward, being gone out of the chamber, the doors being made fast (by the commandment of his mother) for fear of her life. Who [Master Bourne] seeing the said doors made fast, he went on the outside of the windows, beating and breaking down those windows (like a furious bedlam)[5] minding to have come in again upon her.

2. Item: incontinent[6] after, the said Anthony did beat one of his mother's men that was her slaughter man, whereof he never recovered but died, and a little before the fellow's death, he compounded[7] with him.

---

1 Many of these "articles" are described by Mistress Bourne in her petition to the Privy Council (BL, Add. MS 38170, fols. 151–158, 6 December 1582). The date of this document must be within a similar time frame.
2 A note made by Sir John Conway on fol. 8.
3 Sir John Bourne died in 1575.
4 Dorothy Bourne.
5 Bedlam, *n.* †5. An inmate of Bethlehem Hospital, London, or of a lunatic asylum, or one fit for such a place, a madman; *spec.* one of the discharged, but often only half-cured, patients of the former, who were licensed to beg, wearing as a badge a tin plate on their left hand or arm. Also called *Bedlam-beggar* (*Bedlam beggar* at Compounds), *bedlamer* (bedlamer *n.*[1]), *bedlamite* (bedlamite *n.*). *Obsolete.*
6 Incontinent, *adv. arch.* Straightway, forthwith, at once, immediately, without delay.
7 Compound, *v.* II. To compose differences, settle claims. 15. b. To accept terms of settlement in lieu of prosecution: hence the Committee for Compounding with Delinquents (i.e. Royalists) under the Commonwealth.

3. Item: the same Anthony, being at Oxford about two years past, and there he, with one Thomas Powell, who being arrested for the peace by the officers there, the said Anthony did rescue the said T[homas]. P[owell]. Commanding all his men, being about the number of 20 or more to draw their weapons, in which assault the Mayor and the whole town rose against him and drove the said A[nthony] and all his to take house, where he stood swearing, threatening, and railing at the Mayor and the whole town, calling them villains, rascals, knaves, cuckolds: saying also there was neither honest man, woman, nor maid in all the whole town.

4. Item: the said A[nthony] within short span after this, he and his men met with an honest townsman (a capper[8] of Worcester) and fell upon him, beat him, threw him down into a mire[9] puddle and drew him up and down for no cause given by the poor man, and there left him at the point of death.

5. Item: the said A[nthony] falling out with one William Freer of Oxford, Gentleman, after the misdemeanors done at Oxford, coming home to his own house provoked his men every day to kill the said Master Freer, saying with these words, "God's wounds, God's blood, have I never a knave, never a slave that will take a gun or a dag[10] and kill the villain and dispatch him?"

6. Item: the said A[nthony] after his going beyond the sea,[11] returning back into England again, his wife hearing thereof, went to London to meet with him, thinking to have sued to her Majesty and to the [Privy] Council for him when he seeing her there, was very impertinent with her, that she should give Mistress Pagnam there moiety of her living to her maintenance. His wife, denying this unreasonable request, fell out with her, railing, staring, and swearing, calling her whore and all that naught is, and saying further, that he would (with an abominable oath) pull down her pride. He would make her before he left her, to be glad to wear a frieze gown,[12] and before that she[13] should lack he would tear his wife's skin off her back, with his dagger also drawn all this while in his hand like a cruel tyrant. At which time, diverse gentlemen of worship being present, persuading him to forsake and leave his evil life, who [Anthony] answered them again, that it was not five hundred whores would serve him when so ever he did leave her.

---

8   Capper, *n.* 1. A capmaker. *Obsolete.*
9   Miry, *adj.* 2. a. Full of mud or mire; muddy.
10 Dag, *n.* 2. *Obsolete.* A kind of heavy pistol or handgun formerly in use.
11 Anthony Bourne first flees the realm without a warrant c. 18 March 1577. Our last record of his whereabouts makes him a fugitive in May 1595.
12 Frieze, *n.* A kind of coarse woolen cloth, with a nap, usually on one side only.
13 Mistress Pagnam.

7. Item: how at the Greyfriars in London the same time he did protest with great oaths to Sir John Conway and Sir James Mervyn that he hated his wife deadly and that he neither could or ever would find in his heart to live or dwell with her. He said, further, that for the value of 500 crowns he could get some knave to give her a fig[14] to be rid of her. He also to his wife, protesting with great oaths and also hath by his letters since confirmed it, that he would abate her pride, and where her glory is altogether in her house, that he would over blow it with gunpowder and so blow up both her and it. Since which time there hath been great suppositions that there hath wanted but fit opportunity to have these matters accomplished.

8. Item: one Raffe Arrasmythe, his man coming from Calais,[15] from his master [Anthony] unto Chipping Norton with two cases of pistols sent to Sarsden for diverse of his fellows dwelling with his mistress [Elizabeth Bourne] to make merry with him, and when the shot should be paid, every man offering to pay a part, "nay, God's wounds," quoth he, clapping his hands upon his purse, paying with terrible oaths, here is money enough for us all. And also saying unto them, "if I may bring to one feat that I have to do, before I go out of the country, I shall have a hundred marks for my labors, inquiring in what chamber his mistress [Elizabeth Bourne] lay in, and what company lay in the house, and when without."

9. Item: since his coming to the Tower,[16] he doth nothing but rail at his wife, her kindred, and friends that doth anything for her, calling them knaves and whores, threatening to beat them and to kill them. As he threatened to kill Sir John Conway, he cared not how, if it were pissing against a wall.

10. Item: he procured his men to rob pigeon houses and to take them in the fields with nets, the owners finding fault herewith, he swore most detestably to his men "God's wounds, can ye not shoot at the knaves that do find fault?"

[11.] Item: when he would have his wife to sell any land, he would use her divers and often time with threatening words to make his wife sell her land.

---

14 Fig, *n*.1. *Obsolete*. A poisoned fig used as a secret way of destroying an obnoxious person.
15 In BL, Add. 38170, Elizabeth Bourne describes this man as being "burnt in the hand," a mark associated with convicted criminals.
16 Tower of London. The Acts of the Privy Council places Anthony in the Tower in 1578, with a release on bail in May of 1579.

22 6 December 1582, [Mistress Bourne's Petition to the Privy Council]

(© British Library Board, BL, Add. MS 38170, fols. 151–158)

6 December 1582

    Master Bourne, about 16 years past, immediately after we were married, began by some foreign liking of other women to withdraw his chaste love from me.[1]

    My hope of his amendment, when time should teach him the difference between vice and virtue (considering then his young years) made me bury my secret sorrows a long time in silence. But time wrought contrary to my hope. Instead of my wished good and his amendment, I have found nothing but the continual increase of his ill, to a due confirmation of my despair of better.

    Most unkindly, he hath refused to live with me these six years, in breach of his holy vow of chaste matrimony, and hath lived, and still continueth in open sin and shame with harlots, to the ruin and spoil of himself, me, and my children.

    So heavy be these griefs and so unfit a thing it is for a wife publicly to complain against her husband, that, if unwillingly by his own want of God's grace and good consideration I were not compelled, I would rather commit his sins, with my sorrows, to the silence of my grave than to the view and judgement of any living creature.

    But since it becomes me, in satisfying of my betters and the world, to avoid the imputation of an unreasonable creature in myself, and to prove by truth that my husband seeketh to abuse his friends and to spoil me by a false title of a reformed life, I have here underwritten the beginning, proceeding, and continuance of his incontinent life, his slanderous reports, wicked practices, terrors, and tyrannous speeches against me, my friends, kin, and allies, and the reasons growing from the same, which counsel me not to consent to live with him who is so constant in sin, and so imperfect in virtue.

---

1 Elizabeth Horne and Anthony Bourne were married on 27 September 1565 in Holt, Worcester.

74 *Letters and Documents*

Immediately after we were married, he left my company and lived in the liberty of his ranging[2] affections with diverse women.

When I uttered my grief of mind therein unto him, as the general report of his repair[3] to many women and his continual absence from home gave me cause, he said it was all untrue. His absence from me was not for any dislike in me, nor his repair to the company of other women for any unlawful love, but for that his father and he could never agree.

Whatsoever I did know, I accepted of his denial through hope and my patient sufferance to call home his love. Because he alleged that his disagreement with his father bred the cause of his absence from me, I so entreated and obtained that both we and our small number sojourned with my mother.

There he continued for a time in good usage of me, to my great comfort. But the sequel in short time made proof that his continuance with me and increase of love and liking was but dissembled of purpose and policy to win my consent to the sale of a good part of mine inheritance, which should be as he gave the reasons and his promises to my mother and my friends, for the relief of us both during his father's life, and promised that after he would recompense me with as much again.

I agreed to his desire and enjoined with him in the sale of my land. Upon the present receipt of the money, he left me alone as before and continued in London by the space of half a year and spent £500 in vain love with a gentlewoman. Whom I mean and who she was, he knows. I now conceal her name of better consideration than I have cause.

My mother, perceiving him in the way and will to consume all, challenged his promise that she might be privy how he meant to employ the money for our relief which he had received for my lands, but he would not. Whereupon, she, charging him with his loose life and the wrong that he did me, he answered her in these words: that I had nothing in me to content him, that I was unhandsome, a fool, and not the woman that he could love. Yet, for her sake he would use me well.

In these terms, he departed thence and I with him, unto a little lodge of mine inheritance[4] where we kept house by the space of half a year, in which time he allured one, a serving woman of mine, to be naught[5] with him, besides many other by his own report and common speech, which he had abroad.

2 Ranging, *v.*1 I. 4. *intransitive*. To change from one (esp. romantic) attachment to another; to change affections, to be inconstant. *Obsolete*.
3 Repair *v.*1 3. a. *intransitive*. To go habitually or frequently to a place or (occasionally) a person. OR 4. *intransitive*. To resort; to have recourse to a person or thing for aid, guidance, etc. *Now arch*.
4 We are unsure which property she means, but most likely it is Sarsden.
5 Naught *adj*. 2. to be naught with: to have illicit sexual relations with, to commit adultery with. *Obsolete*.

When I was assured of all the ill between him and my maid in his absence from home, I put her away. Wherewith at his return, he was so enraged that unless I would send for her again and suffer her in my house, he swore by great oaths that he would put me away.[6]

Being thus delivered of her, he presently brought me home a common harlot as any in bridewell,[7] one Anne Vaughan, a woman most famous for her ill life, whom out of beggars robes and a bawdy house he decked in brave apparel, to the pleasing of both their fancies, and so kept her in house with me. And notwithstanding he knew she had the French pox[8] yet he lay with her at his pleasure. Of their ills he used no secret, nor she any silence. If it were not sufficiently seen, they both would tell it liberally.

In fear of her loathsome disease and that harm which might come to me from her by Master Bourne, as no creature did live in more fear, sorrow, and danger than I did when I was once assured of their ills and loathsome disease, I would not suffer her in house with me. He then sent her to his man Sale's house by the city of Worcester. There and at Worcester he kept her at his charge so long till she was not able to be removed but in a cart, the pox had so consumed her. He hath said himself that he hath taken the unlawful use of her body in that loathsome state, of purpose to infect me, that he might be rid of me. And he did swear with great oaths upon her going out of my house that I should never have a woman serve me whilst he lived but he would lie with her, or it should cost him £500.

After this he haunted[9] and had one Bess Wood, a common harlot in London and Oxford. But she soon left him in better liking of others.

Then he fell into his open sin and shame with Mistress Pagnam and took her from her husband, as the world can witness, and brought her to a house of mine own.[10] When I would not be persuaded to endure that, neither to suffer her in house with me, he offering me his good will and my liberty to

---

6 Put, *v.* To put away. 2. c. *transitive*. To dismiss or get rid of (a person, occasionally also an animal); to send away from one's presence; to exclude; (frequently) *spec.* to divorce. Now somewhat *archaic*.
7 Bridewell, *n.* Now chiefly *historical*. A prison, a jail; *esp.* a house of correction in which inmates are put to work. Also *figurative*.
8 French pox, *n.* now *historical* = syphilis *n.* 1; cf. morbus gallicus n. and Spanish pox *n.* at Spanish *adj.*, *n.*1, and adv. Compounds 3. Pox, *n.* I. Senses relating to diseases characterized by pocks. 1. a. Any of several infectious diseases characterized by a rash of pustules (pocks), esp. smallpox, cowpox, and chickenpox. See also chickenpox n., cow-pox *n.*, smallpox *n.* b. Syphilis. Frequently with distinguishing word, as French, great pox, etc.: see the first element.
9 Haunt, *v.* 4. To frequent the company of (a person) to associate with habitually; to "run after."
10 7 May 1577, the Privy Council sends several letters to sheriffs in Oxon, Warwick, Worcester, and Gloucester regarding Anthony Bourne who has "very wickedly intysed away the wife of one Robert Pakingham, gentelman" (Calendar of State Papers Foreign: Elizabeth, Volume 11, 1575–1577).

76 *Letters and Documents*

live in as loose order with any man as he did with her, he resolved me and many his good friends that he would never live with me, nor use me as his wife. He bid me therewith satisfy myself, or else I should, whether I would or not. He said to me and them that Mistress Pagnam had for him refused her husband, her natural children[11] and all the world, and he would do for her as much. And thus unkindly departed from me and fled into France with her.[12]

Since, he hath led his sinful life with her now six years to the ruin and spoil of himself, me, and my children. And still she liveth and her bastards on his charge and at his devotion.

And to prove that, he hath in this time aggravated his sin and shame with many others and abateth not, but continueth in the same. I am truly to charge him with these dissolute parts of life, besides his disorder with Mistress Pagnam.

Whilst he was a prisoner in the Tower of London,[13] he had a child by a nurse of Mistress Pagnam.

Item: he hath had one other child in that time that he was prisoner in the Tower by another woman, who was brought to bed of the same, and the child nursed at Newington: one of Master Lieutenant's[14] men was bound that the parish, after the woman's delivery, should be discharged of the mother and child. This bastard remaineth in his[15] charge with the rest.

By this you may see what he profited by imprisonment, towards the reformation of his precedent ills. In that time he had also one bastard by Mistress Pagnam.

Presently, upon his delivery out of the Tower, he allured one Bess, a woman servant of Mistress Blount's, who keepeth the ordinary table,[16] to be naught with him. He and she both confessed their sins, without shame, to many. In short time, she was conveyed thence, and it was thought by Master Bourne.

He did steal away a young wench from one Winnington's in Smithfield, kept her, and payed for her diet in Westminster near half a year, left her

---

11 Natural, *adj.* and *adv.* II. Relating to birth or family; native. 14. †a. Of a person: having a status (esp. of allegiance or authority) by birth; natural-born. Cf. natural subject n. at Compounds. 2. *Obsolete* (historical in later use). b. Of the transfer of a privilege, property, etc.: according to right of heredity. Hence of property, a privilege, etc. (later also a trait): hereditary; possessed by right of birth.
12 Anthony Bourne flees the realm without a warrant c. 18 March 1577.
13 According to the Acts of the Privy Council, Anthony Bourne was in the tower in 1578 and released on bail in May of 1579. Anthony writes to William Cecil, Lord Burghley from the Tower on 28 January 1577/8 (HH, CP 160/117, fol. 186).
14 Likely, Sir Owen Hopton, Lieutenant of the Tower of London from 1570–1590.
15 Anthony Bourne's.
16 Ordinary table, *n.* C.1 (compounds) b. *Obsolete* the table at which an ordinary was served and which was afterwards cleared for gambling; (hence) a gambling-table or gambling-house.

with child, and after she should be delivered, to be sent to him in Ireland to wait upon Mistress Pagnam.

Besides these, since he was delivered out of the Tower, he became in love with one Waste's wife in London, and ran himself into great loss of time and charge to persuade her to leave her husband and to go with him, which, as himself confessed, he brought to pass that she consented to go with him. In this he made his folly so apparent to the world that a merchant of great wealth and good credit told him in open street that Mistress Waste had wasted both his wit and wealth. All this is most true. I myself did see a letter of his own handwritten to a gentleman, a companion of his, from the sea coast, wherein he did challenge him of great discourtesy for alluring her away from him, and in which letter he did greatly threaten to be quittance[17] with him. And so I have heard he was after his return.

Since his return out of Ireland and desire to live with me, he hath kept one Jane Wilson in the Whitefriars, until she warmed him so hot (as it is said) that he was glad to seek water to quench the fire. With some consideration, he became weary of her. Since, he took away one Margaret from Mistress Mask's, who keepeth the Lord Clinton's house in Canon Rowe. After he had kept her a little while, he sent her in the latter part of the last summer to Mistress Pagnam into Wales. But by the way (as it is said) she is proved with child, and upon this chance and challenge, Mistress Pagnam hath left Wales and is retired to Westminster because she may be more near at hand to prevent such wrongs.

About Bartholmewtide[18] last, he had another maid of Mistress Mask's, some call her Welch[19] Anne, some Canam, some Master Bourne's standard bearer. He placed her first at Lambeth, and now she remaineth in Westminster. The woman herself confesseth that she hath been naught with him and boasteth that she hath had three pounds money of Master Bourne at a time to pay for her diet.

Himself hath confessed to many that he hath been naught with one knight's wife in Westminster. At the first, he promised her more to lie [with] than he had to give her. And then she cozened him (as he hath told diverse) of a case of dags[20] and other necessary furnitures, which is spoken of being true, to his great reproof, shame, and folly. Now he useth her in another kind. He maketh her his purveyor and receiver. He taketh the pleasure of her house with Mistress Pagnam, and others daily.

---

17 Quittance, *v.* 3. *transitive*. To give up, cancel, renounce; = quit *v.* 10. *rare*.
18 A festival in honor of Bartholomew, one of the 12 apostles, celebrated on 24 August.
19 Old form of Welsh, *adj.* and *n.*
20 Dag, *n.* 2. *Obsolete*. A kind of heavy pistol or handgun formerly in use.

78   *Letters and Documents*

Since midsummer[21] last, he hath had his part by consent in common with his companions and copartners of one Jane Jackson, besides many others I could particularly name. But these are too many for me to hope that ever he will be reformed. He began so young and hath continued so many years. I note this withal, which increaseth my grief, he taketh no profit of time; experience teacheth him not to be wise. One harm maketh him not to avoid another. In sin he continueth and is not ashamed. Since he hath been dismissed out of the Tower of London, he hath spent his time, being years in passing and repassing Mistress Pagnam from place to place, from England into Ireland and back again. Since his and her return, he hath kept house with her in London, Westminster, Shoreditch, Lambeth, etc. About the first spring of this last year he did ride with her in progress into Worcestershire and Wales. Here he left her behind him, returned to London and to the Court: a man disburdened (as he said to his friends) of his woman and her bastards, reformed in his loose life and desirous to live in good sort with me. All this being a mere device and policy to abuse my Lords of the Council,[22] his friends, and mine, and tending only to the spoil of me and my children. What likelihood is there for the world or myself to believe otherwise? She hath ever since lived at his charge in Wales, and hath been with her there since he sought order of my Lords of the Council to have me restored unto him. And now either he hath removed her nearer him to London again, or else she of her good will hath removed herself to him, in hope to find the supply of many courtesies that she wanted being so far off. So as together I leave them in folly so fast knit as no discretion can divide them, until death dissolve the one or both. For Master Bourne believeth her bastards to be his own pretty sweet children. And this false persuasion of the devil to continue him his servant withholds my help and kills my hope. So in despair of their amendment, whom God hath so long forsaken, I learn to speak farther of their sinful lusts. Now I come to as great, or greater wrongs which he hath done me in harder degrees.

> His terrors and tyrannous speeches, which have made me these many years despair of my life and consume my poor estate greatly to procure my safety against his threatened mischiefs.

Upon diverse good causes and considerations, he infeoffed[23] my friends in lands, goods, and debts, to the recompense and advancement of me and my children.

---

21 Midsummer, *n.* a. The middle of summer; *spec.* (a) Midsummer Day (24 June); (b) the day of the summer solstice (21 or 22 June), or the period around this. Also *fig.*
22 Queen Elizabeth's Privy Council.
23 Enfeoff, *v.* 1.a *transitive*. To invest with a fief; to put (a person) in possession of the fee-simple or fee-tail of lands, tenements, etc. Also *absol.* Const. *in*, *of*, †*on*, later *with*; also *simply*. 2. To hand over as a fief; to surrender, give up entirely. *Figurative.*

Within one quarter of a year next following, through the inconstancy of his mind and his perseverance in ill, he repented the benefit, which he had done us, fled beyond the seas without her Majesty's license of purpose and policy to do all that in him was to make question and forfeiture of the whole.[24] And letted not[25] as one careless of his conscience and soul's health, in malice of me, to give his oath in evidence against the truth and his own deed, to the overthrow of himself, and to the harm of me and my children.

He required of me toward the maintenance of Mistress Pagnam the one half of that portion which he had allotted and, as I thought, assured to me and my children for our relief.

I offered himself the whole, so he would refuse her, and to live with his credit anywhere. But I assured him that I would not yield to mine own wants to maintain such a shameless rig.[26]

He fell so passionate at this my answer, that he reviled me with all the ill words he could devise. He offered me the terror of his dagger (which my father, Sir James Mervyn, saved me from), with solemn oaths vowed he would tear the skin off my back. If he might not, he would blow up me and my house with gunpowder, but he would be revenged and rid of me.

Sir James Mervyn and Sir John Conway, six or seven days after this heat, used friendly persuasions with him that there might be an unity between him and me and that he would leave Mistress Pagnam. He asked to what end, saying with her he was contented. If he should leave her to live with such a moil[27] as I, five score would not serve him a year, protesting with solemn oaths to them, as he had done to myself, that it had been the heaviest burden of mind to conceal his secret hate of me from the first day he married me. And, therefore, he would be rid of me or it should cost him the hazard of his neck.

After this, he did from Calais write to me and Sir James Mervyn that he would come to England again for no other cause but to be revenged of me. He said in his letters that it should not be all the friends my father Mervyn could make, nor my mother's credit in court that should save me from his revenge, nor harm Mistress Pagnam.

He hath, sithence, revenged himself of me by hard degrees that never offended him. Mistress Pagnam liveth with him in peace and pleasure

---

24 According to the Statute of 13 Elizabeth, Ca3, "An act against Fugitives over the Sea," leaving the realm without the permission of the Queen resulted in forfeiture of land and wealth.
25 Let, *n.*1 Hindrance, stoppage, obstruction; also, something that hinders, an impediment. Now *arch.*
26 Rig, *n.*4 Now *rare.* A wanton or loose woman; (in early use esp.) a harlot, a prostitute.
27 Moil, *n.*1 1. Turmoil, confusion, tangle; confusion of sound, hubbub. Also: trouble, vexation. 2. Toil, labor, drudgery. Frequently in toil and moil (cf. to toil and moil at moil *v.* 2). Moil, *n.* and *adj.* Irish English, Welsh English, and English regional (western). † moile, *n.* 1. A pudding, probably molded made of ground rice, almond milk, and other ingredients.

80 Letters and Documents

without any punishment of her ill life. And I live and languish through despair, being assured of the uttermost mischief that she can devise or he intend me if God his providence shield me not. He did swear before Sir James Mervyn, Sir John Conway, and others that if by these means he might not come to be revenged, he would give an ill person 500 pounds to give me an Italian fig.[28]

After all these ill speeches, he sent an ill man, who had been burnt in the hand,[29] out of France to my house.[30] He came to Chipping Norton and there used such speeches and behaviors with my servants as do yield vehement presumption that he came to do me some mischief. In the night he enticed my men unto the tavern, bestowed banquets on them. In the midst of their good cheer, he was very inquisitive to know of my men how many persons I kept, in what places of my house they lay, what number within my gates, and how many without. And also if I did not use ordinarily to walk abroad into my gardens and pastures, and with what company, and at what times of the day. This man was well furnished with dags and stored with money. He would suffer none of mine to pay money. He told them he was sufficiently stored, that he had a thing to do before he departed the country which, being done, would fill his purse better. He never showed himself by day, yet tarried at Chipping Norton seven or eight days. Upon the day of his departure, he came by my house and desired to see and speak with me, (as he said), from Master Bourne. But I durst not speak with him, my fear was such by these reasons I have showed you, through ~~my husband's~~ his threatenings, of which I could set you down a number more. But these be too many and may suffice.

I will now unfold to you some of his unconscionable devices, wicked policies, and slanderous reports, untruly invented and maliciously executed against myself, my friends, kin, and allies.

After he had willfully purchased himself a prisoner's place in her Majesty's Tower of London, he had convenient time to make himself a just audit of his past life and present estate, by wisdom to repair that which by will he had ruined. And so would any man but he. But not tasting of God his grace so far as to accept his imprisonment a divine providence to reform the disorders of his life, he wrought all things to the increase of his own mischief and the spoil of me and my children.

He doubled his sins against me with this wicked device to call my inconstancy and chastity in question, of policy to withdraw the compassion and

---

28 Fig, *n*.1 2. A poisoned fig used as a secret way of destroying an obnoxious person. Often fig of *Spain, Spanish fig, Italian fig. Obsolete.*
29 Burn, *n*.3. 2. a. A mark made by burning, a brand. Convicted criminals were branded. [See also *The Roaring Girl*, Thomas Middleton and Thomas Dekker, where Sir Alexander asks Trapdoor to "Hold thy hand up? What's this? Is't burnt?" (1.2. 208–209)].
30 This man is likely Raffe Arrasmythe, Anthony's man in Calais, identified in BL, Add. MS 23212, fols. 7–8.

good conceit of the virtuous from me, to make his own offenses the more tolerable and my friends to fall from me. The intention proceeded from Satan and the consent proves the same. The man prospers, as the world can witness, as yet untaught to leave sin, to fly shame, to fear God to know himself, to shun his harm, or to embrace virtue. This plot and policy he framed without God's grace and performed it without cause, conscience, or consideration. God can witness, myself never offended him and my friends less. Yet this he put in action as followeth:

In March in the 19th year of her Majesty's reign,[31] he went away with Mistress Pagnam, left me comfortless alone, without compassion of my sorrows, in despair of my life, by reason whereof, I became big, swollen, as if I had been long and quick with child. And yet not so. Such was my state, not able to go without staff and of small hope. For the physicians assured me that I had received some ill thing in my meat or drink.[32] Being thus distressed, I desired for my better stay and comfort Master Richard Hobby, esquire, and his wife,[33] being my cousin-german,[34] to live with me in my life, that I might rely myself upon their good company and counsel in all my needful causes and travails. I found them my good friends. They lived with me in my house and became careful suiters with me to my Lords of the Council for my wellbeing and ~~my husband both~~ Master Bourne likewise. In recompense of their goodwills toward me, being all the offence they ever made, Master Bourne, to cause them to fall from me in their friendship, he railed at them with most spiteful and unreverent words, calling him a villain, knave, and cuckold, his wife arrant whore, saying he was a kestrel kite;[35] he would clip his wings and cut off his head.

Because Sir John Conway, at the request of me and my friends, waged law in proof of his deeds to be good and lawful to such uses as they were truly meant and not as he did indirectly against himself, his true knowledge,

---

31 March 1577.
32 Dropsy, *n.* and *adj.* A. *n.* a. A morbid condition characterized by the accumulation of watery fluid in the serous cavities or the connective tissue of the body. [Dropsy was a malady often confused with pregnancy as Jonathan Gil Harris discusses in "All Swell That End Swell: Dropsy, Phantom Pregnancy, and the Sound of Deconception in *All's Well That Ends Well.*" *Renaissance Drama*, vol. 35, 2006, 169–189.]
33 Elizabeth (Bustard) Hobby.
34 Cousin-german, *n.* Now *archaic*. 1. A child of a full brother or sister of either of one's parents; a first cousin. Cf. cousin *n.* 1b. Cf. germane cousin at germane *adj.* 1.
35 Kite, *n.* 2. *figurative*. A person who preys upon others, a rapacious person; a sharper; also more indefinitely a term of reproach or detestation. Combined with "kestrel," Master Hobby becomes a bird of prey: Kestrel, *n.* 1. a. A species of small hawk (Falco tinnunculus, or Tinnunculus alaudarius), also called stannel or windhover, remarkable for its habit of sustaining itself in the same place in the air with its head to the wind. The name is extended to about 15 foreign species of the restricted genus Tinnunculus.

and conscience (in malice of me) intitle[36] her Majesty by Jury upon his own evidence. For this he railed at him, called him knave, villain, and cozening knave, saying he went about to beguile him of all that ever he had and swore by great oaths that he would kill him though it were pissing against a wall.

When he saw that this indirect course of his took not effect to his will and that Sir John Conway persevered in defense of the cause, he complained to sundry personages of honorable estate, both men and women, that Sir John Conway lived as ill with me as he did with Mistress Pagnam, and that all which he did defend in right of my children, was in wrong of her Majesty, and through unlawful love and affection towards me.

To aggravate this cause and to make his reports the more credible, he informed sundry great estates that my former loose life with one Master Freer of Oxford was cause of his fall and fault with Mistress Pagnam. Otherwise, as he gave forth, he had never gone astray. To confirm this whole, he named Master Freer to be father of my youngest daughter and delivered the substance of all this both in speech and writing to be delivered her Majesty for a truth.

After this, before the right honorable my Lords of the Council, when we both came face to face, I complained my grief of these his reports and desired, in honor of her Majesty being her sworn servant and in good grace of myself, that I might thereof acquit myself or else find no favor. He there denied the whole and justified me, that he had never reported me unhonest of body or, that less was, thought it.

We no sooner were dismissed of that honorable presence by commandment that he, Sir James Mervyn, Sir John Conway, and I should agree within ourselves, to satisfy her Majesty of 1000 pounds, but in going out of the chamber, upon the passion of his mind, he called me arrant whore and said he would use me like a whore for my cunning policy and choice of time to make him justify my honesty to the discredit of himself.

My father Mervyn and Sir John Conway desired him to be silent in that place and for the better regard of his own credit, considering how lately he had denied the knowledge or thought of dishonesty by me, wished him to suppress such rage of speech. With that, he charged Sir John Conway that I was his whore and said that so sufficient a man told him as would avouch it to his face, and that his brother Powell.

He farther said his brother Powell advised him to avouch me a whore to the state of the right honorable Council and publicly to everybody, counseled him to confirm it with his corporal oath, and he would prove it for

---

36 Entitle, *v.* II. From title, *n.* "right to possession." 4. a. To furnish (a person) with a "title" to an estate. Hence gen. to give (a person or thing) a rightful claim to a possession, privilege, designation, mode of treatment, etc. Const. to with *n.* or *infinitive*; also simply. Also *absol.* Now said almost exclusively of circumstances, qualities, or actions; formerly often of personal agents.

him. As he farther said his brother Powell advised him that he had no other means to reduce himself to be pitied and to make his faults seem the less, but to persuade the world that I had led as unchaste a life as he, and that my loose life and ill doings were the chiefest cause of his folly and fall.

Sir John Conway, being thus charged by Master Bourne before diverse of his friends and mine and in open audience of many, charged Master Powell with Master Bourne's words, required of him what reason moved him to speak them, from whom he heard them, or how he conceived so much ill of him. Master Powell protested to Sir John Conway before Master Bromfield and Francis Brace, Esquire, that Master Bourne had therein belied him. He never used any such speech nor heard any such from any other but from Master Bourne himself, who, as he said, sent for him into the Tower and told him that he had devised such a course against me and asked his counsel and help how he might proceed in it, either to prove it true or to make it seem likely, and whether it were not a good device? And he told him, no, and so left him, supposing that would by his counsel and of his own discretion have fallen from it.

That he offered Sir John Conway, his brother Powell, and me this wrong, Sir Francis Walsingham, his Honor, can witness. Francis Brace, Esquire, being cousin and special friend to Master Bourne, did affirm before his honor that he heard words Sir John Conway received of Master Bourne, the charge Sir John Conway gave Master Powell when they met in the fields, and his flat denial of all, and charged Master Bourne that the ill device and speech proceeded from himself and had none other author.

Of this reproof, he nothing abashed, desired of Master Francis Walsingham, his Honor, that he would order Mistress Pagnam to live with him in safety from all unquietness that might be offered by me, my friends, or servants. He said that he would settle himself and her within 12 miles of me at Kidlington. He swore by solemn oaths before his honor that he would never leave to love her and friend her whilst he lived. He protested to his Honor that he loved her little finger better than all my body and that he had a son by her. He held more dear his little toe than both my daughters, that I might assure myself that all he could get for his life should be too little for her and her children, and all he could pluck from me, he would. These cold comforts he gave me in presence of many and added to it this injury, which I bear with greatest grief: he did swear before his Honor that my youngest daughter was Master Freer's bastard and protested, as God should save him, that he could prove it by credible oaths to be true that he said.

After all these ill speeches and broils[37] by the mediation of my Lord Chancellor of England[38] and Sir Francis Walsingham, his Honor, and by the friendly travail of Michael Blount and John Chamberleyn, Esquires,

---

37 Broil, *n*. 1. a. A confused disturbance, tumult, or turmoil; a quarrel. See also brulyie *n*.
38 Thomas Bromley.

he desired an end of all controversies between himself, me, and Sir John Conway: desired that, upon conclusion of all things touching all good, debts, and lands, he and I might live in terms of courtesy and good speech each of other, protested with great oaths that he would do so for his part and entreated Master Blount and Master Chamberleyn to promise so much on his behalf. For my better assurance, thereof, he became bound at the end of all controversies in a 1000-pound band,[39] that he would not molest me in person, lands, goods, nor any ways.

I assented to his reasonable will in all things touching a quiet end. I enjoined with him in consent to do all things that were thought meet[40] by his friends and mine towards Sir John Conway, and so did I absolutely agree with Sir John Conway to satisfy him of all things he desired.

After he had received the full accomplishment of all covenants and promises from me and Sir John Conway, and was to perform reasonable agreements on his part, he refused to do them, grew into rages and railing speeches against Sir John Conway, saying he was a villain, bankrout[41] knave, that he had the French pox by my gift, that Freer of Oxford had given them me for an increase to those my father had left me. Lastly, he swore by great oaths that he would never be quiet nor his conscience satisfied until he had killed me for a whore, Sir John Conway for a villain, and that pocky squire and villain born Freer of Oxford, and my youngest daughter, as he said, Freer's bastard. These things being done, he swore he should have a quiet conscience and never afore. And these all he swore he would do, what time, torment or dissimulation soever he should be urged to abide and suffer.

Lastly, I may assure myself, he doth still entertain these ill speeches and beliefs of me. For since the time, he hath made deceivable show of his reformed life and demanded to have me to live with him. He hath said and sworn that my youngest daughter is Freer's bastard, a wrong most intolerable for a clear conscience to digest that is free from the sin. An untruth conceived in deadly hate, persecuted by such degrees of spite, confirmed and continued by such exchange and length of time, as I am justly moved to leave no considerations of the man, the manner, and matter undisgested[42] through all the wisdom and judgement I may, from whence I receive these

---

39 Band, *n.* 11. a. Security given; a deed legally executed, binding on him who delivers it. *archaic*; now *bond n.1.*

40 Meet, *adj.* 2. a. Suitable, fit, proper for some purpose or occasion, expressed or implied.

41 Bankrupt, *n.* I. An insolvent person, and related senses. †a. A person who defrauds his or her creditors or avoids paying his or her debts. Also: a person whose debts are the result of reckless expenditure. *Obsolete* except as passing into senses 1b, 1c.

42 Digest, *v.* 3. To settle and arrange methodically in the mind; to consider, think or ponder over. 6. a. To bear without resistance; to brook, endure, put up with; to "swallow, stomach."

incident[43] considerations upon the griefs I have unfolded and the peril that may befall me, in agreeing to live with Master Bourne.

But first I protest that, notwithstanding anything which I have before mentioned in ripping up my griefs or any reason, which I shall hereafter allege for my defense in the confirmation of my deliberate purpose not to live with him anymore. I mind not to renounce and forgo those advantages in law, which his demerits have procured unto me against himself. But only desire in the meantime to satisfy the right honorable my very good Lords of the Council, and such as shall be deputed from these Lordships to the hearing of any matters between me and Master Bourne: to that end, that (the truth from them being known to others) those who have thought well of my cause heretofore, may be thoroughly confirmed in their good opinion, and all others who have injuriously wronged me either by their words or thoughts, may alter their minds and correct with discretion their unadvised judgments.

The reasons and considerations, drawn from his dissolute and loose life, which persuade me not to live with him.

1. The laws, which in cases of matrimony and divorces have, at this present, place, and authority in this land have set down this expressly, which also practice and use continually doth confirm, that the honest wife of an adulterous husband, upon her suit and instant[44] petition to be divorced from her husband, and upon manifest and clear proofs of his adultery, or else his own confession of the same, is of the Judge to be heard and her petition to be granted. Since, therefore, truth itself and Master Bourne his own confession to the Right Honorable my Lords of the Council have cleared me, not only from ill, but also from suspicion of ill; since his adultery is and hath been so notorious, as nothing more, and confessed by himself to diverse, of whom some are honorable, there is no doubt but by law I may be divorced from him. Which benefit of law to renounce were in me as great folly and madness as the patient to refuse a sovereign medicine or in the afflicted his aid and comfort. Wherefore, since law hath provided a salve and remedy for my sore, I mean to use it to my good, as God shall give me grace, without injury to Master Bourne, who hath given the cause thereof.
2. Secondly, Master Bourne hath in all likelihood gotten that disease amongst his women, which he professedly[45] sought for, to the end he might infect me therewithal. Which being true, I trust no well advised gentleman will think me worthy blame in fleeing a disease so easy to be

---

43 Incident, *adj.*1 †3. Relating or pertinent to. *Obsolete.*
44 Instant, *adj.* I. Urgent, pressing.
45 Professedly, *adv.* 1. By or according to profession or declaration; by one's own admission; openly, avowedly.

taken and so dangerous being had, as that will not only consume me whilst I live but also bring me more speedily to the grave.

3. Thirdly, since adultery is a vice so loathsome and vile as which by the Parthians[46] and Lydians (being heathen men)[47] and by the word of God in all ages, (practiced also in Geneva[48] at this present) is most severely punished by extreme death, even as also lions and storks do in like kind correct this offence and elephants so detest it that they descry[49] the same in men. I should, doubtless, participate with Master Bourne's adulteries if I should be willing to live with him, whom divine and humane laws and very nature of unreasonable creatures have judged worthy of death.

4. Fourthly, the punishment of adultery by the laws now in use with us is excommunication till the party which offended shall repent his former life, and some such bodily pain or shame as shall be thought meet by the ordinary[50] of the place where the sin is committed. Now since he or she worthily incurreth excommunication, who keepeth company with an excommunicate person, especially such a one as Master Bourne, who maketh a jest at the judgement of God and still growth from worse to worse, waltring[51] and wallowing in his filthy lust: I hold it damnable for me to live with him, whom his demerits have separate, till he amend, from the company of the faithful.

5. Fifthly, if it hath been suffered in him now these six years to disjoin himself from his lawful wife and go about ranging from place to place with another man's wife, divorced publicly from her husband for her adultery,[52] I hope no reasonable gentleman will condemn my purpose lawfully to leave his company hereafter, who hath so long thus unlawfully separated himself from me.

6. Sixthly, since marriage without agreement and love between the parties is nothing else but a continual vexation and hell of torments unto a quiet mind; since Master Bourne's affections have been so estranged from me ever since we were first married, and especially since his familiarity with

---

46 Parthian, *n.* A. 1. A native or inhabitant of Parthia, a region of the Achaemenian empire and later a kingdom in what is now Iran.
47 Lydian, *n.* B. An inhabitant of Lydia. A region in western Asia Minor now part of Turkey.
48 Reference to Calvinism and the religious practices that started in Geneva in the mid-1500s, specifically, the practice of punishing adultery with death. See *Adultery and Divorce in Calvin's Geneva*, by Robert Kingdon. Harvard UP, 1995; and Beam, Sara. "Gender and the Prosecution of Adultery in Geneva, 1550–1700." Women's Criminality in Europe, 1600–1914, edited by Manon Van der Heijden et al., Cambridge UP, Cambridge, 2020, 91–113.
49 Descry, *v.* 7. *transitive.* To denounce, censure; to rebuke, criticize.
50 Ordinary, *n.* I. 1.a. Chiefly *Ecclesiastical Law.* A person who has, of his or her own right and not by the appointment of another, immediate jurisdiction in ecclesiastical cases, such as the archbishop in a province, or the bishop or bishop's deputy in a diocese.
51 Waltering, *v.*1 2. *figurative.* To wallow or revel in (prosperity, pleasure, sin).
52 Mistress Pagnam.

Mistress Pagnam, that he hath not only in his deals made known his hate to me and love to others, but also hath expressly spoken it to some honorable personages in preferring the little toe of her bastard before his lawful children by me, I conceive not in any reason how it is possible for him and me to live together, without giving great offense to all those who shall understand of our domestical disagreements.

7. Moreover, it hath never been seen nor practiced in any place that parties man and wife once disjoined as Master Bourne and I are, each one void of love to the other, did at any time after conjoin themselves again in the [illegible] estate of holy marriage. For Master Bourne hath, not upon any heat or sudden motion of his mind but upon a long and deliberate purpose (yea since his feigned show of desire to live with me), so disposed me of his love (if ever he loved me) and so fixedly hath placed it on Mistress Pagnam, that it is impossible to remove it. And seeing his unchangeable determination in mind and practice (albeit in words he doth sometimes for a while dissemble it) I cannot choose but extinguish that love which I have born him and live to myself contentedly as I may, lamenting my former mishap in joining with such an husband.

Moreover, I am right well assured that those honorable personages who wish us to live together do conceive some hope of Master Bourne's amendment, which upon consideration of these reasons ensuing, may worthily be despaired.

8. Eighthly, ill doings breed ill thinking and of corrupted manners spring perverted judgements. And how? There be in man two special things: man's will, man's mind: where will inclineth to goodness, the mind is bent to truth; where will is carried from goodness to vanity, the mind is soon drawn from truth to false opinion. And so the readiest way to entangle the mind with false doctrine is to entice the will to wanton living. Wherefore Master Bourne's licentious and wanton life doth make me fear lest he be grown into a kind of atheist, a thing most dangerous to them that shall live with him.

1. First, the stinging of the bee mends the sweetness of honey, roses best refresh our senses when we prick our hands to reach them. He that cracks the nut thinks the kernel sweetest. The reason is not for that the goodness of a thing is the better for the evil thereunto belonging, but for that the remembrance of the evil maketh us to hold the good in more reputation, especially in love. The affection of Master Bourne towards his Mistress Pagnam, and hers towards him, hath been begun with both their open shame and namely her divorce from her husband, nourished with experience and charges on his part, even to his utter undoing. And therefore, as he also hath protested, since she hath left her husband for him, he means to hazard the loss of his wife for her and never to leave her during life, whose little finger he more esteemeth than my whole body. So easily did he compass me and her so hardly.

88   Letters and Documents

2. Secondly, as it fareth with diseases in the body, so is it with the infections of the mind. We see in daily experience that a little rottenness in any part of the body. If it be not presently recovered, it will daily increase and spread itself more and more till the whole body be infected and the disease become incurable. Even so sin once crept into the mind of man and finding itself cherished for a long time without controlment,[53] dispossesseth the mind of all reason whereby to master it and maketh the man senseless that he may not perceive it. So little hope is there of Master Bourne's amendment, whose adultery for these 16 years hath continually increased.

3. Thirdly, as they that angle for the tortoise, having once caught him are driven into such litherness[54] that they lose all their spirits, being benumbed,[55] so they that once take hold of wanton love to abandon their bodies to diverse harlots as Master Bourne hath done are driven into such a trance that they let go the hold of their liberty, bewitched like those that view the head of Medusa[56] or like the viper[57] tied to the bow of the beech tree, which keepeth him in a dead sleep, though it begin with sweet slumber. So deadly is Master Bourne in his cursed and wanton love, being tied to his Mistress Pagnam.

4. Fourthly, if there were any hope of amendment, in Master Bourne, it would have appeared in his careful withdrawing of himself from his harlot since the time of his feigned desire to live again with me. But he hath in this meanwhile, as before, frequented her company, and with solemn oaths, protested both his sound love towards her and his corrupt affection towards me. Whereupon I conclude, that vile and wanton love as a sweet venom hath taken such a deep root in his part that he still meaneth to delight therein because it seemeth sweet. And it will still more and more infect his senseless soul, unless God vouchsafe him such grace and favor as may conduct him to true repentance

5. Fifthly, his own confession that five score women would not serve him a year if he should live with such a moil as I, doth sufficiently prove

---

53   Controlment *n.* 3. Restraining, check. Frequently (in the 16th–17th centuries) in *without controlment*. *Obsolete*.
54   Litherness, *n. Obsolete*. 1. Wickedness. 2. Laziness, sloth, indifference; want of spirit, cowardice.
55   Benumb, *v.* 2. To render (the mental powers, the will, or the feelings) senseless or inert; to stupefy, deaden.
56   Medusa, *n.* 1. Greek Mythology. The one of the three Gorgons who was immortal (see Gorgon n. 1a): (more generally) each of the three Gorgons. Also *allusively* with reference to any of the attributes of a Gorgon. Hence: a person who resembles Medusa; a terrifying or ugly woman.
57   Viper, *n.* 1. a. The small ovo-viviparous snake *Pelias berus* (formerly *Coluber berus* or *Vipera communis*), abundant in Europe and the only venomous snake found in Great Britain; the adder; in general use, any venomous, dangerous, or repulsive snake or serpent.

the little hope of his amendment, albeit I should add no further proof thereto.

All which considered, first, the law which granteth unto me a divorce from him for his notorious adultery; secondly, the danger of the disease, which in likelihood his women have bestowed upon him; thirdly, the vileness of his sin; fourthly, his hard estate being excommunicate (if not yet by course of law, yet by desert) and remaining unrepentant; fifthly, his six years absence from me and willful refusal to dwell with me; sixthly, the bitter debate waring between us through want of love if we do live together; seventhly, the rareness of this example, that we two should rejoin in marriage, since neither of us doth love the other, he willfully renouncing me and I upon just cause refusing him; eighthly, the fear of his atheism; nine,[58] the small hope of his amendment, first by reason of his exceeding and constant love upon her, upon whom he hath consumed his wit and treasure, [and] secondly, because of his disease through length is become either altogether or wellnigh[59] incurable; thirdly, because he is become dead in sin; and fourthly, for that having once or twice or oftener professed his meaning to repent him of his evils, he, notwithstanding, still continueth and runneth on headlong in as great misliking of me or liking of his Mistress Pagnam as ever he did before. Lastly his own confession that five score women would not serve him a year, if he should live with me. I am persuaded in conscience that I may lawfully deny to live with him, who hath defiled his body and soul with so manifest adulteries.

Now it remaineth that I briefly set down the reasons and considerations which move me to not to consent to live with him in regard of that fear which I stand in of my life.

The reasons and considerations, drawn from his tyrannous speeches and deeds, which persuade me not to dwell with him.

1. First, the laws (now in use and practice in England in cases of matrimony and divorce) do grant me a divorce from him for the great cruelty, which he hath practiced against me by word and deed as shall appear more particularly in that which followeth.
2. Secondly, he hath sworn with solemn oaths that he would tear the skin off my back and if he might not, then that he would blow up me and my house with gun-powder, but he would be revenged and rid of me; that it had been the heaviest burden of his ~~conscience~~ mind to conceal his secret hate of me from the first day he married me. And, therefore, he would be rid of me or it should cost him the hazard of his neck. That

---

58 This number is written as "9" in the original and inserted. This is her ninth justification for divorce, in which there are five grounds not to hope for Anthony's amendment.
59 Well-nigh, *adv*. Very nearly; almost wholly or entirely.

he would give an ill person five hundred pounds to give me an Italian fig. That he would never be quiet, nor his conscience satisfied until he had killed me for a whore. These things and some others being done, he swore he should have a quiet conscience and never afore. And these all he swore he would do, what time, torment, or dissimulation soever he should be urged to abide and suffer. All which threatening speeches confirmed with solemn oaths makes me assure myself of death through his means if once, by consenting to live with him, I offer him so convenient a means to exercise on me his purposed ~~malicious~~ malice and bloody cruelty. Neither can I assure myself of safety upon any bond or oath of his whatsoever. For either he hath sworn truly in his tyrannous protestations that he would kill me or otherwise cause me to be made away, and then meaneth to omit no means whereby to perform the same or else he is willfully and solemnly perjured. If so, then what credit may be given in a matter of so great importance unto him, or trust to his bond, who hath so often committed willful perjury? For he hath even solemnly sworn my death since the time that he hath feigned a desire to live with me.

3. Thirdly, he did himself once offer me the terror of his dagger, which my father Sir James Mervyn saved me at that time, or else no doubt he had sped me to his desire. Also in March, in the 19th year of her Majesty's reign,[60] he went away with Mistress Pagnam and left me comfortless, alone, without compassions of my sorrows, in despair of my life, by reason whereof, I became big swollen. Such was my state, not able to go without staff, and of small hope. For the physicians assured me that I had received some ill thing in my meat or drink. Out of which two points I conceive that much: first the laws will, that the purpose to hurt made manifest by some open attempt, be no less punished, then the effect itself already executed. Whereby appeareth my danger to live with Master Bourne, who hath both threatened and assayed to kill and murder mee. For as I am not to esteem him the less my friend, who himself made against his will? So must I of necessity think him my mortal foe who practiceth my death continually, albeit he be not able to compass the same. Secondly, in all probability it is true, albeit expressly I cannot charge him, that Master Bourne, either himself gave me some venomous thing before his departure from me, or else left some other to perform the same. For he threatened it before and departed from me in great displeasure. Which two considerations the rather enforce the same.

4. Fourthly, Master Bourne sent an ill man, who had been burnt in the hand, out of France to my house. He came to Chipping Norton, and there used such speeches and behaviors with my servants as do yield a

---

60 Likely, March 1577/8.

vehement presumption that he came to do me some mischief. What his speeches and behaviors were is expressed in the second part of the griefs before mentioned

Wherefore, since Master Bourne hath not only by injurious speeches sought my utter discredit and by tyrannous words threatened to kill me, but also hath practiced the same both by himself and by others. Since the law doth grant me for the same a divorce from him, to the end I may live in better safety and assurance of my life, I cannot without extreme folly refuse this lawful means to be in less danger of his bloody practices against my life, nor could [I] stand to live with him whom I have descried to be my mortal enemy, unless I would myself consent to mine own death and utter ruin.

5. Fifthly, he hath done what he could to bring my name and honesty in question, to make me infamous through the world, to have my children, as bastards, dispossessed of their lawful inheritance: the which what injury may beg greater or hate more perfect, I cannot possibly imagine.

To conclude, as there is no sound reason in my judgement (under the correction of my betters) that may lead me to consent to dwell with Master Bourne, so are the considerations many and grounded upon law and reason, which dissuade me from the same.

23 [Undated], Master Julius Caesar's Response to Mistress Elizabeth Bourne's Petition

(© British Library Board, BL, Add. MS 38170, fols. 176–178)

[Summary of Master Julius Caesar's Latin commentary on Mistress Elizabeth Bourne's petition to the Privy Council for a divorce from her husband.][1]

Drawing on a rich medieval canonical and theological tradition,[2] Julius Caesar explains that both a husband and a wife can leave a spouse because of adultery and that even though it seems in one sense that a wife sins more gravely in adultery because she sins against the "good of offspring" (one of the three goods of marriage extolled by Saint Augustine) in another way the man sins more because of his greater power of reason, in a third way they sin equally against the good of faith which spouses owed each other regardless of gender.

Each can leave the other because of adultery but neither can remarry while the other lives. The author then explains how accusations can be made and on what basis, (being caught in the nude, a naked man with a naked woman in bed together, or after many secret meetings in suspect places, at suspicious times), that spouse can lawfully be left, that according to the laws and the canons anyone of good reputation can normally bring an accusation of adultery, but in seeking a legal separation only a husband can accuse a wife or a wife against a husband. A husband wanting to accuse a wife of adultery in secular court must make a written libel according to the penal law, and must oblige himself to the talionic[3] punishment. He is not allowed to act by a representative, but he must do it himself. Furthermore, if he

---

1 Julius Caesar begins his commentary in Latin in fol. 176. The rest of his commentary is in English. The editors wish to acknowledge and thank Sara McDougall for this summary of Caesar's Latin commentary. Since Caesar is responding to Mistress Elizabeth Bourne's Petition to the Privy Council (BL, Add. MS 38170, fols. 151–158), it is likely that this document can be dated around the same time, c. December 1582.
2 Largely, Raymond of Peñafort, Thomas Aquinas, etc. and citations to medieval canon law and some Roman Laws.
3 Talionic, *adj. rare*. Of or pertaining to the law of talion, or to the rendering of like for like. Talion, *n*.1 = retaliation n.; esp. in the Mosaic, Roman, and other systems of Law, the Lex talionis, or †talion law, the principle of exacting compensation, "eye for eye, tooth for tooth;" also, the infliction of the same penalty on the accuser who failed to prove his case as would have fallen upon the accused if found guilty.

wants to accuse before an ecclesiastical justice, he has to do so according to the law on separation of bed, that is to say he has to give a libel of accusation, but he does not have to oblige himself to the penalty of talion.

In a case of carnal fornication a man is not compelled to take back a wife who has been chastised, nor a wife a man, but in "spiritual fornication," meaning apostacy, he is compelled to take back a reformed wife. Caesar explains that these are different because one corrupts the body and the other the soul. If a wife shows a similar case, that is to say one why the man should be suspected of having done harm to her, the judge must take care, by sufficient guarantee, that he will treat her well and honestly as a man shall treat his wife, and that he will not hurt her in her person or her goods. And he shall give an oath of this caution, if the wife is not confident about this oath of her husband, that he shall give actual money bond or provide someone to serve as a guarantor for him subject to a money penalty, and he will not contest, and beyond that he is not prosecuting her for good reasons.

There are three goods of marriage namely faith (fidelity), offspring, and the sacrament. In fidelity it is expected that neither the man with another nor the wife with other should join themselves. In offspring, that they be loved, raised up from weakness, and instructed in religion. With respect to the sacrament, that they should not be separated from the marriage, but rather it should be preserved indissolubly until death. That said, although the church can make a divorce on account of the impediments to marriage and on account of fornication or by common consent or ordination or religious life, marriage among the faithful after it has been contracted and consummated shall last inseparably until death.

[End of Latin, beginning of English commentary.]

Whether the laws of the holy church and the cannon laws of this realm do, at this day, admit a divorce between a man and his wife, and whether the ease do as well lie on the woman's side to challenge and have a separation from a husband being an open adulterer, as for the man to put away his wife being an offender.

Item: whether the laws of our Church of England have so certain proceedings in this cause and so absolute a power as neither against injustice they may be hindered through an obstinate will of the husband, that will not obey the laws of the church in that behalf, or overruled by any other court or authority.

If a wife be admitted to divide herself from an evil lying husband by the spiritual law upon just proof of his mislaying, in what manner must the proof be made? What substance, matter, and circumstance must be proved, by how many witnesses?

Item: whether must the wife herself persecute the cause in her own person against the husband, and write down and give the libel[4] of the accusation, or may she do it by her proctor[5] or other substitute?

If the law enjoin her to prosecute the action in person and the woman despair of violence or death to be given her through the malice of her husband by reason of his hate conceived, what security will the laws of the church give the woman to warrant her liberty and life, that she may without fear prosecute the cause?

If the laws of the Church of England admit the wife of her petition to be divorced from her husband, being proved an adulterer, and have the right and custom a due course therein, after upon due cause objected and proved, whether that any of the spiritual court will undertake within a set time, and for certain consideration of their pains and travail to bring to pass the same so as by sentence and order, the wife may live apart in peace and security from her ill husband both in body and substance.

A man having forsaken his wife's company by the space of seven years, having lived in open sin and shame with diverse lewd women hath in actions sought the uttermost spoil and overthrow both of her good name and substance, and put her in bodily fear of her life by diverse malicious practices, menacings, and threatenings, do desire to be restored to her again.

Whether have the Spiritual Jurisdiction power and authority to sequester or settle the wife in any safety and indifferent men's protection, free from the husband's violence? If the wife have just cause through probable likelihood to despair of her life through her husband's threatened mischiefs and pretended purposes.

May not the woman refuse to live with him until he have reformed his ill life and made her such satisfaction of the injuries done her as the assurance thereof may increase God's fear and due love in them both?

Is there any authority can compel her to accept of him until she have sufficient security offered and made her, that he shall use her in all things as a loving husband should his wife; and that she may live in safety of her life and limbs and also that he shall not consume nor waste any part of her goods and revenues, nor intermeddle therein further than what through his good usage of himself and her she shall vouchsafe to yield him?

If the husband have broken his faith of matrimony in wrong of his wife; if he have done a reasonable act in law in advancement of his children and to

---

4 Libel, *n*. 2. A formal document, a written declaration or statement. *Obsolete exc. Historical* (as occasional rendering of Latin *libellus*), and Law (see 3). 3. a. *Civil Law*. The writing or document of the plaintiff containing his allegations and instituting a suit. b. *Ecclesiastical Law*. The first plea, or the plaintiff's written declaration or charges, in a cause.

5 Proctor, *n*.1 1. a. A person employed to manage the affairs of someone else; an agent, proxy, attorney. Cf. Procurator *n*. 1 1C. Now *hist* and *rare*.

make his wife some amends and after will against truth take his corporal to undo the same through an ill conscience and increasing malice towards his wife; if he have utterly wasted his estate of goodness and lands that in himself his bond is nothing worth, nor any man of credit will be bound for him.

What assurance can he give his wife for her safety to live with him or by what reason can any authority enjoin the woman to live with him?

If the woman can prove his faith and vow of matrimony broken, and that he hath taken a foolish oath to wrong her in life or living, and have probably reason to cause her to despair of her life through his malicious threatenings, otherwise, upon her complaint ought not the ministers of the ecclesiastical laws to make a separation between them so as it might be lawful for the woman to be defended and relieved by her kin, allies, and friends, and he without a power to do her spoil or hurt?

Mistress Bourne's questions:[6]

Brief answers to certain questions
demanded on the behalf of Mistress Elizabeth Bourne.

1. The canon laws of this Realm do at this day admit a divorce between a man and his wife. And in the case doth as well lie on the woman's side to challenge and have a separation from her husband being an open adulterer, as on the man's side to have a separation from his wife being an adulteress.
2. Albeit the proceedings of the canon laws touching divorces are of themselves most certain; yet, the power thereof is not so great, but that it may be crossed, hindered, and the course thereof stopped for a time either by corruption or friendship, things no less incident to other laws then to the said canons.
3. For a woman to be divorced by law from an adulterous husband it is sufficient for her to prove that oftentimes or once, at least, he hath had the use of another woman's body besides hers since the time of their marriage; the proof whereof will be sufficient if either himself upon his oath shall confess it before the judge or else shall she do prove it by the oath of two honest and credible persons.
4. The wife may prosecute the cause of divorce against her husband and give in the libel of the accusation by her proctor or lawful attorney.
5. And if in case that her pursual[7] answers to any matter laid into the court by her husband, be necessarily required, she shall be safely

---

6 This line occupies all of fol. 177v, and is written down the side of the folio.
7 Pursual, *n.* = pursuance *n.* (in various senses); the action or fact of pursuing someone or something.

sequestrated[8] and committed for the time to the custody and safeguard of some credit and good countenance (whom she shall like of) by the order of law; where she shall not need to fear the violence of her husband.

6. Albeit the laws admit the wife to be divorced from her husband being proved an adulterer; and have in right and custom a due course therein, yet will no wise lawyer undertake to bring to pass the same within a set time because some things, perhaps, may be alleged and proved in the husband's behalf, why sentence should not pass against him.

7. If the wife have just cause through probable likelihood to despair of her life through her husband's threatened mischiefs, and portended purposes, the Ecclesiastical Judge hath authority and power to separate the wife from the husband in place of safety, unless that the husband can put in so sufficient security as the judge can like of that he shall not offend or hurt her. And no authority can compel her to accept of him if she do once resist for the cause above said to live with him until she have sufficient security offered and made her, that she may live with him in safety of her life and limbs. Which sufficient security if he cannot give, the ecclesiastical judge may separate them. And then it may be lawful for the woman to be defended and relieved by her kin, allies, and friends and he without lawful power to do her spoil or hurt.

Jul. Caesar

---

8 Sequestrate, *v.* 1.a. *transitive.* To remove, put away; to seclude, keep away from general access or intercourse; to put in a place of concealment or confinement.

24 27 January [No Year], Master Anthony Bourne to Mistress Elizabeth Bourne

(© British Library Board, BL, Add. MS 23212, fols. 9–10)

To the worshipful, my wished willing good wife, Mistress Elizabeth Bourne, be these.
    Master Bourne's his letter to his wife.[1]
Mistress Bess,
    It was held fit by my lords of her Majesty's most Honorable Privy Council, and of my part very earnestly wished, that we should have had your presence at this meeting. I, hoping (by conference) to have moved your conformity to my reasonable desires. They holding it commendable in me to offer, and no less due in you to have entertained what should be honestly offered and intended. But since it hath pleased you to determine of yourself contrary to their wills, and my desire, I am yet resolved not to use the advantages {...}[2] you which my complaints of your obstinacy i{...} possibly yield me, but rather determined to mollify your hard resolution, by time, sufferance, acceptance of that cold end for me which do the rather endure in hope that my {...} (here in) may give you hope of my disposition and so be as it were, and entry in to that {...} commendable course which (in protection of your {...} honor, and to the recovery of my poor credit) would, you would more calmly consider of, th{...} hitherto it seemeth you do. As to Sir John, and myself, we stand resolved in a {...} So as I believe (according to his faithful pro[mise]) {...} that (as he that tendereth both his own and our {...}tions[3]) he will deal faithfully in his discourse {...} with you. I therefore (for the time) leave you to his advice and hope (in time) you will hold fit to yield me that, which I dare now challenge for my right, and with all more carefully show your own wrongs. And so with wishes of your good, I leave you I hope better minded than you seem, but freed from all fears of me. If you will accept my faith, and play {...} meaning for your warrant, which as I hope to {...} saved. I freely and simply give you. God bless you and yours. And then fare you well. Chipping Norton, this 27th of January,
                                  Your h[usband] and desirous {...}
                                  Anthony [Bourne] {...}

1 This is written in the left margin of fol. 9r in an unknown hand.
2 The tears on fol. 9r are down the right margin.
3 The tear makes it difficult to know what this word might have been, perhaps [ac]tions?

25 20 February [1582/3][1], Mistress Elizabeth Bourne to Master Anthony Bourne

(© British Library Board, BL, Add. MS 23212, fols. 11–16)

Mistress Bourne's letter to her husband, etc.[2]
    Bourne's letter[3]
    The true copy of my answer to Master Bourne's letter, wherein he wisheth reconciliation between us. Good son Conway, after you have perused my letter with this copy, set your hand to the same with Master Caesar's[4] and return it to me safe. If Master Bourne ill report my writing or misconster[5] my meaning, you may hereby satisfy yourself and his friends.
    Mistress Bourne her answer:
Master Bourne,
    I perceive by your letter there hath been a late meeting of some gentlemen upon causes between you and Sir John Conway, and that not altogether done by your own consent, but by order from the Lords of her Majesty's most Honorable Council: you say it was by their honors held fit, and of you desired that I should have been there.

---

1 We have dated this letter based on the signature in witness of Julius Caesar, who enters the Bourne dispute in August of 1582. Elizabeth Bourne's petition for divorce and Caesar's comments on it are dated December of 1582. We believe that this letter is sent to Anthony as a kind of warning of things to come. As Mistress Bourne warns him, "I seek by due course of law to live in more safety and quiet than is yet offered or can be assured on by any other agreement" (fol. 15r). Later in this letter, she seems to refer to the indenture witnessed and signed by arbitrators, found in NA, SP 12/158, fols. 140–146, January [1583/4]. If the date of that document is correct (see our note on the date in our transcription), then this letter would be post-petition.
2 This note is on fol. 16v, written in John Conway's hand as his usual notation of the contents of the document.
3 This is likely written by Edward Conway. His father always noted the name of the writer and a short description of the letter's contents. Here Edward only notes the author. Following is a note from Mistress Bourne witnessing that the letter is a copy and asking Edward to sign it as a witness with Julius Caesar and to return it to her.
4 Julius Caesar.
5 Misconstrue, *v*. 1. a. *transitive*. To put a wrong interpretation upon (a word, action, etc.); to mistake the meaning of (a person); to take in a wrong sense (in modern use often intentionally).

I have been a long time enforced to secret myself from the eye of the world and the knowledge of all my good friends, kin, and allies. Thereby to [indecipherable] your extremities in myself, and to avoid my{...}[6] trouble. By reason whereof, I could not {...} advertised of the cause, nor required to the {...} so as my ignorance in that point, I hope {...} excuse my absence.

It seemeth very strange to me how you could {...} a ground of complaint, either against me or S[ir] John Conway, to trouble any magistrate or othe[r] {...} you have by yourself, and your friends taken {...} and strict accompt from us both of all {...} you could could demand. There was nothing {...} out of question and all things in difference {...} ended upon your own desire, offer, and like {...} and with the consideration and consent of the {...} Chancellor[7] your honorable friend, the privet{...} of Sir Francis Walsingham, his honor, an[d] {...} many other of your, and my friends, kin, and a[llies] {...} so as there can be no such error, nor indire{...} dealing proved in the cause, and conclusion {...} I hear you suggested. No doubt you were {...} perfect state, abled by the laws of the realm {...} of years, discretion, and freedom, to dispose {...} of all that was yours. The liberty of {...} your person being restrained by her Majesty for punishment of your obedience and disorders {...} towards her Highness yields you no advantage {...} to cavil[8] with you credit, neither to seek to [falsify] your own deeds which you have done with {...} appearance to the world. Upon good consideration {...} by good assurance of law consent of friends, sealing covenant and acknowledgment of great bonds for confirmation of the same.

If these your deeds, already done by law, suffice not to bind you, and to quiet all things, it shall little avail to have any farther conclusions with you, by law or arbitrament. I see let law be what it will, you will not obey it, nor fear to break it. I hope your willfulness therein shall not much hinder me. I would be sorry it should hurt yourself.

I am not very interested in anything that is in difference between you, neither intend to make myself a party to any of your new devices. I followed the advice of my learned counsel, in satisfying myself of that was intended me by your former agreements. I see now they advised and I took the safest course in trusting myself best, and in consenting with you to assure Sir John Conway absolutely, all lands and goods, with the education and benefit of both my daughters' marriages according to the words of your conveyance, without any trust or interest preserved or intended to my use.

This being done orderly upon good consideration by both our consent and deeds in as sure wise as law can devise it. I wonder that you, against

---

6 All tears in this letter are located in the right margin of each recto folio.
7 Likely Thomas Bromley, Lord Chancellor, 1579.
8 Cavil, *v.* 1. a. *intransitive.* "To raise captious and frivolous objections" (Johnson); to object, dispute, or find fault unfairly or without good reason. Const. at, about (formerly also against, with, on).

your credit, seek to break it, especially considering you have several deeds under your own hand, and seal, and persons of good credit to witness against you.

I grieve to see your weak consideration, and great inconstancy to be such as that you will still be made the shaft[9] of envy, the scourge of yourself, and the plague of me and my children, who have not offended you.

I may justly say this, for the world sees it, and I do know it, your love is still settled in others and your hate determined upon me.

If you did intend yourself credit and me quietness, you would not continue in sin, [use] one war upon another and break every peace you consider, by covenant, by bond, by solemn vow, and oaths.

Your want of judgement in these points, and your careless accompt of your conscience and credit, are cause I hold it vain for me to believe your outward shows of amendment and well-meaning toward me.

If you had a will and desire to recover my love, to be yours {...} which unkindly you have despised, and of right given me cause to settle in myself, you would seek me by the degrees of courtesy and not of cruelty, by performance of that {...} you promise, and not by falsifying your faith; you would not pluck from me the maintenance of me and my children, to consume it and your own, to maintain your sin and shame: Mistress Pagnam and her bastards[.] Be these means to reconcile love? If you had a [conscience] to judge, your wisdom that did direct you {...} to do no wrong, and grace to raise yourse[lf] {...} Since you would not (in satisfying those that a {...} of your reputation) make yourself thi {...} the gaze of the world, to live in contention w[ith y] {...} wife that hath ever held faith and peace with you, {...} seek to relieve such as are hated of God,[10] and {...} said of the world to beggar me and your rightful children.

Whilst you continue this course, what do you {...} else but still revive your sin and shame? {...} any man of grace and judgment would rat[her] {...} labor to make a grave of forgetfulness than [a] {...} tree of remembrance.

I beseech you take a better course in ease of [your] {...} self and me. Peace would better become us {...} profit both, than dissention.

That I cannot accept such truce as you offer, nor {...} dare not offer that I wish[.] I had cause[.] [B]lame [your] {...} self. Your fair speeches and solemn oaths ha[ve] {...} been so often falsified to me as you may in {...} own reason hold me excused that I dare not trust. {...} Since I have been your wife, you have never held {...} faith with me in your chastity, nor remained constant in any good mind towards me three months. {...} How should I resolve myself to believe your words, {...} to put trust in your promises? Or to think you can thus suddenly love me now? That this {...} sixteen years have constantly but hated me by [continual] and increasing degrees being

---

9 †Shaft, *n.*1 2. That which is created; a creature.
10 The bastard children of Anthony Bourne and Mistress Pagnam.

brought by dispraise to the ebb of this care from whence shall I draw the hope of any better comfort?

Your honorable friends' bonds, or any other you can offer in performance of your promise to use me well, are as small security to me as your own assurance, whereof I have too much proof. Myself am no person abled in law to take or sue any bond for my benefit or safety. If I were, I would not meddle with my betters, my friends will be as loath and for me to rely a trust upon them in anything touching you.

They are so much wearied and afraid of your inconstancy and clamorous speeches, as I have no reason to require them, and they great cause to deny me. But chiefly, I am discouraged by your own words and deed from accepting any further by any bonds. I had relied myself on [if I] [indecipherable] your bond, your faith, and my friends' trust. You have broken your bonds, and those I trusted have failed in their faith and my trust reposed. Shall I trust you that have more than 300 times beguiled me? And shall I repose a second trust in any friend when I am once deceived where I believed best? I should with repentance sorrow hit all too late. Therefore, blame me not if I take the safest course for my quiet.

The remembrance of these your speeches to myself discourage and despair me. I offered to live with you under condition you would bind yourself from the love of Mistress Pagnam and her bastards, and to use me well. You answered, no King, no Caesar should bind you from her unless they bound you in darby bands.[11] If they did, you did swear, you would have another and so many more as should make them weary of binding you for your being bound to well use me; that you said you would, and you asked me withal what it would avail me when you had me[?] I was your wife[.] You might and would keep me as you thought good: and that you swear should be in a frieze[12] gown, with bread and water and close enough for having any mean to complain of you either to her Majesty, the Lords of her Highness Council, or to any my friends.

Blame me not that I fear your threatening. I have found you by many degrees so constant in performing your hate towards me.

I am most assured it is not any remorse of conscience, repentance of your sin, or love of me that moves you now to desire to live with me. It is bare need, wanting the benefit of a better mind to relieve yourself, Mistress Pagnam, and her unrighteous children, that makes you seek by the spoil of me to succor her and hers.

---

11 Darby, 1. Darby's bands *n*. (also Father Darby's bands) apparently some rigid form of bond by which a debtor was bound and put within the power of a moneylender. (It has been suggested that the term was derived from the name of some noted usurer of the 16th century.)

12 Frieze, *n*.1 1. A kind of course woolen cloth, with a nap, usually on one side only; now *esp.* of Irish manufacture.

The world sees this manifest and I know you [still] {...} hold her and hers in your love and liking an[d] {...} [indecipherable] me unto you without love or affection[n]. I would my Lords of the Council did truly u[nder]stand your abuses of me, the ungodly life you {...} lead and your deceivable shows you make of ame[nd]ment, and all but devices to blind their honors {...} and to entrap me. I would not doubt but they {...} would refer you to a better reformed life before {...} they would entreat an unity between us. No d[o] you assure their honors that you are quite disch{...} of Mistress Pagnam and her bastards, and that y{...} put on a sorrowful mind of your offences past {...} and intend to sin no more.

They know not, Master Bourne, how little profit you {...} took by God's providence, and her Majesty's merciful {...} correction of your disordered life by imprisonment, nor {...} how many misbegotten bastards you had in the present {...} time of your restraint by Mistress Pagnam and others, nor {...} how you have increased them by many sundry women {...} since your enlargement. Is your carrying Mistress Pagnam into Ireland? Your bringing her back? Your living with her in London? Your placing her in Wales? and your reducing her thence to London where she now liveth in your daily company and charge? And your loose life with many other women without any forbearance or intermission of time from your sins—a mean[s] to assure me of your amendment? I have nothing else to persuade me but your own words which you deliver at ease; and I should dearly buy them, if I should trust them.

Your solemn oaths have passed so largely in slander of me, as I that do assure myself it is more than the good mind of a man would have consented without cause, or can now disgest[13] though hit be untrue.

The manner of the mischief, the nature of the wound is such, and the grief so cureless, as the remembrance cannot die but may be of right an eating corrige[14] in your conscience, as well as continual martyrdom to me thorough my whole life. I say it is the only enemy of our peace and the canker of despair that consumes my outward life, though my clear conscience gives solace to my inward soul.

I would you had compared that consent of cruelty with the clog[15] of your conscience, before you had wrongfully impeached my chastity. You might as well yourself, and in less harm for me, have taken my life to have given you liberty (so I wish, and much better had it been) than careless of my

---

13 Digest, *v.* 3. To settle and arrange methodically in the mind; to consider, think or ponder over.
14 Corrige, *n.* (Etimology, French corriger, <Latin corrigĕre to correct *v.*) To correct, chastise, punish. [Our reading is that Mistress Bourne suggests that this memory should, could, work as a corrective or chastisement eating into Master Bourne's mind.]
15 Clog, *n.* 3. *figurative.* Anything that impedes action or progress; an impediment, encumbrance, hindrance.

destruction, and your soul's health to have consented the willful murder of my reputation and innocency, as you have done to make your fault seem the less towards me, and the world, and to bereave me the good opinion of the virtuous. The policy was ill and the consent worse.

To determine this you have taken 16 year's space. It is no sudden deed rashly attempted, but considerately executed.

Therefore, I fear the more to live with you, since your malice towards me is so continuing and constant; I dread to sleep with you because you have sworn my death and destruction; and I more than fear to make you governor of me, and my children, that hates me for naught and holds them to be none of yours. I would you had never done yourself, and me, that wrong. It is that drowneth my desire, that despaireth my mind, and discomforteth my heart to live with you. How shall I believe that your mind will suffer you to joy to live with me, since yourself hath openly reported to be dishonest, and confirmed the same with solemn oaths before honorable personages, in such sort as it may settle a belief in several minds. That you would never have spoken it in such a presence without a surety of truth? Or fr[om] {...} whence shall I draw any hope at all, of happy {...} you when it is lack and not love which moves you {...} me: since your belief of women is so loose an{...} think we all sinners and write to me to live for the repair of my credit and your [indecipherable] I hope you shall not be imputed my shame, [then] I trust [when] {...} one shall answer their own offenses. I shall not {...} found guilty of your faults.

I thank God of this special benefit he hath ordained {...} just renown of the innocent shall stand upon the [testimony] {...} of their own conscience and not upon the wick[ed] {...} imagination, and untrue speech of the ungodly {...} malicious.

Though you have broken your only vow of chaste ma[trimo]ny,[16] gone astray this sixteen years, and lived in open view, and loathsome lust with Mistress Pagnam, and others, and so continue[,] I have not falsified my faith with you, neither done any act to impeach my credit, to call my life in comparison with yours, or in disgrace to be anything, if truth may judge me.

Therefore, good Master Bourne, do me right, reduce yourself to a better mind, and belief of me. And I will pray to God to settle in you his better grace: for of this I am most assured: where malice is covered by policy and love enforced by necessity that state cannot long stand in perfect peace, and therefore I will not consent to live with you until time and your unfeigned retire from sin to virtue, and your continuance in the same, make me assurance of a better quiet than yet you offer me and that others think they have consented for me. Therefore, pardon me if in the meantime I seek by due course of law to live in more safety and quiet than is yet offered or can be assured on by any other agreement.

---

16 There is a tear here, separating the words, "trimo" is missing, but the meaning is clear.

Sir John Conway, by his letter dated the 22nd day of January which came to my hands with yours the 13th day of this month of February, hath acquainted me with the conditions of your new award, which profit me nothing, and assure me as little, either to live with you contentedly or from you quietly; and therefore, as it is concluded without my consent, it shall be fulfilled without my help.

It may be so very well without your offense, for he is sufficient with whom you deal, and wise enough to satisfy you and himself with the reason of his own doing. I mislike not with any benefit he hath assured you; for he hath not in his power to dispose of anything that mine is.

Therefore, if your benefit were more, I should be more glad. So it would move you the rather to give me quiet. I protest to you and God, I wish not to live and see you lack, so I had the mean[s] to help you, and you the measure to make it do you good. Neither have I written anything in this letter with will to offend you, but only to lay before you the reasons of my grief and to satisfy you that I refuse not to live with you but by more just cause than I wish I had to allege in that behalf, wherein I beseech you urge me not to object, and prove that I can.

Good Master Bourne, call your secret conscience to witness, and since that may assure you in the truth of that I allege, mislike me not; though I seek an orderly course of law without the which I cannot be warranted to live in quiet from the trouble you may still offer me. You know, and have reason to judge that all is nothing when God shall work, and we shall agree to live together as we ought.

I pray you, Sir, therefore, be as willing to consent to my quietness, without farther trouble to yourself, and me. As I shall be willing (by your God's grace) to live with you in his fear, and due obedience when time, and your perfect amendment shall assure me your chaste love, and unfeigned repentance of my wrongs.

If I should sooner consent to live with you, it would but work in short time that we should the farther off divide ourselves asunder.

When you have taken an infallible truce[17] with all your foreign affections: when time hath assured, and confirmed in you a better conceit of me and mine, and when I may repose myself wholly in your chaste, and constant love, and may commit mys[elf] {...} and mine only in trust upon your own {...} faith without other bonds or surety. The {...} I joy to live with you: otherwise, it is a dr{...} and dangerous life for us to live in so near [fel-]{...}lowship as man and wife. If only love, g{...} belief each of the other, and the fear of God wou{...} not in us always our safeties and do frame {...} in us

---

17 Truce, *n*. 3. a. Hence, Respite or intermission (more loosely, freedom or liberty) from something irksome, painful, or oppressive. Our reading is that in her conditions for reconciliation, Mistress Bourne lists first that Anthony must be free of his foreign affections, that is from his commitment to Mistress Pagnam.

one life, one love, and one liking of all th[e] {...} and one continuing care in both our hearts to th{...} increase of our good, and lessening of our grief. {...} If I may live to enjoy this happiness, I shall {...} the sufferance of all my sorrows well satisfy {...} which I have endured or shall until a happier {...}.

Whereof, wanting the present assurance, I rest {...} myself in hope of that which God may hereafter work to my farther comfort, and your better cre-{...} dit, and leave to trouble you with my ill hand: humbly beseeching you to consent, and not mislike the course I seek for my safety, and I will not fail to pray to God daily to increase his favors, and your good fortunes in whose safe-keeping I leave you, written this 20th day of February.

By her that wisheth you the daily increase of God his grace & the good of all your desires.

A true copy of a letter sent by Mistress Elizabeth Bourne to Master Anthony Bourne Esquire. Witnesses,   Edward Conway
J. Caesar

26 [Undated],[1] [A written opinion by one Daffarne finding that Master Anthony Bourne has no right to "demand or make title unto any the manors, lands, hereditary goods, or chattels conveyed to the said Sir John Conway"]

(© British Library Board, BL, Add. MS 23212, fols. 26–27)[2]

Upon the two first Indenture dated 18 March 19 Eliz.[3] which contain the grant of all the lands and goods specified in the signed Indenture, I take it without doubt that all the said feoffees[4] and donees[5] named in the said Indentures were seized of the land and possessed of the goods only in trust and to implied[6] trust[7] of E.B.[8] for life, and after to the use of Amy and Mary

---

1 This document appears to be a legal opinion that might have been sought just prior to the Indenture clearing John Conway of any wrongdoing and barring Anthony Bourne from reclaiming any properties (NA, SP 13c, fol. 28). The indenture also protects both Sir John Conway and Mistress Elizabeth Bourne from all harassment Anthony might devise. The date of Daffarne's opinion, therefore, would precede 18 January 1583.
2 There is no address or indication for whom the recipient of this opinion was meant.
3 1576/7.
4 Feoffee, *n.* 1. The person to whom a freehold estate in land is conveyed by a feoffment. 2. a. (More fully feoffee in or of trust.) A trustee invested with a freehold estate in land. Now chiefly applied in plural to certain boards of elected or nominated trustees holding land for charitable or other public purposes.
5 Donee, *n.* One to whom anything is given; esp. in *Law*, (a) one to whom anything is given gratuitously; (b) one to whom land is conveyed in fee tail; (c) one to whom a "power" is given for execution.
6 Implied, *adj.* Contained or stated by implication; involved in what is expressed; necessarily intended though not expressed: see imply *v.* Often in legal phrases as implied contract, implied trust, implied warranty, etc.: see these words.
7 Trust, *n.* 4. †a. *Law*. The confidence or faith placed in a person or persons into whose possession assets, property, etc., are put, to be held or administered for the benefit of another. Chiefly in upon trust. *Obsolete*.
8 Elizabeth Bourne.

B[9]., the two daughters according to the estates limited in the feoffees and donees, but A.B.[10] is utterly concluded[11] to claim anything to his own use:

By the indenture Tripartite dated 14 October 21 Eliz.,[12] I take it that also all the right or claim which A.B. could claim in the premises as in the right of Eliz. B., his wife, is by that Indenture granted and released by A.B. and all feoffees and donees unto Sir J.C.[13] and so that thereby the said A.B. is concluded to claim anything in the premises to the use of his said wife. But I suspect notwithstanding that Sir J.C. standeth seized of the land and possessed of the goods to the first use specified to be implied in the two first Indentures of 18 March, 19 Eliz. by reason that he was privy of her first use so implied.

By the grant of A.B. in the said tripartite Indenture of the education and marriage of his two daughters, the said A.B. is utterly barred to claim the education or marriage of his said daughters. But that notwithstanding the daughters be at liberty to marry when and whom they will.

Likewise, by the last release of all actions etc., A.B. is utterly barred of all actions etc. but yet I suspect that the right and interest of E.B., his wife, and of his daughters do still remain to the [indecipherable] impeached by all the said reasons of A.B.

My opinion is clearly that by reason of the divorce[14] and several conveyances made by Master Anthony Bourne and his feoffees and donees and others to Sir John Conway, Knight, the said Anthony Bourne is in law equity or conscience utterly barred to herein demand or make title unto any the manors, lands, hereditary goods or chattels conveyed to the said Sir John Conway or to have or claim the education or marriage of Amy or Mary, his daughters.

Daffarne

9 Bourne.
10 Anthony Bourne.
11 Conclude, *v*. †3. a. To shut up *from* a course of action, etc.; to preclude, debar, restrain, 'estop'. *Obsolete*. b. To shut up *to* a course of action, etc.; to bind, oblige. Still in legal use.
12 1579.
13 Sir John Conway.
14 The reference to a divorce is significant and does not occur again. Documents refer to the Bourne marriage as one in which they have determined to live separately.

27 January [1583/4],[1] [Report of Arbitrators Appointed by the Privy Council]
(NA, SP 12/158, fols. 140–146)

To the right honorable our very good Lordship: and the rest of her Majesty's most honorable Privy Council.

A brief of the beginning, proceeding, and conclusion of all things between Sir John Conway, Knight, and Anthony Bourne, Esquire

Anthony Bourne, Esquire, by his several deeds, dated the 18th of March in the 19th year of her Majesty's reign, in consideration of £300 by year of the inheritance of Mistress Bourne, sold in consideration also that she should join with Master Bourne in fine[2] of the manor of Holt and Battenhall, sold by him to extinguish[3] her title of Dower, therein, for the knowledging whereof by her he stood bound in great and straight bonds. And in consideration of amends and better satisfaction to his wife and her friends in the wrong she had received by Master Bourne for the casting her off and taking the other gentlewoman into his society, determining to live with her in consideration of the relief and stay of his wife and children, and in consideration of a marriage before concluded to be had between the son of Sir John Conway, Knight, and one of the daughters of the said Anthony Bourne, did give, grant, and assure and release all his lands in possession and reversion[4] with all his goods, chattels, debts, duties sums of monies and

---

1 This date is provided by the Calendar of State Papers as "Date: Jan.? 1583." Folio 146v includes that date and question mark in a modern hand.
2 Fine, *n*.1 †III. Senses denoting an agreement, contract, or settlement. *Obsolete*. 9. b. A compromise made between parties in a fictitious or collusive lawsuit for the possession of land, formerly in use as a means of conveyance in cases where the ordinary means were unavailable or less effective. *Obsolete*. c. gen. An amicable settlement of a lawsuit. *Obsolete*. P1. in (†the) fine. Formerly also: †at fine. Cf. affine adv. a. In the end; at last. Now *rare*.
3 Extinguish, *v*. 3. b. To render void (a bill, claim, right, etc). In *Law* sometimes *spec*. c. To discharge, obtain total acquittance of, "wipe out" by full payment or composition.
4 Reversion, *n*.1 I. Senses relating to succession of ownership or office. 1. *Law*. A. An estate granted to one party and subsequently granted in turn or transferable to another, esp. upon the death of the original grantee; the right of succeeding to, or next occupying, such an estate. b. The return of an estate to the original owner, or his or her heirs, after the expiry of

demands to Sir John Danvers, Sir James Mervyn, Sir John Conway, Knight, and John Chamberleyn and William Clarke, Esquires, to have and enjoy the same freely and absolutely without any condition to their proper uses[5] during the life of Elizabeth Bourne, wife of the said Anthony, and after her decease to remain to Amy Bourne and Mary Bourne, daughters of the said Anthony and their heirs and assigns, forever.

Master Bourne, the second day of June next following the date of his deeds, aforesaid, fled out of England without her Majesty's license, contrary to the laws of parliament, arrived at Callais and from there directed his letters to Sir James Mervyn and Sir John Conway to send him over certain household stuff, plate, and several sums of money to the value of one thousand pounds for the better maintenance of himself and his woman. For as much as Sir John Conway, in due consideration of his duty toward her Majesty, to move him through want to repair home the sooner refused to satisfy his request in these points of so large demands only sent him that might supply his necessary charges for a time with his best advice to seek in duty his reconciliation to her Majesty, my Lords of the Honorable Council, and the liberty of his country. Hereupon, Master Bourne took so great mislike that presently showed a sorrowful and repining[6] mind against the covenant which he had made in advancement of his [children] under th{...}[7] and due considerations aforesaid exclaiming [agai]nst all those whom he had assured his children's right [entitled] her{...} the whole state, suggesting it done by fraud and coven[8] to her Majesty. Whereupon grew long question, suit, and great charges in law between her Majesty, Master Bourne, and his {...} and the said Sir James Mervyn, Sir John Conway, and others.

But in fine, it pleased her Highness of her great clemency by [the] Lords of her Honorable Privy Council to command Anthony Bo[urne,] Esquire, and Elizabeth, his wife, Sir James Mervyn, and Sir John Conway to agree within themselves of all controversies, and to satisfy Master Thomas West of 1000 pounds, which her Highness had given him, and was pleased of her gracious {...} in consideration thereof and for the better relief of the

---

    a grant or death of the grantee; the right to such a return; an estate thus returned. 3. *a*. The right of succeeding to the possession of something, or of obtaining something at a future time; the action or process of transferring something in this way. Also: a thing or possession which a person expects to obtain.
5 Use, *n*. 15 c. A trust vested in a person for the holding of land or other property, of which another receives or is entitled to the profits or benefits. [This term is used throughout this document as well as NA, SP 13c, fol. 28. In particular, we learn that Elizabeth Bourne is left with the use of properties which are hers while Sir John Conway receives all the profits.]
6 Repining, adj. B. Given to repining, discontented; characterized by or of the nature of repining.
7 The tears in this document are located in the margin of the right margin of each verso folio.
8 Perhaps short for covenant? But also: coven | covin, *n*. a. An assembly, meeting, or company. Obs. b. spec. A gathering of witches; a "convent" or company of 13 witches; cf. convent *n*. 1, 2.

110 *Letters and Documents*

gentlewo[man] to grant her Highness's free pardon of all other forfeitures by Master Bourne's flight to such persons and the said Anthony Bourne, Elizabeth his wife, Sir James Mervyn, and Sir John Conway should, within themselves it should pass unto.

It fortuned they could not agree within themselves whereupon her Highness commanded Sir Francis Walsingham, Knight, {...} Principal Secretary to hear and determine all grie[vances between] {...} all the said parties, which his Honor could not, although his persuasion and travail were great. But in short time, [Anthony] Bourne, drawing himself to better remembrance of h{...} and reason than he had showed before his Honor procured {...} Chancellor's letters to Sir Francis Walsingham, his Honor, to [Michael] Blount and John Chamberleyn, Esquires, to travel to Elizabeth Bourne, his wife, and also to Sir John Conway, and made them offer in writing for a small end of all controversies, which being thought reasonable and indifferent for all parties by their hon{...} the offer and end was accordingly accepted.

And, thereupon, the said Anthony Bourne, finding no able means in himself to satisfy the 1000 pounds to her Majesty by the time required or to procure sufficient sureties for Satisfaction thereof neither in himself able to pay his {...} charge and debts to Master Lieutenant of the Tower for his diet and other duties of the house, nor yet to sue out h{...} Highness letters patents for the pardon of his flight and of all his goods and chattel forfeited, and, furthermore, being unable to wage law for recovery of all such debts and right which her Highness had pardoned and ought to be due to him or to his wife and children to be holpen[9] in these extremities, and to have a certain benefit and competent person assured and paid him for his maintenance, whereas the estate of debts stayed doubtful and in danger of utter loss or at the least, long suit in law, experiences, and trouble. And desiring presently to travel into Ireland with a resolute mind to spend the rest of his life apart from his wife with his woman and for a full agreement and final determination between his wife, himself, and Sir John Conway of all controversies touching their several rights in and to all the whole state of lands, goods, and debts, conveyed and assured by his several deeds of conveyance[10] bearing date the 18th day of March in the 19th year of the Queen's Majesty's reign, the said Anthony and Elizabeth, and the kin and friends of them both, made special suit to the said Sir John Conway to take upon him to pay her Majesty 1000 pounds and also to become bound to pay [Master] Bourne two thousand pounds by a day certain to assure him also the receipt

---

9 Holp(e) | holpen, *n.* past tense and participle of help *v.* Also occasionally used as present tense and infinitive.
10 Conveyance, *n.* 7. a. *Law.* The transference of property (esp. real property) from one person to another by any lawful act (in modern use only by deed or writing between living persons).

of threescore and twelve pounds of arrearage[11] of Cutteslowe and Cumnor in the hands of Master Chamberleyn. And that his wife should confess[12] a fine[13] to extinguish her right of 50 pounds a year in Cumnor, being joint purchaser with him for the same and in consideration that the said Anthony might reserve to himself and enjoy the whole right and accompt of two thousand pounds debt, due from the Lord Chancellor of England, then by virtue of two recognizances[14] as also in consideration that he enjoy one jewel of one hundred and fifty pounds price that sometime was his wife's, then in the hands of the Lord Compton, together with all other debts due from the said Lord Compton and Francis Stafford. And lastly, in consideration that Sir John Conway was content that the said Anthony Bourne shall reduce the portion of 5000 pounds, assured by him unto Amy Bourne, his daughter, in her advancement of marriage with Sir John Conway's son, to one thousand, one hundred pounds and thereof clearly to acquit the said Anthony. And that the said Sir John should be pleased to accept the payment thereof at the hands of Elizabeth Bourne, wife of the said Anthony as the said Sir John and Elizabeth could agree of. Under all those aforesaid considerations, it was and is fully and plainly concluded, accorded, covenanted, and agreed.

That the said Anthony Bourne, Sir John Danvers, Sir James Mervyn, Knight, William Clarke and John Chamberleyn, Esquires should give, grant, and absolutely release jointly and severally unto the said Sir John Conway, his heirs, executors, and assigns, without any trust, confidence, interest, use, or property reserved to the said Anthony and Elizabeth the manors of Cutteslowe, Sarsden, and Upton-upon-Severn in possession and reversion with all their profits and appurtenances[15] during the life of Elizabeth Bourne and after her decease to the use [of] Amy and Mary Bourne, forever according to the true meaning of one book of conveyance made by the said Anthony unto Sir John Danvers, Sir James Mervyn, and others be{...} date the 18th day of March in the 19th year of the [Queen's] {...} Majesty's

---

11 Arrearage, *n.* †1. b. The state or condition of being behind, or *in arrear*, with a payment due; indebtedness, debt. *Obsolete.* 3. a. *concrete.* That which is in arrear; an amount overdue, an outstanding or unpaid sum or balance.
12 Confess, *v.* II. spec. 7. *Law.* b. *transitive.* To admit (a thing) as proved, or legally valid.
13 Fine, *n.1* †III. Senses denoting an agreement, contract, or settlement. *Obsolete.* 9.b. A compromise made between parties in a fictitious or collusive lawsuit for the possession of land, formerly in use as a means of conveyance in cases where the ordinary means were unavailable or less effective. *Obsolete.*
14 Recognizance, *n.* 1. *Law.* A bond or obligation by which a person undertakes before a court or magistrate to perform some act or observe some condition, such as to pay a debt, or appear when summoned; the action or process of entering such a bond. Also: a sum of money pledged as a surety for such a bond, and forfeited by a failure to fulfil it. Also in extended use.
15 Appurtenance, *n.* 1. *Law* and *gen.* A thing that belongs to another, a "belonging"; a minor property, right, or privilege, belonging to another more important, and passing in possession with it; an appendage.

reign. And also according to one other Indenture trip[artite][16] {...} bearing date, the 14th day of October in the 21st year of [her] {...} Majesty's reign made, sealed, and delivered by the said Anthony of t[he first] {...} part, Sir John Conway, Knight, of the second part, {...} Sir James Mervyn, Knight, William Clarke, and J[ohn Chamberleyn] {...} Esquires of the third part, and also all goods, debts, ch{...} duties, plate, household stuff, rights and demands {...} mentioned and expressed in another indenture made by Anthony to all the foresaid persons, bearing date as aforesaid {...} 18th day of March, in the 19th year of the Queen's Majesty's reign. And also all other his goods, debts, chattels, rights, duties, and demands, which the said Anthony had at any time before. To have and to hold the same goods, debts, rights, and demands whatsoever unto the said Sir John Conway, his heirs {...} executors, and assigns, forever, and to the only use, behoof, {...} benefit of the said Sir John without any use, trust, or confidence, reserved to the said Anthony or Elizabeth[.] A{...} by the said indenture appeareth.

And also under the consideration aforesaid and for divers other reasonable causes her moving, the said Elizabeth consented and agreed and the said Anthony did give and grant as much as in him and her was unto Sir John Conway the custody, education, and bringing up of Amy Bourne and Mary Bourne, daughters of the said Anthony during their minorities, and until they shall be married. And also the bestowing and marriages of them and all commodities and profits growing thereof, at his liberty, appointment, and pleasure without any let, taking away suit, action, impeachment, trouble, disturbance, hinderance, gainsaying, molestation, or interruption of the said Anthony Bourne or of any other person or persons, by his or their means, assent, consent, or procurement. To the performance of all which covenants the said Anthony Bourne standeth bound in five thousand pounds by statute of the staple.[17]

And also in covenant and under the same penalty, that the said Anthony shall not nor any man for, by, or under him or by his knowledge, consent, or sufferance, claim, challenge, or sue for or demand in any court or courts or before any judge, chancellor, or the most Honorable Council of the Queen's Majesty, her heirs or successors, or elsewhere or otherwise, anything specified in the said conveyance and assured or meant to be assured to the said Sir John Conway.

And also that he hath not nor shall not do, procure, suffer, nor consent unto any act or acts, thing or things, or any devise, conveyance, or otherwise

---

16 Tripartite, A. *adj.* 2. Made in three corresponding parts or copies, as an indenture n. (q.v.) drawn up between three persons or parties, each of whom preserves one of the copies. "B. n." A tripartite indenture (see A. 2). *Obs.*
17 Statute of the staple, *n.* †1. *Law.* = statute staple n. *Obsolete.* 2. The statute 27 Edw. III, which established staples (staple *n.*² 1a) in various English towns, and at Carmarthen, Dublin, Waterford, Cork, and Drogheda, and contained regulations for their form of government and the conduct of their business. Chiefly with *the* and capital initials. *historical.*

whereby the estates, limitations, or uses in the said deeds of conveyances made or assured or mentioned or meant to be made or assured are, shall, or may be by any man of means discontinued, avoided, defeated, altered, weakened, or impaired.

And, furthermore, that the said Anthony shall at all time and times whensoever he shall be required thereunto at the charges of Sir John Conway do acknowledge, perform, execute, and cause and suffer to be done all acts, things, devises, conveyances, and assurances in law be it by fine, recovery[18] with double or single voucher[19] release[20] with warrantize[21] deeds enrolled or otherwise and by all or so many of the said ways or means as from time to time shall be advised or devised by the council of the said Sir John Conway for the more better assurance and sure making of the whole.

And for the clear discharge of the said Sir John Conway against the said Anthony Bourne of all manners of matters, actions, and demands, whatsoever, the said Anthony Bourne by the said Indenture doth remiss and release unto the said Sir John Conway all actions accompts, debts, duties, uses, trusts, confidences, suits, demands and all other things and matters from the beginning of the wor[ld] {…} until the day of the date thereof.

And also the said Anthony Bourne hath by one other his deed of release bearing date the 22nd day of April in the 23rd year of the Queen's Majesty's reign, remised, exonerated, and quitclaimed[22] Sir John Conway of all actions, duties, debts, and demands for any manner of matter, cause, or color whatsoever from the beginning of the world until the day of the date thereof, except one anuity or annual r{…} of fourscore pounds a year, to be paid to Master Bo[ourne] during his life by Sir John Conway, his heirs, execu[tors,] or assigns.

Unto all which covenants, concords, and agreements, Elizabeth Bourne, wife to the said Anthony Bourne, did give her {…} full and willing consent

---

18 Recovery, 2. *Law. a.* The fact or process of gaining or regaining possession of or a right to property, compensation, etc., by a legal process or judgment; spec. (also common recovery) a process by which entailed estate may be transferred from one person to another, based on a legal fiction involving the collusive default of a third party (now *historical*). Cf. fine n.1 9b, fine and recovery at fine *n.1* Phrases 5.
19 Voucher, *n.*[1] 1. a. *Law.* The summoning of a person into court to warrant the title to a property.
20 Release, *n.* 2. b. A written discharge or receipt attesting the settlement of a debt, etc. 3. a. The relinquishment of a right or claim; spec. surrender of the right of legal action against another. Also: an instance of this, or a document affirming it.
21 Warrantise, *n.* 1. *Law.* = warranty n. 1a. clause of warrantise (also used *figuratively*); plea of warrantise. 2. a. gen. The action of warranting, guaranteeing, or giving assurance; the state or fact of being guaranteed. to hold, clepe, bind, call to warrantise; on, with, by warrantise.
22 Quitclaim, *v.* 1. *transitive.* To declare (a person) free; to release, acquit, or discharge. Also intransitive. Now archaic and historical. 2. *transitive.* Chiefly *Law.* To renounce, resign, give up (a possession, claim, right, pursuit, etc.).

as appeareth by a particular under {...} her own hand and by a joint consent in writing with {...} husband as followeth:

> For as much as Sir John Conway is content to take {...} to satisfy the Queen's Majesty one thousand pounds and {...} Bourne two thousand pounds and all other things agreed {...} which Master Bourne requireth, and for as much as he is {...} to stand to the charge in calling in the debts and to the adve{...} what may be lost of them and for as much as he is further c{...} to stand to the perils of all encumbrance and charge which may come upon the lands by Master Bourne or otherwise, and for as much as he is moreover content to acquit me of the £1500 which ought to be paid to him by Master Bourne's covenant, and of all other things, I am content and well pleased a[nd] do give my free and full consent that Master Bourne assure all things absolutely, without any trust, condition, limitation, or use to be reserved to me or to any person for me, and am further contented and well pleased that according to the plain word and covenants of an Indenture of three parts, bearing date 14th day of October in the 21st year of the Queen's {...} reign, that Sir John Conway shall enjoy all {...} to his own proper use and benefit, according to the express words of the Indenture. In witness of which truth and my willing consent to the same, I have written this note of remembrance with my own hand, faithfully promising Sir John Conway to set my hand and seal to a joint and sufficient warranty with Master Bourne, to authorize Sir John Danvers, Sir James Mervyn, Knights, John Chamberleyn and William Clarke, Esquires, to release to Sir John Conway absolutely all their right, interests, state,[23] and claim into the whole state of lands, good, debts etc., conveyed to them and every of them by Master Bourne's several deeds bearing date the 18th day of March in the 19th year of the Queen's Majesty's reign that now is, and that he may and shall quietly enjoy without any trust, use, limitation, or meaning of any part of it to be intended or reserved to my use or behalf. I bind myself by my faith and my truth always to acquit and discharge him of all trusts of or for any part of anything that is, or shall be, conveyed and assured by Master Bourne and intended to me by any meaning, bill, book, agreement, or writing.
>
> E. Bourne

In confirmation whereof the said Anthony Bourne and Elizabeth his wife by her and his letters of warrant and request did authorize Sir James Mervyn, Sir John Danvers, Knights, John Chamberleyn and William Clarke, Esquires, jointly with the said Anthony by one Indenture tripartite bearing date the 14th day of October in the 21st year of her Majesty's reign to give,

---

23 State, *n.* †(c) With reference to livelihood, wealth, or possessions. *Obsolete.* Cf. estate *n.* 2.

grant, convey, release, assure, sign, seal, and set over unto Sir John Conway, Knight, absolutely all things within the several deeds of conveyance specified as appeareath plainly by the said deeds at large, as by his and her letter of warrant in these words under written, viz.

> After my very hardy commendations, whereas by my several deeds indented bearing date 18th day of March in the 19th year of her Majesty's reign, I did assure and convey unto you my very loving friends, Sir James Mervyn, Knight, Sir John Danvers, Knight, Sir John Conway, Knight, John Chamberleyn and William Clarke, Esquires, all those my manors and Lordships of Cutteslowe and Sarsden in the County of Oxford and diverse other hereditaments,[24] mentioned in my deed therewith. And, likewise, by the other of my said deeds {...} assure and convey to you, the persons aforesaid, all my goods, chattels, jewels, and household stuff, among other things mentioned in the same deed to the uses contained in the said deed. For as much as since diverse questions in law hath grown my occasion touching the forfeiture of all the said goods and chattels and as well touching the same as for the preservat[ion] {...} of the inheritance of the said lands according to the trust mentioned in my said deed, the said Sir John Conway, Knight, hath greatly traveled and hath therein fully satisfied my expectation and my wife's, besides travail and suit {...} to her Majesty touching the forfeiture therein pretended, and thereupon, the said Sir John Conway, my wife, and I [have] upon full agreement in all respects entered into full conclusion and composition touching all the promises, the counterpane[25] of the Indentures, thereof, made between {...} may appear. My hardy request and also hers, therefore, {...} you, the said Sir James Mervyn, Sir John Danvers, John Cham[berleyn,] and William Clarke is that upon the request of the said John Conway, you will absolutely release and assure to {...} Sir John Conway all such right and titles and estate and {...} as to you together with the said Sir John Conway {...} the promises by the deeds aforesaid. And this my {...} with my own hand and sealed with my seal, shall be {...} a satisfaction to you towards me of all trust reposed {...} forever. As a full warrant and discharge on her part {...} in the promises to all intents and purposes, for which you do {...} both she and I shall be thankful unto you. And thus I commit you to the tuition of the Almighty. From London this 18th of February 1579.
> Your willing friends,
> Anthony Bourne & E. Bourne

---

24 Hereditament, *n.*1 a. *Law.* Any item of property that can be inherited; something either corporeal (such as land or a building) or incorporeal (such as a rent) that can be passed to an heir; real property.*corporeal, incorporeal hereditament*: see the first element.
25 †Counterpane, *n.*1 Obsolete. 1. *Law.* The counterpart of an indenture.

116 *Letters and Documents*

Now after the full and perfect agreement, conclusion, sealing, and delivering of this Indenture tripartite to Sir John Conway by Master Bourne, Sir John Danvers, and Sir James Mervyn, John Chamberleyn, and William Clarke, Esquires, absolutely without any condition, trust, limitation, use right, purport,[26] intent, or meaning reserved to Master Bourne, his wife, or any person, but only the right of the lands to descend to Amy and Mary Bourne his two daughters. And after Master Bourne of his part had acknowledged a statute of £5000 for the performance of the whole, and after Sir John Conway on his part had performed all covenants in the said indentures and every other book, bill article, or agreement with Master Bourne, or any man to his use:

Sir John Conway of a friendly consideration and care of his well doing, and withal to further a quiet state between him and his wife,[27] they being agreed then upon actions to lead their lives separately asunder until by their further assents they should with good liking be fully determined to live in one dear society and company; in the mean[28] that Mistress Bourne might live quietly, in person, without violence to be offered by Master Bourne or by any his procurement, and that she might have and use the custody, commodity, and profit of all lands and tenants, revenues, and profits, and also all goods, apparels, and household stuff, or any other benefit or meet thing which by any of her friends and allies should be lent, given, or sold her toward her maintenance without seizure, intermeddling or disturbance of[29] Master Bourne or any other by his means. In this consideration partly and chiefly as it may further appear by an Indenture bearing date of 29th day of June in the 22nd year of her Majesty's reign that Sir John Conway should quietly enjoy all profits, lands, and goods conveyed. Sir John Conway did covenant and bind himself, his heirs, and executors to pay after the life of the Lady Anne, Countess of Warwick, wife of Sir Edward Unton, fourscore pounds of yearly pension to Master Bourne, during his life in manner and format in the said Indenture is expressed.

Hereupon, Master Bourne by his deed dated the 22nd day of April In the 23rd year of the Queen's Majesty's reign, hath remised,[30] exonerated, and quitclaimed Sir John Conway of all actions, duties, debts, and demands for any manner of matter, cause or color whatsoever from the beginning of the world until the day of the date thereof. Except this one annuity or annual

---

26 Purport, *n.* 1. a. That which is conveyed or expressed, esp. by a formal document or speech; effect, tenor, import; meaning, substance, sense.
27 Anthony and Elizabeth Bourne.
28 Mean, *n.*3 1. b. An intermediary tenancy between a lord and a second tenant. Only in mene: in such a tenancy; writ of mene: = writ of mesne at mesne *n.* 2a. *Obsolete. rare.*
29 By.
30 Remise *v.*1 1. *Trans. Law.* To give up, surrender, transfer, or release (a right, property, etc). Also to release (a person) from an obligation, etc. Frequently in legal formulas.

rent of fourscore pounds yearly paid to Master Bourne during his life by Sir John Conway, his heirs, executors, or assigns.

Upon all these agreements there accrued Master Bourne £1743, 13ˢ 4ᵈ [31]

Master Bourne of these sums was fully satisfied and paid the {...} day of March, anno 1580, before March 1582, having {...} wasted all or the most part of this benefit and state of {...} aforesaid, through his continuance and charge with Mistress Pagnam. He suggested a new complaint against Sir John Conway before the Lords of the Honorable Council, and the Chancellor of England, that he withheld from {...} of certain lands, goods, tenants, in right {...} of his wife, and also the body of Mary Bourne {...} youngest daughter and co-heir.

Here upon, there was by letters of warrant {...} Lords of the Council and by commiss[ion of] {...} her Majesty's Court of Chancery under the great seal {...} date the 22nd day of November in the 25th year of her {...} Majesty's reign, authority and power given to Henry Unton, James Croft, Henry Goodere, and John Chamberleyn, Esquires, to hear, execute, determine, and certify all causes {...} and controversies, whatsoever, between the said Anthony Bourne, plaintiff, and Sir John Conway, Knight, defendant, when upon grew a final end of all griefs and demands whatsoever. Viz.

It appeareth by Indenture tripartite dated the 18th of January, in the 25th year her Majesty's reign made between Henry Unton, James Croft, Henry Goodere, and John Chamberleyn, Esquires, of the one part, Sir John Conway, Knight of the second part, and Anthony Bourne, Esquire, of the third part, concluding and determining all controversies between Anthony Bourne, Esquire, and Sir John Conway, Knight, surmised[32] by the said Anthony Bourne as well before the Lords of her Majesty's Privy Council, the Court of Chancery as elsewhere, that the said Sir John Conway had not performed the trust and confidence reposed in him by certain several Indentures, articles, and other writings. After many and diverse objections, allegations, and defenses as could or might on either side be inferred and alleged, and after a full hearing of all manner of causes and controversies, whatsoever, between them, the said parties, the said arbitrators do with the free and full consent and willing submission of both parties, now order unto and determine all causes, griefs, complaints, controversies, debates, surmised[33] trusts, and suits whatsoever between them, in manner and form following, viz.

---

31 1743 pounds, 13 shillings, 4 pence.
32 Surmise, *v.* †1. a. *transitive*. To put upon someone as a charge or accusation; to charge on or upon, allege against a person; spec. in Law, to submit as a charge or information, allege formally. *Obsolete.*
33 Surmised, *adj.* †1. Submitted as a charge or information to a court of law; charged upon or alleged against someone; more generally, alleged, supposed. *Obs.* †2. Devised falsely, feigned. *Obs.* †3. Imagined, supposed, fancied. *Obs.*

118   Letters and Documents

First, the said arbitrators do order and award, for as much as the said Sir John Conway, by his former proceedings and conformity to this final Ind[enture] hath effectually performed and discharged the trust that Anthony Bourne hath any way reposed in him, and hath not done, or gone about to put in ure[34] or practice any act or devise for his own private benefit to defraud or impeach the said Anthony Bourne or his heirs, the said arbitrators do first order, arbitrate, and award and the said Anthony Bourne for him, his executors, and assigns, doth covenant and grant to and with the said Sir John Conway, his heirs, executors, administrators, and assigns and every other person claiming [for], by, or from him, them, or any of them shall be freely acquitted and discharged against the said Anthony Bourne, his executors and administrators of, for, and concerning all manner of suits and quarrels, griefs and complaints, trusts, accompts, reckonings, controversies, and demands in any wise concerning either any goods, chattels, debts, lands tenants, or hereditaments or otherwise, except the breach of some covenant[s] in these points contained, or for the nonpayment of £80 by the year, granted by Sir John Conway by a deed indented dated the 29th day of June in the 22nd year of her Majesty's reign.

And the said arbitrators do award that although they do not find any cause in law to enforce the said Sir John Conway thereunto, yet in respect of the present estate of the said Anthony Bourne, and in consideration, that it is condescended[35] by the said Anthony Bourne that the said Sir John Conway shall have by the intent of this award the education and free disposing in marriage of Amy Bourne and Mary Bourne, daughters and heirs apparent of the said Anthony Bourne and Elizabeth, his wife, according to the purport[36] and effects of a pair of indentures tripartite dated the 14th [day of] {...} October in the 21st year of her Majesty's reign, and in consid[eration] {...} of the avoiding of all charges, expenses, and suits which may {...} to the great losses of the said Sir John Conway and to the {...} and impairing of the estate of the said Anthony Bourne {...} and award, and it is agreed by the said Sir John Conway (at {...} mediation of the said arbitrators[)] that the said Anthony Bou[rne] {...} have and enjoy the manors of Cutteslowe with the appurtenances[37] {...} the feast of the Annunciation of our Lady, next [& etc.] for the {...} of 80 years (if the same Anthony and Elizabeth shall both

---

34   †Ure, *n.*1 *Obsolete*. I. in ure: 1. a. In or into use, practice, or performance. Often with verbs, as *bring, come, have,* and esp. *put*. Also rarely with *into*.
35   Condescend, *v.* †9. to be condescended: to be agreed. *Obsolete*.
36   Purport, *n.* 1. a. That which is conveyed or expressed, esp. by a formal document or speech; effect, tenor, import; meaning, substance, sense.
37   Appurtenance, *n.* 1. *Law* and *gen*. A thing that belongs to another, a "belonging"; a minor property, right, or privilege, belonging to another more important, and passing in possession with it; an appendage.

live) and upon the yearly rent of £90 to be paid to Sir John Conway, his heirs, or assigns, in manner and for[m] hereafter following, and under such conditions {...} Indentures mentioned.

And that the said Sir John Conway and Ed[ward his] son and heir apparent of the said Sir John, before {...} day of this instant month shall become bound by {...} obligatory to Henry Unton, James Croft, Esquires {...} of £600 with condition there upon endorsed for the {...} of £300 at midsummer in the year of our Lord God {...} the new College Hall in Oxford and doth coven[ant] {...} pay Anthony Bourne before the annunciation of our Lady a {...} £100.

And the said Sir John Conway for the consideration aforesaid by these presents hath devised[38] to the said Anthony Bourne the said manor of Cutteslowe with the appurtenances (excepting woodland and underwoods) to give and to hold the same from the annunciation of our Lady next for 24 years, [(]if the said Anthony Bourne and Elizabeth, his wife, shall fortune both so long to live) paying therefore yearly to the said Sir John Conway, his heirs, and assigns £90 at the feast of St. Michael and the annunciation of our Lady by even portions.

Provided always that if the rent of £90 be not paid after any of the said feasts by the space of six weeks, or if the said Anthony Bourne or any other by his consent, means, or procurement or under his title shall any time hereafter in any court of the Queen's Majesty or elsewhere, before any judge, justice, chancellor, or any other person or persons sue, implead,[39] molest, vex, grieve or trouble the said Sir John Conway, his heirs, executors, or assigns, or any claiming by, from, or under them for any debts, duty, trust, confidence, or demands or other matter, contrary to any article in this award had or moved or contrary to the meanings and intent thereof (except upon the breech of any article or covenant contained in these Indentures or non-payments of the yearly rent of £90 or shall before reconciliation had and made with his wife, molest, vex, sue disquiet, or trouble by any means whatsoever the said Elizabeth, his wife, either in person or in goods, or chattels, lands, or rents, which be, shall be, or may hereafter happen to be in {...}, use or receipt, of the said Elizabeth, his wife or of any other for her or under her title or possession. That then and from thenceforth the said lease of the said Manor of Cutteslowe and one covenant hereafter in the said Indentures for the payment of the yearly rent of £90 and all things herein contained touching the assurance of the lease and rent of £80 to be utterly void and of non-effect.

38 Devise, *v*. †3. To assign, appoint, order, direct. (*absol.* or *transitive* with simple object or object clause.) *Obsolete*. 4. *Law*. To assign or give by will. Now technically used only of realty, but formerly of all kinds of property that could be disposed of by will, = bequeath.
39 Implead, *v*. 1. a. *trans*. To sue (a person, etc.) in a court of justice, raise an action against. †2. To arraign, accuse, impeach. Const. *of*. *Obsolete*.

120   Letters and Documents

[B]etween these parties to revive any new or further suit concerning these causes now determined by us, whereby your Lordships or others might again be driven to further trouble in the hearing of any new complaints, and for as much as notwithstanding some former agreements heretofore concluded and by great good advice set down, there hath been from time to time matter found to renew strife between them. For the avoiding whereof, in time to come and for the former reasons by us alleged, we have thought it good also to let your Lordships know that we have made this order as well with the willing assent and voluntary submission of {...} themselves to the same, as by virtue of the said co{...} to us directed. And therefore, are most humble {...} to your Lordships that it will please you by your lette[rs] {...} parties to signify your favorable acceptance of or serv{...} in this agreement with your express commandment {...} them both for the due observing of the same and them desisting from all further differences in that be {...}. And lastly, that by your Lordships' order, this commission {...} order may be returned into her Majesty's court of {...} Chancery there to remain of Record {...} of the parties which shall at any time hereafter {...} the infringing of the same.

And so with our most humble duties to your g{...} leave to trouble the same, Chipping Norton {...} day of January.[40]

Your Lordships' most humble at commandment {...}
H. Goodere and John Chamberleyn

---

40   "1583?" is written in a more modern hand on the center top of fol. 146v. It seems to be the source of the date given in the Calendar of State Papers.

28 18 January 1583[/4], [Arbitrators' Report, Indenture of Award]
(NA, SP 13/c, fol. 28)

This Indenture of Award tripartite[1] made the eighteenth day of January in the five and twentieth year of the reign of our sovereign lady, Elizabeth, by the grace of God, Queen of England, France, and Ireland, defender of the faith, etc., between Henry Unton, James Croft, Henry Goodere, and John Chamberleyn, Esquires of the first part; Sir John Conway, Knight, of the second part; and Anthony Bourne, Esquire, of the third part, WITNESSETH[2] that whereas diverse indentures, articles, and writings of agreements and conveyances have been heretofore had, made, and sealed between the said Anthony Bourne, Sir John Conway, and others, whereby as well the goods, chattels, as the lands, tenements, and hereditaments of the said Anthony Bourne have been assured and conveyed to diverse uses as by the said conveyance may appear, whereupon (and by reasons of the flying of the said Anthony Bourne beyond the seas without her Majesty's license, contrary to the statute in that case provided) diverse controversies are arisen and grown between the said Anthony Bourne and the said Sir John Conway upon the surmise of the said Anthony Bourne, as well before the lords of the Queen's Majesty's most honorable privy council, as in the Court of Chancery and elsewhere, suggesting that the said Sir John Conway had not effectually performed the trust and confidence reposed in him by the said several indentures, articles, and other writings. The [indecipherable][3] matters in controversy by virtue of her Majesty's commission, bearing date the two and twentieth day of November last past, under the great seal of England, hath been referred to the hearing and determination of the said Henry Unton, James Croft, Henry Goodere, and John Chamberleyn, being Arbitrators indifferently elected and chosen by and between the said parties of and by their own voluntary and free consent to hear and determine all manner of

---

1 Tripartite, *adj.* and *n.* A. adj. 1. a. Divided into or composed of three parts or kinds; threefold, triple. 2. Made in three corresponding parts or copies, as an indenture *n.* (q.v.) drawn up between three persons or parties, each of whom preserves one of the copies.
2 All capitalized words in the original have been retained.
3 There is a fold that obscures the word, which may be "chief," but only the "f" is visible.

controversies whatsoever moved or depending between them. NOW, therefore, as well assembling themselves at Chipping Norton, within the County of Oxford, the day and year aforesaid as the parties themselves, after many diverse and sundry objections, allegations, and defenses as could or might be on either side then before them, declared, produced, inferred, and alleged, and after full and ample hearing of all manner of causes and controversies whatsoever between them, the said parties HAVE AND DO by these persons with the free and full consent and willing submission of both the said parties, set down and pronounce their order, rule, arbitrament and determination of all causes, griefs, complaints, controversies, debates, surmised trusts and suits whatsoever between them, the said parties. As also they, the said parties, do by these presently covenant and grant for them either with the other in manner and form following: (that is to say), FORASMUCH as the said Sir John Conway as well by his former proceedings as by his [good] conformity to this final end, hath well and effectually performed and discharged the trust and confidence that the said Anthony Bourne hath heretofore any way reposed in him and hath not done or gone about to put in ure[4] or practice any act or acts, devise or devises, for his own private benefit whereby to defraud, impair, or impeach the said Anthony Bourne or his heirs. Therefore, as well they, the said Arbitrators, do first order, arbitrate, adjudge, and award as also the said Anthony Bourne, for him, his executors and assigns doth covenant and grant to and with the said Sir John Conway, his executors and assigns by these presents, that the said Sir John Conway, his heirs, executors, administrators, and assigns and every other person claiming in, by, from, or under him, them, or any of them shall from henceforth be forever fully and freely acquitted and discharged against the said Anthony Bourne, his executors and administrators of, for, and concerning all manner of suits and quarrels, griefs, complaints, trusts, accompts, reckonings, controversies, and demands in anywise concerning either any goods, chattels, debts, lands, tenants, or hereditaments or otherwise (except only for or concerning one annuity of fourscore pounds by the year hereafter in these presents mentioned) and except also for such interest and benefit as to him, the said Anthony Bourne, is ordered and assigned in this present award and agreement. AND that the said Anthony Bourne, his executors or administrators, shall not at any time hereafter in any court of the Queen's Majesty or elsewhere before any judge, justice, chancellor, or other person or persons, either by course of Equity or Common Law sue, implead, molest, vex, grieve, or trouble the said Sir John Conway, his heirs, executors, administrators, or assigns or any claiming in, by, from, or under them, or any of them for, by reason or any way concerning any other debt, duty, trust, confidence, or demand (except upon the breach of some of the covenants, articles

---

4 † Ure, *n.*1 *Obsolete.* I. in ure: a. In or into use, practice, or performance. Often with verbs, as *bring, come, have,* and esp. *put.* Also rarely with *into.*

or agreements contained in these Indentures or for the nonpayment of the annuity or yearly rent aforesaid of fourscore pounds by the year granted unto him, the said Anthony Bourne, by the said Sir John Conway by a certain deed indented[5] bearing date the nine and twentieth day of June in the two and twentieth year of the reign of the Queen's Majesty that now is.[)] AND FURTHERMORE, as well, they, the said Arbitrators, do award that although they do not find any cause in law to enforce the said Sir John Conway there unto, YET NEVERTHELESS in respect of the present estate of the said Anthony Bourne, and in consideration that it is now full and freely granted and condescended unto by the said Anthony Bourne, that the said Sir John Conway, his executors and assigns shall have by the intent of this, our present award, the marriage, education, bringing up, and free disposition in marriage of Amy Bourne and Mary Bourne, daughters and heir apparent of the said Anthony Bourne and Elizabeth Bourne, his wife, according to the express words, effect, and purport of a pair of indentures tripartite had and made between the said Anthony Bourne of the first part, Sir John Conway of the second part, and Sir James Mervyn, Knight, and others of the third part, bearing the date the fourteenth day of October, in the one and twentieth year of the reign of our sovereign Lady Elizabeth, the Queen's Majesty that now is. AND in consideration also of the avoiding of all such charges and expenses in suits of law, which otherwise might arise to the great vexation, trouble, charge, and losses of the said Sir John Conway and to the great hinderance and impairing of the good estate of the said Anthony Bourne, DO by this award order and judge, and also it is agreed by him and the said Sir John Conway (at the mediation of the said arbitrators between them) and the said Sir John Conway doth for him, his heirs, executors, and assigns covenant and grant to and with the said Anthony Bourne, his executors and assigns, by these presents that the said Anthony Bourne shall and may have, hold, occupy and enjoy the Manor of Cutteslowe with the appurtenances in the County of Oxford from the feast of the Annunciation[6] of our Lady now next coming, for and during the term of fourscore years then next following (if the said Anthony Bourne and Elizabeth his wife shall both fortune so long to live) for and upon the yearly rent of fourscore and ten pounds to be paid by the said Sir John Conway, his heirs, executors, and assigns in the manner and form as is hereafter following, and under such articles, and conditions as is hereafter in these Indentures mentioned. AND that the said Sir John Conway with one Edward Conway, Esquire, son and heir apparent of the said Sir John Conway shall before the five and twentieth day of this instant month become bound by

---

5 Indent, $v.^1$. †3. a. *intransitive*. To enter into an engagement by indentures; hence, to make a formal or express agreement; to covenant (*with* a person *for* a thing); to engage. Also *figurative*. *Obsolete*.
6 25 March.

their writing obligatory to Henry Unton and James Croft, Esquires, in the sum of 600 pounds with condition there on endorsed for the payment of the sum of 300 pounds to the said Henry Unton and James Croft, their executors and assigns on the Feast of the Nativity of Saint John Baptist,[7] which shall be in the year of our Lord God one thousand five hundred fourscore and four in the Common Hall of the College of Oxford, which is called the New College, AND doth also covenant to and with the said Anthony Bourne, his executors and assigns, to pay unto the said Anthony Bourne, his executors and assigns, 100 pounds at or before the Feast of the Annunciation of our Lady, now next ensuing, the date hereof in the said hall of the college aforesaid. AND THE SAID Sir John Conway for and in consideration aforesaid hath demised,[8] granted, and to farm letten,[9] and by these presents doth demise, grant, and to farm let unto the said Anthony Bourne, the Manor and Lordship of Cutteslowe aforesaid with the appurtenances in the County of Oxford with all profit and commodities to the said Manor or Lordship belonging or appertaining (excepting and reserving unto the said Sir John Conway, his heirs and assigns, all woods and underwoods standing or growing in or upon the same[)], TO HAVE AND TO HOLD the said Manor and Lordship of Cutteslowe with the appurtenances and all profit and commodities to the said Manor and Lordship belonging or appertaining (except before excepted unto the said Anthony Bourne and his assigns[)] from the feast of the Annunciation of our Lady now next coming, after the date of these presents for and during the term of fourscore years then next following and fully to be complete and ended (if he the said Anthony Bourne and Elizabeth his wife shall fortune both so long to live), YEILDING AND PAYING, therefore, yearly during the said term unto the said Sir John Conway his heirs and assigns fourscore and ten pounds of good and lawful money of England at two terms or feasts in the year usual (that is to say) at the feast of Saint Michael the Archangel and the Annunciation of our Lady by even portions provided always that if it fortune the said yearly rent of fourscore and ten pounds to be behind and unpaid in part in all over or after any of the said feast days in the which the same ought to be paid by the space of six weeks, OR if the said Anthony Bourne or any other by his consent, means, procurement, or under his title shall at any time hereafter in any court of the Queen's Majesty or elsewhere before any Judge, Justice, Chancellor or any person or persons sue, implead, molest, vex, grieve, or trouble the said Sir John Conway, his heirs, executors, administrators, or

---

7 24 June.
8 Demise, *v.* 1. a. *Law (transitive)*. To give, grant, convey, or transfer (an estate) by will or by lease. †2. gen. To convey, transmit; to "lease." *Obsolete*.
9 † Letten, *adj. North American. Obsolete*. Of a property: leased, let. While this definition does not correspond to England or our period, the sense is correct. John Conway will rent the property of Cutteslowe to Antony Bourne.

assigns or any claiming in, by, from, or under them or any of them for any debt, duty, trust, confidence, demand or other matter contrary to any article before in this present award in that behalf had and made or contrary to the true intent and meaning of any part of this present award (except upon the breach of any covenant, article or agreement contained in these Indentures) or for the nonpayment of the yearly rent of fourscore and ten pounds aforesaid, OR shall at any time before reconciliation had or made with his said wife molest, vex, sue, disquiet, or trouble by any means whatsoever the said Elizabeth, his wife, either in her own person, or in any the goods, chattels, lands, or tenants' profits or possessions which be, shall be, or may happen to be in the hands, possession, use, or receipt of the said Elizabeth, his wife, or of any other for her, or to her use, or by, from, or under her title, state, or possession. That then and from henceforth the said lease of the manor of Cutteslowe, and also one covenant hereafter for the payment of the yearly sum of threescore pounds and all and every article, clause, and sentence herein contained touching the assurance of the said lease and rent of threescore pounds to be utterly void and of non-effect. AND THE SAID Anthony Bourne doth covenant and promise to and with the said Sir John Conway, his heirs, executors, and assigns by these presents, that he will not at any time hereafter let or set the said Manor of Cutteslowe or any part thereof without sufficient provision made by the consent of the said Sir John Conway or his heirs for the preservation of the houses, buildings, and mounds of the said Manor from any waste, spoil, or destruction, AND IF IT HAPPEN the said Elizabeth Bourne to decease or depart this natural life before the said Anthony Bourne, then the said Sir John Conway for him, his heirs, executors, and assigns covenanteth, and granteth to and with the said Anthony Bourne, his executors, administrators, and assigns to pay or cause to be paid to the said Anthony Bourne, his executors and assigns, so long as the said Anthony Bourne, his executors or assigns shall well and truly perform, observe, and keep all and every the provisos and conditions before in these presents mentioned and contained which on his and their part are to be performed and kept, the yearly rent or sum of threescore pounds of good and lawful money of England within the Common Hall of the college aforesaid called the New College in Oxford at the feast of Saint Michael the Archangel and the Annunciation of our Lady by even and equal portions. The first payment, thereof, to begin at such of the feast which shall first happen next after the decease of the said Elizabeth Bourne. AND FURTHER, the said Anthony Bourne doth covenant and promise to and with the said Arbitrators and any of them, and to and with the said Sir John Conway, his executors and assigns, that if it happen any reconciliation to be had between the said Anthony Bourne and Elizabeth, his wife, (as the said arbitrators hope and wish and the said Anthony Bourne himself doth pretend and faithfully promiseth to endeavor and seek) that then the said Anthony Bourne will give and perform good and sufficient assurance as well for the security and good usage of the person of the said Elizabeth, his wife, to her liking, as of her goods and lands. AND THE SAID Anthony Bourne doth further faithfully covenant and promise, and the said Arbitrators do likewise award and order, that the said Anthony Bourne shall by way of humble suit move the Right Honorable the now Lord Chancellor of England to annihilate[10] and make void one recognizance of 1500 pounds wherein the said Sir John Conway and Sir James Mervyn stand bound to his Lordship, to save him harmless against her Majesty for 1000 pounds. AND ALSO the said Arbitrators do award that the said Anthony Bourne shall sue unto the Right Honorable the Lord Treasurer of England to take some order for the discharge of the said Sir John Conway touching certain bonds made for or concerning the pretended grant heretofore claimed by William Lane and Edward Lane of the goods of the said Anthony Bourne supposed to be forfeited by his flight of the seas without her Majesty's license. AND ALSO that the said Anthony Bourne shall with effect make most humble suit unto the Lords of her Majesty's most Honorable Privy Council for their Lordships' furtherance and honorable favors in the due execution of her Highness's letters patents heretofore made touching the goods and debts of the said Anthony Bourne, and especially for a debt of 1000 pounds withholden by James Cressy, Esquire, and all other debts by the said letters patents granted or assigned over. AND for that the said Arbitrators verily trust and hope all causes and strifes between the said Sir John Conway and Anthony Bourne are now finally decided and ended, do order, and the said Sir John Conway and Anthony Bourne do covenant and agree each with other, that their several bonds or obligations taken before the Lords of the most Honorable Privy Council be utterly void and delivered up to the parties to be cancelled. AND that nothing in these presents contained be prejudicial to the said Anthony Bourne touching such promise of a surplusage of the said debt of James Cressy, as Sir John Conway hath heretofore made to the said Anthony Bourne. AND it is not withstanding this award fully intended by the said Arbitrators that nothing comprised herein shall extend to, exonerate, or discharge the said Sir John Conway from any trust or confidence reposed in him (if any such be) touching any portion of lands or other substance whatsoever due, limited,[11] or appointed for the maintenance of the said Elizabeth Bourne during her sole life or separation from the said Anthony, her husband,[12] nor after the decease of the said Anthony from any benefit she

---

10 Annihilate, *v.* 2. To make null and void, make of none effect, annul, cancel, abrogate (laws, treaties, rights, etc.). Two examples use the spelling found here. 1525 Ld. Berners tr. J. Froissart *Chron.* II. cliii. 421 "That shulde breke or adnychilate ... the alyances that hath been sworne." 1579 W. Fulke *Confut. Treat. N. Sander* in D. Heskins *Ouerthrowne* 558 "To adnihilate the sacraments ministred by heretikes."
11 2. *transitive* Limit, *v.* †a. To appoint (a person) to an office; to prescribe (a penalty) *upon* or *for* someone; to appoint, direct (a person *to* do something). *Obsolete.*
12 This moment in the Indenture of Award indicates clearly that Elizabeth Bourne was legally named a *femme sole, n.* "*Law.* Now *historical.* An unmarried woman; (sometimes) *spec.*

may reap by virtue of any trust at any time heretofore committed unto him (if any such trust was so repos[ed]). IN WITNESS WHEREOF to the first part of these Indentures tripartite annexed unto the said Commission and certified to the Lords of her Majesty's most Honorable Privy Council by the said Commissioners, they, the said Commissioners together with the said Sir John Conway and Anthony Bourne severally have set their hands and seals. And to the second part of the said Indenture remaining with the said Sir John Conway and to him delivered by the said Anthony Bourne as the deed of the same Anthony, he, the same Anthony Bourne, and the said Commissioners severally have set their hands and seals. And to the third part of the said Indentures remaining with the said Anthony Bourne and to him delivered by the said Sir John Conway as the deed of the said Sir John, he the same Sir John Conway and the said Commissioners severally have set their hands and seals, given the day and year first above written.

[H]enry Unton, James Croft, H Goodere, Esquire, John Chamberleyn, John Conway[, Knight], Anthony Bourne[, Esquire]

Witnessed that they within named Sir John Conway and Edward Conway have the [twentieth] day of January, [Her] Reign Elizabeth, [viginti] quinto, infrascriptis sealed and delivered on obligation of 600 pounds for the payment of the 300 pounds according to the covenant within written.

1583
Sir John Conway
Master Anthony Bourne, Esquire.
[John Chamberleyn][13]

---

one who is divorced or widowed. Also in the English and other common law legal systems: a married woman whose legal status, esp. with regard to her right to own property or to carry on a business, is that of an unmarried woman."

13 The signatures are below but upside down beneath this confirmation of action by John Conway and Edward Conway. The final signature is extremely faint.

29 28 August 1584, Lucia, Lady Audley to Mistress Elizabeth Bourne

(NA, SP 12/172, fol. 174)

To my very loving sister, Mistress Bourne, give these.

    Nature (my good sister) should be greatly weakened of her wonted forces, if I should not, by all convenient means desire to know of your well doing and good contentment. And for that all occasions of assurance are taken away by your strange abodes, these are to desire you in regard of my satisfaction, and other more of your well hoping friends, to return me some few lines to witness unto us what state you now remain in and what course of life you have resolved on. If to abandon yourself from your well-wishing friends, then grieved shall we be to foresee how strangers that love and live with spoil[1] will in the end reject you. Yet thus much (sweet sister) I am to let you understand that my home shall ever be to you as your own. And if you would but put on the mind once to make trial of me and it, I doubt not then but both would answer your expectation. And withal you shall do me a great curtesy, who am fain for want of a household companion to go the oftener abroad, which is the only impairing of my good housewifery. Thus wishing in you all good affects I end unsatisfied till I see you. Fonthill,[2] this 28th day of August, 1584.

                                    Your assured friend and loving sister,
                                                      Lucia Audley

---

1 Spoil, *n.* †8. a. An act or instance of spoiling, damaging, injuring, etc.; a damage, impairment, or injury; a piece or work of destruction. *Obsolete*.
2 Fonthill Gifford in the County of Wiltshire was the Mervyn family home.

30 November 1584, Mistress Elizabeth Bourne to Lucia, Lady Audley
(NA, SP 12/175, fol. 24)

To my very loving sister, Mistress E. Bourne give this.[1]

    I that live my good sister, far off from consort[2] and company, may well at {...} to examine and consider what I am, of whom descended, how nature works in you, myself, and others, and how my misfortunes grow, which acquaint me with strangers, and divide my natural friends from me. I find I was rightfully begotten and brought forth without nature's imperfection, the child of such a father as the memory of his worthiness lives in many his acts without blemish. And his special love in me by the estate he left for me to inherit.[3] In this much of my first entry into the world, you may witness with me that I was brought forth with {...} hope of any happy estate. If I have lived to do any act {...} the same, or my first liberty, it hath grown through {...} love towards my husband, and from a natural affection {...} to increase you and yours, and to assure your love and theirs of {...} we are both descended, to be my more thankful friends than they have been.

    In these few words, I have told you the sum of all my sorrows, which kills the pleasures of my life and divides me from my natural friends that should be. God knows it is their cause, not my choice nor ca{...} that I live amongst strangers, sequestered, divided from them. {...} Further, my mother or any my natural friends or allies {...} earnest request and reasonable offer, received me and mine {...} protection and care, or had assisted me but with their counsel and {...} when I was distressed. [I] had never bound myself to the curtesy of strangers, neither occasion had ever grown for you or them

---

1 This is one of two letters written to Lucia Audley by Elizabeth Bourne (though the hands are significantly different) in reply to Lucia's letter. The torn sections of the letter come at the right side of the folio and often obscure important information. This version seems to have been written on the back of a letter from Lucia Audley to Elizabeth Bourne. We are unsure which letter is a draft and which the one actually sent. We chose this letter because the other letter is written in a more modern hand.

2 Consort, *n*.1 3. a. A partner in wedded or parental relations; a husband or wife, a spouse. Used in collocation with some titles, as queen-consort, the wife of a king; thus, also king-consort, prince-consort (the latter the title of Prince Albert, husband of Queen Victoria).

3 Sarsden, left to Elizabeth Bourne by her father.

to send letters over far countries to be advertised of my health, my course of life or strange abodes. I had lived amongst them and joyed in them. But being wronged by an unkind husband, refused {...} nature by such as should have been my best friends and ill {...} by no other, I was urged to seek foreign relief, and sithen {...} reason have sequestered myself from the world's gaze, and Master Bourne's hard purposes, until it may please God to give me a better estate of comfort.

In Sarsden I am resolved to live if Master Bourne will give me peace and thereto attend God's providence in the event of conflicting days. If you and my well-hoping friends should forsee and better regard my spoil and ruin (as you write) my {...} that you will faithfully, plainly, and friendly adu{...} aid me, against so great an inconvenience. You shall find m{...} receive good, willing, to eschew ill and very thankful of your good will. And so receive me, sweet sister, and from me a million of thanks for the curtesy of your loving letter. Desire my humble [illegible] my mother and my hardy commendations to yourself. Sarsden this [blank] of November 1584.

Your loving sister and assured {...}
though most unfortunate {...}

31 1 June [No Year],[1] Mistress Elizabeth Bourne to Eleanor, Lady Conway

(© British Library Board, BL, Add. MS 23212, fols. 178–179)

To the right worshipful, my Lady Conway, these.
Madam,

    I pray you forget not the courtesies I have done you. I have helped you and yours with all I have had or could get, which I now find the want of. I pray you help me, therefore, with ten pounds to supply my want and pay my debts before I go out of the country[side], which shall be on Saturday, but Friday I hope, which I do to the quiet of my own mind. And to that end you should not need to disperse my children about the country. You are amongst your friends. And I have lost all mine for friending you: there for your own credit. You will help me with so little a sum, knowing I have helped you with a great deal more. I pray you take order I may have the bowls and salts and spoons I have here to serve my turn at home, which is but a small 300 or 400 pounds worth, which you have had. And this praying God you requite the next friends you have better than you do me. I end, the first of June from Arrow.

                      Your too sure friend till your discourtesies altered me,
                                            E. Bourne

---

1 This letter is certainly written before November 1588, when Lady Conway dies. Perhaps the date is sometime between 1586–1587 when John Conway is in Flanders?

32 [1585],[1] Eleanor, Lady Conway to Robert Dudley, Earl of Leicester

(NA, SP 46/17, fol. 239)

To the right honorable Lord Robert Dudley of Leicestershire, Knight of the most noble order of the garter, Baron of Denbigh, Lieutenant General of the Q[ueen] Majesty's Army and Forces in the low countries beyond the seas, and one of her Highness's noble Privy Council

In humbleness,

She woth[1] unto your right honorable lordship, your humble supplicant, Eleanor Conway, wife of Sir John Conway, Knight, that whereas he, at his departure over the seas in her Majesty's service under your honor's conduct did take order and suffered an extent[2] to be levied upon his manor of Cutteslowe in the county of Oxford £500 the year to satisfy the Queen's Majesty's debt of £300 unpaid residue of 1000 pounds lost to her Highness for the unlawful departure of Anthony Bourne, heretofore beyond the seas without license and during the said Sir John Conway his said dutiful service, further extents being granted against other his lands for the said £300 to the great hinderance, trouble, and impoverishment of your supplicant and their children in his absence. It may therefore please your honor of your accustomed clemency to move her highness and the right honorable Lord Treasurer that the payment of the said £300 may be stalled upon in the said Manor of Cutteslowe and that all other his lands, goods, and chattels for time of the said Sir John Conway his [service] may be protected and

---

1 Form of wit, †3. Passing into the sense: To become aware of, gain knowledge of, get or come to know; to find out, ascertain, discover; to be informed of, learn, "hear" (at or of a person), esp. in answer to inquiry; hence sometimes virtually equivalent to "inquire, ask." Cf. know *v.* 14, to know of —— 2 at phrasal verbs (obsolete uses). *Obsolete*.
2 Extent, *n.* I. Senses relating to valuation and debt. 1. *Historical*. a. The valuation of land or other property; *esp.* such a valuation made for the purpose of taxation; assessment; an instance of this. †c. A tax levied on such a valuation. *Obsolete*. 2. *Law*. a. (In full writ of extent): A writ to recover debts of record due to the Crown, under which the body, lands, and goods of the debtor may be all seized at once to compel payment of the debt. extent in aid, extent in chief (see quots.).

defended by your Lordship's honorable authority and commission from her Majesty without molestation or [indecipherable]. And your said supplicant with their children here in England as especially bound will daily pray to God for perduration[3] of your honor in health, long life, and felicity. And the said Sir John Conway the more bound to do the like and better to be able to serve in her Highness's affairs beyond the seas at your Lordship's good directions.

---

3 Perduration, *n*. The action of enduring or capacity to endure indefinitely; continuous duration; existence having neither beginning nor end.

33 [Undated],[1] [Mistress Elizabeth Bourne's Demands of Sir John Conway]

(© British Library Board, BL, Add. MS 23212, fol. 68)

These be my demands from Sir John Conway

First, to have my daughter, Mary delivered to me or to those I shall appoint.

Secondly, to have all my books of covenants that have passed between Master Bourne and Sir John Conway delivered me and all his interest in them made over to my friend as I shall appoint.

Thirdly, to have my house at Sarsden delivered to me with a letter of attorney to sue the bond for cutting down my woods and not repairing my house according to the covenants of the lease.

Fourthly, to have my plate and household stuff and cattle delivered to me and my cousin Hobby's bond and a bond that Master Bourne made to my uncle, Sir Roland Clarke, and a letter of attorney to sue Bate's bond.

These my demands to be presently performed or else Sir John Conway's resolute answer.

34 3 February [1586/7],[1] Mistress Elizabeth Bourne to Sir John Conway

(© British Library Board, BL, Add. MS 23212, fols. 129–130)

To the right worshipful, Sir John Conway, Knight in Flanders, these.
Sir,
   I am sorry you will force me to complain and to desire redress of my wrongs from other than yourself. As you may assure yourself by my long sufferance of your wife's injuries offered me, who durst not make claims to all my living, but most discourteously, nay rather Judasly[2] stolen my daughter, Mary, from me. I putting myself in your hands, with children, goods, and living, as for my best safety, and now I am spoiled of all to my great grief and your great shame.
   All which I have forborne to complain of for that you swear to me in many letters that you are neither consenting nor privy to any your wife's doings against me, offering me (in them) to right me in all things else that I could desire from you. I did assure myself that Sir John Conway did love his reputation too well ever to say or write but that he would perform. As I have born all wrongs to my great discontentment, and I have often advertised to you thereof, to my great charge, so am I credibly informed my messengers came safely to you, specially my own man, Anthony Wilson, which was the last messenger I sent to you. For Sir John Norris hath acknowledged to my Lord his father,[3] the receipt of his letters by my man three weeks since. But I can hear nothing, neither of my man, nor answer of my letters from you, and yet there is come over at three several times above 40 sail of ships since

---

1 We date this letter based on notes from the Acts of the Privy Council records of 1586–1587, which chronicle the dispute between Lady Conway and Elizabeth. The Privy Council discussed whether Lady Conway should deliver Mary to her mother or keep her, until "their Lordships should have answer out of Flanders as aforesaid from Sir John Conwaye concerning the true intent and meaning of certain writings of conveyance of the landes, goodes and marriage of the said daughter of _____ [sic.] Bourne, esquire, by him made unto Sir John" (229). Further, a bond of £2000 was entered that forbade Lady Conway from contracting any marriage for Mary.
2 Judasly, *adv*. In the manner of Judas Iscariot; with terrible treachery or betrayal; traitorously.
3 Henry Norris, Baron of Rycote, father of John Norris.

Christmas, so I do assure myself there is some indirect dealing such as I did not look for from you; else would you in all this time either have come or sent over, that my child and living might be out of their hands that seek the spoil both of me and mine.

I have sufficiently made known to you in my other letter the many wrongs I have received in your absence both of your wife and brother Greville, my tenant. But it pleases you not to amend it. I think you have greater matters that makes you so careless of mine. But it is to me so near and stands upon my undoing so as I must of force make my own known to be mine, and crave aid of the higher powers to make your wife deliver my child and conveyance her out of her hands, which she takes as her own and sayeth she knows no trust, but hath absolute books to show that all is hers.

I had better hope in you that you would not have gone in so great danger of your life, without disburdening your soul of all that you ought to do and not to leave me and my children and living in their hands that I never trusted. And they assure me I shall find none. I think your conscience is not so bad to spoil those that trust you and have with great charge and travail put all in your hands as my safest place.

You know my daughter, Mary, cost me 1000 pounds, which was to me 100 pounds a year, which was no small matter to put one in trust with. And can there be a more unconscionable part than to steal her from me out of your own house, I putting myself and children there, as for my most assured place. It were pity so bad a part should be unknown.

I will believe you never consented to it, and so sayeth all my friends that hath seen your letters to me, which I will acquaint these with as I do assure myself will cause my lady to deliver my child and writings out of her hands. Since she hath married one of my children with bad devises and without your knowledge,[4] it is no reason she be suffered to do so with the other. I had rather you should right me than any other. But I see you are in such a place as you cannot. I must, therefore, do as I may. I have lost so much time, already, in looking to hear from you as being loath to do that I now am forced to. Therefore, if it please you to redress my wrongs, you must take present order, for I can bear no longer delays.

I am sure my letter shall be delivered to you within this sennight,[5] so as you may send answer with another week if it please you, you shall have me at my father's[6] house in London, so as you shall not need for to look me. I will stay so long for your answer.

---

4 Amy Bourne was married to Fulke Conway, the youngest son of John and Eleanor Conway rather than to Edward, the eldest son, as was contracted between Anthony Bourne and John Conway. See BL, Add. MS 23212, fols. 71–72.
5 Sennight, *n. a.* A period of seven (days and) nights; a week.
6 James Mervyn, Elizabeth's stepfather.

This in hope you will right yourself and me, I leave your trouble with my friendly commendations and praying God to send you safe return home. From Rycote, the 3rd of February.

Your assured friend, proof you know
E. Bourne
Mistress E.B. Master B.[7]

---

7 This is one of the most brief and puzzling of John Conway's notes. Does it mean he shared the contents with Anthony? We cannot say.

35 5 October 1587, Sir John Conway to Mistress Elizabeth Bourne

(© British Library Board, BL, Add. MS 23212, fols. 81–82)[1]

Mistress Bourne,

I have sent, and you have received many letters from, me. I have in them made you sundry offers to do you right in all things without any cause for you to trouble my Lords of her Majesty's most Honorable Privy Council. I see you little regard them and me less that truly well deserved. If I should write you whole volumes, I can say no more in an answer of all your demands than I have done.[2]

You know in the [indecipherable][3] of your own conscience if you have any feeling and fear of God in your heart, your youngest daughter's education and free disposition of marriage is in me by your husband's absolute deed and your free consent.

I would not witness this upon my conscience unduly for any benefit under heaven. Neither will I, for all I have ten times worth, withheld from you anything which in law you can challenge in equity you ought to have, or in any honest regard of friendship I am bound to perform you.

My desire is that you will hold the same correspondence of good proceeding with me. Seek not to call in question my honest reputation before an honorable state without a cause, neither wrong your friend, who hath dealt more friendly with you than with himself. I have performed you all honest parleys of a friend that ever you have needed or I have promised. You did, upon a good belief that I would never see you nor your children want, free[ly] consent that Master Bourne should convey all your lands, goods, and debts absolutely to me, according to the express words of his several deeds without any trust, confidence, limitation, or use reserved, intended or meant, to himself, to you or to any other to either of your uses. If I have failed you in any one [jot] of your beliefs or have, through your consent,

---

1 There is no address.
2 This letter seems to reply directly to Elizabeth Bourne's list of demands in BL, Add. MS 23212, fol. 68 and to correspondence in BL, Add. MS 23212, fols. 129–130 and BL, Add. MS 23212, fols.131–132.
3 The combination of John Conway's difficult handwriting and an archival stamp ("Conway Papers") placed across two lines makes this section impossible to read.

received one penny of profit that I have not truly answered you, prove it and I will never be taken for an honest man.

I did upon honest and friendly considerations take your lands to my use as my own for your life at my peril, to stand to it in court [indecipherable] which should come against them. I did also take upon me at my charge and peril to call in all Master Bourne of debts to my own use and bound myself to pay her Majesty one thousand pounds and two thousand pounds to Master Bourne. The land which Master Bourne conveyed to me and I ought to enjoy I do not enjoy and yet as though I did enjoy them I have and do give you 40 pounds a year out of my own land to make up that Master Bourne holds from me. I have paid her Majesty the greatest part of one thousand pounds. My lands are in present charge to her majesty for the rest.

I have paid Master Bourne two thousand pounds and a great deal more. Yet have I not had any assistance in all these payments but only of £1233 from Sir James Mervyn and three hundred pounds from Master Talbot. The rest of the whole estate Master Bourne hath received and concluded[4] me of contrary to my right and his covenants. Reprove me in either of these two points before my lords of the council or in any part of this I write, and I will never be taken for honest man. If these things be true, I leave it to their honorable considerations whether I have dealt well with Master Bourne and you, or truly you deal ill with me. I would to God I were as free from Master Bourne's and you estate and his children as you could wish and that I have given you a thousand pounds to the rest of I have spent and paid, so as I had but my time before me which I have only spent in his and your causes. I accompt it the most hardest fortune of all my life, that time I have lost in your causes, and the doubtful opinion which the magistrates have conceived of me for you and your causes.

God and yourself knows my honest proceeding wherein having a sensible feeling of my own harm and yours without defect, I did take the first time and open [indecipherable] that was offered me to repair your credit and to move my lords of the council to a better judgment of me than your husband's untrue speeches had brought them in suspicion of.

I had not come into these wars if you had had any friend of yours that would have received you and your company, whereby you might have lived without that increase of the world's ill opinion.

In the point for your relief and my own good I consented to leave my wife and children, friends, country, and what else with all pleasures and profits. And for my honest consideration I find myself unthankfully requited by you. Yet I thank you for the occasion, for I hope the course I have taken shall be, through my time employed, better accepted of her Majesty and my Lords of the Council than when I lived in the loss of my time through your occasions

---

4 Conclude, *v.* †3. a. To shut up *from* a course of action, etc.; to preclude, debar, restrain, "estop." *Obsolete.* b. To shut up *to* a course of action, etc.; to bind, oblige. Still in legal use.

and without doing her Majesty's service that might justly witness my true loyalty and faithful heart.

What resteth for me to do right of you, assure yourself what wrong so ever you offer me, yet you shall find me herein honest. If you would be reclaimed through reason to love your children for my love, the rather and to agree thusly, you should find me thankful and your friend with regard of your good and theirs. If otherwise it seem you good to run on your violent course begun in trouble of my Lords of the Council, I cannot help it. I am glad you have amongst them such good friends as you threaten me with. I am made afraid no way in what shall be offered me from so honorable a presence until my own conscience and deeds accuse me. What I deserve that I assure myself of amongst them and so may you according to your letter. I have signified to their Lordships what right I have to your youngest daughter,[5] and by what degrees I am ready to satisfy you, in all other things. I pray you, suppress these violent courses and passionate proceedings to their Lordships' troubles. You may get more at my hands by a friendly means than by this unfit proceeding. And thus wishing God to put a due remembrance of this fear in your heart. I commit you to his safe protection, Ostend, 5 October 1587.

Your willing friend if please you to deserve it.
John Conway

---

5 Mary Bourne. Amy Bourne, the eldest daughter, was to marry Edward Conway, see BL, Add. MS 23212, fols. 71–72. Instead, she was married to the younger Conway son, Fulke. This angered Elizabeth greatly, as is shown in BL, Add. MS 23212, fol. 129. In the same letter, Elizabeth addresses what she believes is her right to Mary, her youngest daughter, for whom she paid £1000 to keep with her. Here, John Conway clearly states his belief in his right to Mary's education and marriage.

36 November 1587, Eleanor, Lady Conway to the Lords of her Majesty's Privy Council
(NA, SP 12/205, fol. 124)

November
1587

To the Right Honorable Lords of her Majesty's
most honorable Privy Council

Right honorable,

According to your Honors' order, set down the first of this month, I have labored with Master D. Ford and Master Owen that they might effectually understand the case between my husband, Sir John Conway, and Master Anthony Bourne. These learned men having well considered of it, have been many days ready to deliver their several opinions what the law is touching the same. Mistress Bourne on her part hath used such slackness, that there hath not been any meeting or conference between those chosen by her, neither are hers as yet made acquainted therewith. It seemeth she hath little respect to your Honors and less regard of these affairs. Seeking to excuse it by you that lack of her writings,[1] which she pretendeth to be in the country with her husband, a matter unlike to be true. For it cannot reasonably be thought that she would have strived so far in the cause without having her writings ready that should be necessary to inform her council. But she, finding advantage by your Honors, crediting her exclamation and my willingness to satisfy your Honors in all duty by giving my son's bond for the not contracting of the young maid,[2] seeketh all delays possible to frustrate my husband of the bestowing of her daughter, which in all right and equity appertaineth to him both by covenant[3] and

---

1 These papers are mentioned by Elizabeth Bourne in BL, Add. MS 23212, fols. 129–130 as being in Lady Conway's possession.
2 Amy Bourne.
3 Covenant, *n.* 1. *a.* A mutual agreement between two or more persons to do or refrain from doing certain acts; a compact, contract, bargain; sometimes, the undertaking, pledge, or promise of one of the parties. Phrases, to make or enter into a covenant; to hold, keep, break covenant (No longer in ordinary use, except when colored by legal or theological associa-

arbitrament[4] as may appear by the same. Hoping, therefore, your Honors will not suffer my husband to be prejudiced by her herein in his absence; Wherewith, most humble suit and petition to your Honors is, that, in respect of my weak estate and being, a lone woman, destitute of him that should defend his rightful cause, and in regard of my husband's lawful right and of his absence in her Majesty's service (whither he draweth no small portion of his living, having left another part of that to the payment of his debts that grew by obtaining their children for his sons), and for that my children and family are nourished in the country, and myself and servants lie here at great charge about this business, it would please your Honors favorably to consider of me, and to be umpires of these causes (to whose order and judgement I submit myself) or to dismiss the same, as it was, and leave it to the law or respite it till my husband return, who will then answer Mistress Bourne whatsoever she can in law or equity demand of him. And thus craving your Honors' good opinions, in all humbleness I beseech you, that through her delays, I may no longer be driven to consume my husband's substance in maintaining the right he hath so dearly bought. And for such your goodness, he shall be bound in all humble service to your Honors, and we both to win in prayer for your happier increase in honors.

X[5]

Your Honors in all humble duty.

tions.) [Lady Conway refers to the Arbitrators' Report, Indenture of Award of 1583[/4].]
4 Arbitrament | arbitrement, *n.* 3. a. The deciding of a dispute by an authority to whom the conflicting parties agree to refer their claims in order to reach an equitable settlement. [See above.]
5 We are not sure of this mark. It is a kind of squiggle. We wonder if Lady Conway could not sign her name though this seems unlikely given her status. We note, however, that there is no signature in BL, Add. MS 23212, fol. 191, which is another document under her name.

37 27 February [No Year][1], Mistress Elizabeth Bourne to Sir John Conway

(© British Library Board, BL, Add. MS 23212, fols. 133–134)

To the right worshipful, Sir John Conway, Knight, at Ostend, these. In Flanders.[2]

Sir,

I did assure myself of better satisfaction from you. I would not have been at so much charge as to send my man to you but I thought, verily, when you wrote to me that I should have what I could demand and that I should not need to try my friends to come by anything from you. For you, knowing my mind, would yield it me willingly. These words cost me 20 pounds because I did assure myself you would perform whatsoever you write. I can but be deceived and when you can put on a mind to take all my living children and goods, the rest you can do is nothing.

I wonder how this covetous mind is come to you. You never yet took anything from me but what I let you have. Neither have you let nor set any my living but by my consent. And now you say all is your own and I shall neither have house to dwell in nor living to live on, but what please you to give me. And you already find fault with my asking, so as I think I come to live a beggar where I am taught to beg before I meant to begin.

You say I ask everything as though I might command it. And I say let me have my living child and goods as my own, or else, do you keep it if you can. For as long as I have breath, I will say you do me the ~~most~~ wrong. You say you have done much for me and mine and oft tell me of the money travails and charge you have been at for the assurance of my living. But I shall have very little cause to think myself beholding to you if you take all to yourself.

---

1   We believe that throughout this letter, Elizabeth Bourne continues her references to BL, Add. MS 23212, fols. 81–82 in which John Conway makes these claims. BL, Add. MS 23212, fols. 24–25 also seem to confirm John Conway's claims to the education and marriages of the Bourne daughters as well as to properties held by Anthony Bourne. We include it because it is characteristic of her style and lays out clearly how she believes she has been betrayed by her trusted advocate.
2   The folio which includes the address is distinguished with what appears to be the shadow of a stamp "E."

I am well assured, and can bring forth good witness, that your charge was with my money so long as the troubles lasted. And can you with good conscience take 600 pounds land from me for the charge you have been at? You say you have paid many sums of money to Master Bourne. You have paid him none, nor anybody else but what his own debts hath and must answer, saving the last four hundred pounds whereof you know I paid 50. And will you take the benefit of both my daughters from me for that? And I have paid 1000 pounds for the younger? The older, I take to be no less worth, will be a sufficient recompense for all the charge and trouble you have been at.

These things are so well known as it is not you nor I can deceive each other. Neither of us shall be our own judges. Of this I am well assured that some of your dear friends shall lose the reputations they now hold or else they shall witness against you if you take all as your own as you say in your letters you will.

And yet you say I seek your undoing if I have my own from you, if your undoing [hang][3] upon losing of mine, you must pardon me. I must not beg. You have of your own. And I have no more but that is assured to you. So as if you keep that from me, hit is you that seek my undoing and I seek but my own, nor all that [be]neath. You say that it is but upon color[4] that your son would have my daughter. I know no such great preferment by your son['s] match.[5] But if my daughter had not been stolen from me, I could have bestowed her better. So as with that I know no cause to be offended.

But the treacherous dealing in stealing away my other daughter, I committing myself, children, goods, and living into your hands as my sure place, is that which made me see that which now I find. So does it bring me to my mind the many means you have used to come by all I have, telling me ever that it was surest for me to have but one feofee[6] and that I must not acknowledge any trust because Master Bourne would take advantage of it. But since it is come to this extremity that either Master Bourne must have it or you, I will rather trust to him that hath given it me already than you that put me out of doubt I shall have nothing.

---

3 The word is partly in the fold of the folio. We have chosen "hang" based upon the two first letters which we can see are "ha."

4 Color, *n*.1 P2. †a. †under (a) color: by a pretext or fiction; under a pretense. Also occasionally upon color, with color. *Obsolete*. [It is difficult determine what she means by this or what John Conway would have meant by the word.]

5 Elizabeth Bourne refers to her eldest daughter, Amy, who was to marry John Conway's eldest, Edward. She was married, instead, to his younger son, Fulke, which was a violation of the contract John Conway made with Anthony (BL, Add. MS 23212, fols. 71–72).

6 Feofee, *n*. 1. The person to whom a freehold estate in land is conveyed by a feoffment. 2. spec. a. (More fully feoffee in or of trust.) A trustee invested with a freehold estate in land. Now chiefly applied in plural to certain boards of elected or nominated trustees holding land for charitable or other public purposes.

I pray consider it is this extremity that forceth me to do that I do with the extreme dealing I have received from your wife and brother Greville. But all the means you make me [indecipherable] you lay the fault in myself. Indeed, if I had never come in your house, I had never been deceived nor so used, which is the greatest fault I ever committed. I take God to my witness. But I will mend all as well as I may and leave you to your will either to right me or wrong me. For I will leave either complaining or desiring your help.

I cannot forget that you have made my daughter Mary three year and more younger than she is.[7] I imagine the cause and leave you to your better remembrance both of my daughter's age and of my desert. And say not to me you desire to hold friendship with me, and tell me withal you will hold all from me, for the veryest enemy I have can do no more so. I must think of you till you give me better assurance. And when all I have done for you and that you have done for me shall come to be manifested, then it will be known which of us is most beholding each to other. To which I leave all as unwilling as you may see by my long forbearance.

From Broken Warf, the 27th of February.
Your friend, or other, as you use me,
E. Bourne

---

7 Mary Bourne was to be legally of age at 14. Elizabeth Bourne accuses John Conway of having stated Mary's age as younger than she is.

38 7 March [No Year],[1] Mistress Elizabeth Bourne to Sir John Conway

(© British Library Board, BL, Add. MS 23212, fols. 131–132)

To the right worshipful, Sir John Conway, Knight, these, in Flanders. At Ostend.[2]

I did assure myself to have it [indecipherable] by [indecipherable] not to me. I should not need to trouble my friends, for you, knowing what I would have, would yield it me willingly. Else would I not have troubled you and charged myself to send to you. But in the place of performing me all my demands, you have performed me not one, which is more than I looked for. I had a better hope in your good conscience. Else would I not have trusted you. Neither would I have born all the wrongs I have received in your absence, but in hope you would right me. But instead of that, you lay the fault in myself.[3] Indeed, it is true. For if I had not committed my living children and goods into your custody, I could not have been so dealt with. I have the wrong and others have the shame. So do I hope to find equity although you do me none.

You tell me you did take order for me before you went. Indeed, you promised me so, but I did not look it should be such as you now write of, which is to hold all as your own, according to the naked words of the books.[4] This were ~~very hard~~ a very bad order for me that was born to some-

---

1 Like BL, Add. 23212, fols. 129–130, this letter addresses matters chronicled in the Acts of the Privy Council records of 1586–1587, but we cannot say definitively the year in which this letter was written.

2 "At Ostend" is written in another hand, not John Conway's. Interestingly, Conway's usual notes are missing from this letter.

3 We believe that Elizabeth Bourne refers to BL, Add. MS 23212, fols. 81–82 in which John Conway makes these claims. BL, Add. MS 23212, fols. 24–25 also seem to confirm John Conway's claims to the education and marriages of the Bourne daughters as well as to properties held by Anthony Bourne.

4 Elizabeth Bourne's view of the agreement between Anthony Bourne and John Conway, in which all property, including Elizabeth's own, and the rearing, education, and marriages of the Bourne daughters, is clearly not according to the "naked words" of the agreement, which is to say she believed that the words were a formality and that she would retain control of her lands, money, and her children. When John Conway asserts he has the right to all of it, he is legally correct. The dispute here is whether he is also ethically correct according to other, perhaps unwritten, understandings.

thing and must come to nothing. And all because I trusted you. Have I been at charge and trouble this nine years to make my living sure, and am I now most unsure? This were enough to discomfort me greatly, but my right is too well known for you to wrong me. Therefore, I wish you in regard of yourself to do me right and to let me have those things I have entreated my Lord of Buckhurst and my cousin Clarke to demand of you.

And I pray you, let me have my daughter delivered me as most meet and right she should. For she cost me too much to trust anybody with her. And dispose of your son as please you, for nothing will satisfy me but the having of my child, as you know. And the best is my Lord Chancellor[5] knows how I hold her from her father's sale, and because I would have the comfort and company of her, paid a thousand pounds for her. Therefore, think not to have everything as you will because nobody can reprieve you therefore of yourself. Do me right. I desire it earnestly as you may see by my long forbearance, which works nothing to me but hardy and good to you.

This, leaving all to your wise consideration, I end from Broken Warf the 6th of March.

The same {...}[6] to be
E. Bourne

---

5 Likely, Thomas Bromley, Lord Chancellor (1579–1587).
6 This is the only tear, middle of the folio.

39 [Undated], [Sir John Conway to Mistress Elizabeth Bourne]

(© British Library Board, BL, Add. MS 23212, fol. 135)[1]

Me thinks I see you sit sad and solitary after your weary journey. Put sadness away, though the man have broken promise, and he will keep it well the rest of his life. Wot[2] you why he did it? To try your patience and love. You must take it a little unkindly. He will be greatly sorry, and, thereof, more love will increase than was before.

Thus, I see how time will work, and how lovers delight to dally one with another. You shall do well to take the perfect and pleasure of time for times tarryeth nobody. There is nothing more hurtful in these causes than delays and nothing more perilous than haste. Therefore, you must not stand still now you have begun, nor make too much haste lest you overgo yourself, which measures and means proceed, and proves the ends. If my good will, simple will, or poor wealth, may further your desires and good, I am ready ever to use my travails. And I shall thank you that you will put me to any exercise, through want thereof I grow fat. I can sweat as hard through the light of the morn, in the cool night, as other can wither heat of the summer in the hot day.

I did of late withdraw myself from company. And all alone I wandered abroad in wild wilderness woods, where all things was at rest. By favor and fortune, having lost myself and knowledge where I was, I met with a bird of diverse colors, so pleasant to behold as the wonder of her beauty, and the joy of my good fortune lead me to follow which way she did fly. In treading which track, I did feed my eyes so full with delight at the sight of her as that I could well describe to you her manner, her markings, her mirth, mildness, and modesty. But ho! Alas, her name I know not. She brought me, amidst

---

1 While this letter is unsigned and has no address page, the handwriting matches John Conway's other letters. This letter seems to follow Elizabeth Bourne's three angry letters (BL, Add. MS 23212, fols. 129–130, BL, Add. MS 23212, fols. 131–132, BL, Add. MS 23212, fols. 133–134) and shifts the tenor of their correspondence going forward. Whether John Conway is sincere in his declaration of love or claims it as a strategic move, we cannot say for sure. Such questions are treated in our introduction.

2 Wit, *v*.1 *archaic* except in legal use: see 10c(b). I. Simple uses. 1. *transitive*. To have cognizance or knowledge of; to be aware of; to know (as a fact or an existing thing).

the wild woods, to a house where it seemed there dwelt nobody. Yet she gave me to comfort my body, over-wearied with travel, most delicate wines to drink, sundry fruits of the wood and most sweet and savory breads to eat. From heaven, I think, she and all the rest came. For in heaven, for the time, there was no one saveth joyed more than I did in my good fortunes and her good favors.

Good God, I wished you there so oft and so heartily that at length I fell into imagination, and believed with myself that I had my wish, that you were there, that I did drink to and eat to you of everything that was there, and that your joys and mine were equal. Was it so? Or is it but a dream? A dream it cannot be. Therefore, since by my well-wishing and hardy prayer you came thither, as a ghost. Tell me, who she was, where she is, and how she doth that I mean and cannot name? I long to know and wish she may know me better. If you will send me word when and wither I shall travel once again to see her if she be not a Goddess that knows the secret thought of everybody, I will devise a means and make a shift to bring myself to her presence and not make it known to anybody your good will and furtherance therein.

Let me receive your answer to this. Let me know if you can read this bad hand of mine. If you need me and will want me, the fault is yours. You know one penny in one Paternoster while will fetch me whether you will humor me. Farewell to nobody but yourself. I wish you all your own desires.

This much I have translated out of the Latin history I read you of late, which you liked so well.[3] If the English please you, and that you can read my ill hand, I will translate the whole and send it you.

---

3 We believe that this added note acts as a cover for the inappropriate nature of the letter in the event it should fall into the wrong hands.

40 [Undated], Mistress Elizabeth Bourne to [Sir John Conway]

(© British Library Board, BL, Add. MS 23212, fol. 136)[1]

My own good Knight,

You lead me with courtesy so as I cannot tell what to say. Thanks is too mean, for you have so over compassed[2] me with surmounting joy as I think nobody so happy as I. I will live to love and honor and employ my time to do you true service. This is all I can do and this will never cease to do so long as I have life.

I told you, you should find me a reasonable woman. Now you tell me you stay my daughter for my better good, I am satisfied and contented to stay your leisure and will, both in this and all other things.

Do you not think good I should write to Master Grey? I think I had need to make him privy of it that I may know whether he will be willing I should lie in his house. If he will not I must seek further. How shall we devise a place for me to be in when you go to London for I think you must not know where I am certainly, for fear you be put to your oath. I must leave all my trouble upon you as you bid me. So I do and no other wish, will I do willingly.

My rent of attainder[3] is £6 but I must bate[4] him for the rabbits I had at Easter, five pence a couple, but I know how many they be. I think they be not past a dozen couple, as Hawkins can tell. You may take what please you to bear the man's charges that must go to London when, I pray you, send so

---

1 This letter has no address.
2 Compass, *v*. 11. a. To attain to or achieve (an end or object aimed at; to accomplish. b. To get at, attain, obtain, win (an object). Our reading is that she means something closer to "overcome." 2. *transitive. a*. Chiefly in passive. Of an emotion, physical condition, etc.: to overpower or overwhelm; to exhaust or render helpless; to affect or influence excessively. Also of alcoholic drink: to intoxicate (a person). Frequently with by, with.
3 We have found no reference for "rent of attainder," but we assume this is what she means ("rente of taynter"). "Attainment" comes the closest to a meaning having to do with lands or property, "†1. Encroachment. (Cf. attain *v*. 4) *Obsolete*. Charter of London in R. Arnold Chron. f. vi/2 Landis and tenementis ... free and quyt of alle maner axions axing & attenementz."
4 Bate, *n*.2. 2. Deduction, diminution, abatement.

soon as you can. I think the doctor[5] had best to hire on to serve the process,[6] for it must be none of your men, or else my son Conway[7] could help you to one in London, for he knows a many that can do it. You may say to him you promised me to see it done for me, and that I should not care for it.

This you may see, my family's shows that I must come in with my five [eggs]. I persuade myself you take all in good part. I know it can do a wise man no harm to hear a fowl speak well. Take me as any for so you are like to do. Loving, constant, and faithful you shall ever find me. This, as one revived, all joying in my own sweet Knight. I end wishing us[8] all that our loves deserves and desires. Send me your last, and I will make it as large and as mete as my love is for you.

Your E. Bourne

---

5 Elizabeth Bourne may refer to Julius Caesar here, but may also refer to another lawyer that she and John Conway were working with.
6 Process, *v*.1 1. *transitive*. Chiefly Scottish and Irish English. To institute a process or legal action against, to sue, prosecute; to obtain a process or summons against; to serve a process on. Now *rare*.
7 Here Elizabeth Bourne returns to calling Edward Conway, "son Conway" in anticipation of his marriage to her daughter, a practice she suspended in BL, Add. MS 23212, fols. 131–132 and BL, Add. MS 23212, fols. 133–134.
8 Elizabeth Bourne crosses out "you" and amends to "us" in a sign of alliance with John Conway.

41 [Undated], Mistress Elizabeth Bourne to [Sir John Conway]

(© British Library Board, BL, Add. MS 23212, fols. 143–144)[1]

Now, I perceive you love me with such perfectness as I desire and do deserve. I can say but few words, but I am yours. I live to love you, honor, and serve you, and yet more, if I could tell how to say it. Your love and kind offers are such as I rejoice in you more than I am able to express. Oh, happy thing of this life, oh joy of our age. What creature can be more happier than I who loves and is loved interchangeable, unrevocable. By this time do you not think I live, love, and joy that I have such a self as sayeth I shall have all things as will content me and no lady shall withhold him from me?[2]

Although I have a far greater desire than ever I had to see you, yet the consideration is so needful and so reasonable which withholds you from me as I am and must be content. But yet I must needs say so much against my will and liking as ever was anything. I did not know of this bond before now, which made me fear knowing that which I do: that you shall be persuades it were not for your credit to see me or speak with me.

If you will know, the words that Tacey did speak were these: she told Meg that I had done her more harm than 40 pounds could make her amends by procuring her Uncle Whitney's displeasure against her. She could say somewhat that could hurt me, too, for she knew what I meant to do and where I meant to be between this and Christmas, for all Sir John Conway and I kept it so close from her. But she would say nothing that would hurt me because I had been her good mistress.

This in effect was all she said, as Meg Prest[all] can tell you, who told it to Mistress Alice and she told it to Humphrey Osboston, your man. And between them two they made a good matter of it and sent it abroad that it never should cease till it came to the carters.[3] And because I should be sure to hear it, everybody told it me the last time I was at Arrow, and at

---

1 The date of this letter must be before Lady Conway's death in 1588, but after the argument about property and daughters. While there is no address for this letter, we do know the author is Elizabeth Bourne. We assume the recipient is John Conway.
2 Elizabeth Bourne refers to previous letters in which she accused him of loving someone else because he did not write often enough. Though we do not have a letter, John Conway must have reassured her on this score.
3 Carter, *n*. 1 *b*. As a type of low birth or breeding; a rude, uncultured man, a clown.

the last Mistress Elizabeth Conway told me that the carters of Luddington and Arrow had no other word in their mouths but that my maid could tell such tales of you and me as shall make us blush and be ashamed. She told me enough of this, I warrant you. And so did everybody else. Whether this chaffed me, I leave to you to judge. So do I the using of this matter. So as you must not be known you have it of me. The joy that some of them made that they had this to say, past whereby it showed to me the right picture of their good wills.

If it were not for your [sake], I would never come in any of your houses, which is the cause that makes me desire that you should set down in writing between us for my daughter because my lady may know what you and I are agreed on. For she said that neither my maid nor I should have anything to do with my daughter, neither would she have me see them when I was last at Arrow, which grieved me not a little.

I pray you as you love me say nothing but devise ways and means to bring us to live together in friendship as we ought to do to our comforts, as I know you can do if you list, and love me as I know you do. You had drawn a book once for my daughter, which had pretty covenants in it. I think you mean not that which you sent me to Warwick shall stand because it is imperfect as I think I do not remember anything in it that was agreed on between you and me, but a release of all living and children to satisfy the council with.[4] Therefore, I think you mean to make another, but what or how I cannot tell. But all to your wisdom and will I leave it assuring myself you love me and care to maintain for me and, therefore, I assure myself you will devise ways and means that we may enjoy one another.

If you will know the cause why Blythe is I think Blythe is suspected. I understand by him my lady is very desirous to know the letters that pass between you and me, and asks him what he carries and brings. This comes of some suspicion she hath. Therefore, you had need to take great heed. She asked him whether I desired to speak with you. You know her wise. Yesterday Master Francis asked me whether I would send never a token to my friend Blythe. He said you made him safe that he cared for nobody. I am so careful and so fearful, as I do mistrust everything. You know there is an old saying: to be sure, mistrust. If it be a fate in me, correct me for it, and anything else that you mislike, you and I will mend it.

Am I not a good girl, then, and so I will be ever and always to you, ever as you would have me. For Sarsden the author of Hawkins' letter, I pray you do by it as you would by your own, for I make no difference.

I pray you, take order the corn be ended.[5] You may sell some of it if you can have reason. But I would have some kept for myself in hope that within this 12 months I may use it. I could wish that no further grant were made

---

4 There must have been a verbal agreement which is not reflected in written documents John Conway sent Elizabeth Bourne.
5 End, *v.* 2. *Obsolete. Transitive.* To put (corn, hay, etc.) into (a barn, stack, etc.); to "get in."

of the house. But you will reserve it for yourself. I could be content that so much of the groundmen set for years as will answer my mother's rent. And the rest I may spend as my own in my house which will content me best for the enjoying of myself, to my best liking so let it be my own.

This, for pity, I had need to end. This receive my hardy and good will forever to remain forever. a: I would I could attain to make such fine verses as you do that be so properly conveyed, that nobody can perceive it to [indecipherable] for me to understand. Thy treacherous be lady.[6] I am sure I praise you gaily.

More yours than her own,
E. Bourne

---

6 Be-, *prefix*. 4. Making verbs transitive, by adding a prepositional relation: primarily "about," as in bespeak *v.*, speak about (or for, to), bemoan *v.*, moan about (or over); which sense can usually be detected under the various against, at, for, to, on, upon, over, by, etc., required by modern idiom: *c*. To call, to style, to dub with the title of, etc. Often with a depreciatory or contemptuous force ... be-lady, *v.*

42 [Undated], [Sir John Conway to Mistress Elizabeth Bourne]

(© British Library Board, BL, Add. MS 23212, fol. 149)

Kind letters Mistress Bourne.[1]

I see dreams are but things of fancy's follies and fallacies. I leave them to fearful or sound minds to believe them. It is another thing which moveth Saints and subdueth men that now delighteth me. Ask you what it is? Love it is. And of yourself. Not begun, conceived, and wrought in me without cause and consideration. I will not here seem sick of a common disease, which men call falsely. I could allege my reason sufficient that breeds my affection. But I will not. Virtue needs no other [boast]. I do take you for no other: if I did or could, myself should be my own where now I am content to be as much yours.

This, I make you the offer and [surcrease][2] of my unfeigned love. If the worth thereof is your liking, where deserve a just recompense, I desire you give me as good show and assurance of the same, under the witness of your handwriting, as I am pleased to yield you in these few lines. I need not to [dissemble] the pleasure of a true friend to you. Though in the first part of your life you have not had need of a friend, hereafter you may. There neither hath been, is, nor shall be any creature so happy as always to live without the help of others or to pass their life without some adversity and need to try their friends. I wish you may, yet I would you should not live without the occasion and means to try how far, how friendly, and how faithfully I love you.

Through professions of my unfeigned love, I do promise myself your constant love. Therefore, I would wish you should try me. And so to avoid ingratitude in yourself, I wish you to love me as much and to write me the same. For your letter is the image of yourself. This is most true that in the

---

1 While there is no signature, the handwriting is unmistakably that of John Conway. What would usually be an address page seems to be more of a label or identification of a packet of letters to/from Mistress Bourne. We believe the date of the letter is prior to Lady Conway's death since John Conway says he is less free than Elizabeth Bourne.

2 † Surcrease, *v. Obsolete.* 1. *intransitive.* To grow greater or more numerous; to increase to excess.

letter of a very friend, the heart is delighted, the eyes pleased, the understanding comforted, and all the spirits rejoiced.

Therefore, I do with this, all the good will I can, send you my letter at your request, hoping you will do everything worthy of my unfeigned love. Ever as I find so I determined to continue. I reserve the cause and consideration to your use. Tell me how much you would have me yours and how much you will be mine in this or I will give you assurance. In the other, I will repose the same. Let this suffice, for once, to tell you how much I am yours and how much I desire to have you mine. In the meantime, remember that there is nothing more grieveth than lack that one loves. I know not what more to say, but it is long since I saw you. And I shall think it these more long till I see you. So oft as you shall devise to please me, you shall delight yourself. Wish me with you and I was at your will though my liberty be not so much as yours. My love and will shall be ever more than yours. This being [indecipherable] myself to or only yours if I find you all mine. I did for this time and hope of a better. So [indecipherable] yours as pleases yourself.

43 [Undated], Sir John Conway to the Lords of the Privy Council

(© British Library Board, BL, Add. MS 23212, fol. 183)[1]

My duty most humbly remembered,

I was long since solicited by letters from my wife to write to your Lordships touching my interest and right of Master Anthony Bourne's youngest daughter and to be a humble petitioner that the child may remain in her possession according to the father's contract and the mother's consent.

I have forborne[2] a long time to write to your Lordships in this cause by reason I have had more care in the well proceeding of her Majesty's Service, than my particular causes. I hope there is no time overpassed to acquaint you with my right and request, and to obtain that justice with equity to myself which you give all others.

When I was last before your Lordships at the honorable Council table, Master Bourne, then complaining against me, and I unjustly did withhold from him, in right of his wife, his youngest daughters and the property of his lands.

Although I was interested in the whole by his several covenants, contracts, and lands sufficient in laws and equity to defend his complaints, and warrant my possession, yet for the better satisfaction of your Lordships and my honest acquittal, I yielded that such men as seemed to you best for the true decision of the cause might examine and [unrip][3] matters in difference between him and me, and also between him and his wife.

The proceeding thence was then ordered, by your Lordships that a commission should go out of the honorable Courts of Chancery to be executed by others for the more strict and true proofs of all allegations and defenses.

Within this time limited, all the commissions had meeting, the commission was executed, and a final end made of all the controversies, questions, and demands. It was returned before your Lordships with a letter

---

1 Likely a draft or copy of an original. According to the Acts of the Privy Council, disputes between the Bournes and Conways continued even past the time when we believe Conway and Elizabeth had an affair.
2 Forbear, *past participle* forborne, *v.* 5. To abstain or refrain from (some action or procedure).
3 unrip, *v.* 3. †a. *transitive*. To bring to light or notice; to expose to view; to raupdateke up. *Obsolete*.

158   *Letters and Documents*

of certification, what they had done from thence to be certified into the Chancery to remain of record against other parties, which should at any time attempt to infringe the same, to the [renewing[4]] of your Lordships' farther trouble or answer.

The award is triparted.[5] The one part requireth in the council chest. It appeareth therein, and by the letter of certification, that Master Bourne failed in the proofs of all things he challenged, and unjustly charged me with. Yet nevertheless, through the earnest mediation of the Arbitrators, and upon his relenting mind before them in the wrongs he had offered me, and his offer to assure, and [indecipherable] me [quittance] in all causes from the beginning of the world to that day. And that I should enjoy the education and protection of both his daughters and their marriages, according to the words of his former covenants. I was moved and did consent by the award to give Master Bourne £400 and having thereto his wife's good will and free consent, I have truly paid the money through an honest desire to provide for my sequel, all which I trust shall well stand with your Lordships good liking that I might enjoy the same. Considering the great sums of money I have paid, that the [matter] was of whole mind and memory enabled by the laws of the Realm to do my lawful act with his own.

Besides there hath no covenant passed between us repugnant to law: many contracts and concords stand in force sufficient to warrant my quiet enjoying the education and marriage of his daughters, and the law heretofore. And good in laws by judgement of many and chiefly by Master Owen, a special appointment made by your Lordships upon whose judgement the cause was put, at which time the Lord Chamberlain sent to make doubt whether a man might, by the laws, sell his children.

Upon sight of Master Owen's opinion, upon my contrivances, it pleased your Lordships to give order to the Shriver of the counties to proceed no further in the execution of like letters of your commandment then directed to me as now to my wife for the delivery of the same children out of my possession.

If it seems right to your Lordships in laws, reason, and equity and that it was lawful for me to hold the education and marriages of the children against their father's challenges in his own right and his uses, before of his own acts. I hope it shall now seem more reasonable that I enjoin her. By reason through order and commission from your Lordships there hath proceeded an award that hath enjoined me to pay £400 for the same consideration since that time. Which is not my whole charge that I have yielded to enjoin her by 40 pounds a year, which I have and do give her mother in

---

4   Renew, *v*.1. 4. a. *transitive*. To resume (an activity, practice, etc.) after an interruption or lull; to re-establish (a relationship). b. *intransitive*. To begin again, recommence.
5   Conway refers to the Arbitrators' Report, Indenture of Award, NA, SP 13c, fol. 28, of 18 January 1583[/4].

her better maintenance, having no other reason thereto but because she gave me for good will therein, and bequeathed herself to my trust through good belief that I would not see her want.

    I do here protest to your Lordships before her Majesty of God. When I was unwillingly drawn by Sir James Mervyn, Sir John Danvers, Master William Clarke, and Mistress Bourne to be a party to Master Bourne's conveyances I had a thousand pounds in my purse, which I had then received of Master John Cooper for the lands I had sold him [indecipherable]. I did disburse that whole sum in penalty and expense for Master Bourne, within nine months. In my life to this day I have never had penny paid me for any money lent him, paid for him, or laid out in charges since those causes began. The defense of Master Bourne particularly to undo his wife and children; the answering his sundry complaints before your Lordships I in diverse courts of record against me, touching these causes, and my charges and trouble this eight years[6] to call his state of debts, with the money paid for him and not repaid again riseth to about three thousand pounds by particular accompts. Whereunto I would I had added the gift of Mary Bourne to her mother and the benefit of a thousand pounds to Mistress Bourne, now to repair his estate. So as that whole of all this were my less loss through these causes.

    My Lordships, if I had spent 6 years' time in her Majesty's service, or in managing of my own estate, I should have condemned myself of great thought and negligence if I had not deserved more, or made better purchase with less charge.

---

6 It is hard to say when John Conway begins this time period. If he counts it from 1583/4, the date of the Indenture, then this document is dated c. 1591, which seems unlikely. The date is more likely to be in the 1587–1589 period during which these disputes were heard by the Privy Council.

44 [Undated],[1] Mistress Elizabeth Bourne to [Sir John Conway]
(© British Library Board, BL, Add. MS 23212, fol. 157)

After the writing of my letter, and I gone to bed, I find myself something troubled, so as I can take no rest till I have imparted it to you.[2]

I had thought to have kept it till I did speak with you. But I perceive that shall be God knows when. I know never if some may let it. But you offer me so friendly and assure me so certainly as I assure myself ~~I may be bold to that~~ that nobody can withdraw your loving from me.

Yet I know all the devices that may be shall not want performance. If slanderous speech of the world or evil persuading of my ill meaning can avail you shall not want them. The slanderous speech which they said my maid should leave behind her of you and me was most untrue. She said no such thing as Meg Prestall and Androse can tell you.[3] But devised of purpose to slander you and me of your own folks, and carried wondrously, as you shall know, when I speak with you. Therefore, good my own, pardon me if I fear to lose you and know I have sundry enemies. I am afraid when I think of anything that may breed any cause of discord between us.

And, therefore, I pray you, let everything be set down between us for my daughter, Mary. ~~Where I ha~~ I have once received so great a grief for her as I would not have such a one again, not for a king's ransom. Therefore, good sweetheart, as you love, let not her be no cause of the breach of our love. I

---

1 In this letter, Elizabeth Bourne notes that she sued for two years before her daughter could even come to see her. We know that in 1590, when Mary turns 14, orders are given by the Privy Council that Mary be released. If the suits took up 1586–1588, then this letter may be dated 1588–1590.
2 Elizabeth's reference is unclear.
3 Elizabeth Bourne refers to gossip between servants that worried both her and John Conway. In BL, Add. MS 23212, fols. 143–144, she recounts an encounter she had with Mistress Elizabeth Conway who was told about them by a servant. Whatever the motives of either Elizabeth Bourne or John Conway in regard to their affair (see our introduction in which we argue it may have been more calculated on both sides than sincere), there seems to have been some gossip that was worrying. At the same time, we include this letter primarily because of the opportunity Elizabeth Bourne takes to ask John Conway once more to put in writing agreements between them having to do with the custody of her daughter, Mary.

had rather she were very and yet, I love her and must have that care of her as in nature I ought to have of her.

You must think it cannot but grieve me to have my child denied me and have evil will for my good will. I do not speak this to come from you. I know who hath determined it if you and I help it not, and therefore, I pray you, let me have it set down that I may have the bringing up of my daughter. When I will, that others may be beholding to me and not I to seek them for my own child to come to me as I was fain to sue two years for my daughter before she could have leave to come see me. And therefore, if you love me as you say you do, let all things be set in such order as there be no cause of unkindness between us hereafter.

By this time I have made another myself of you. Use me as you love me, for I am bound to say to you anything that troubles me, and to you I seek for ease of mind, laying all my troubles upon you, assuring myself you are to me so sure as nothing can nor shall later nor draw you from me. And the same good belief I rest and remain commending to you my heart in love, as one wholly satisfied and quieted now I have shown you my whole mind.

Yours ever and ever,
E. Bourne

45 [Undated], Mistress Elizabeth Bourne to [Sir John Conway]

(© British Library Board, BL, Add. MS 23212, fols. 165–166)[1]

My own,

I see well what this world is by this ill fortune of mine. I have experience enough. Now Hawkins and my tenants see that I cannot come to see my harvest myself, they will get that they can, everyone for himself and leave me to shift for myself with Thomas Thayer's good dispositions. If you think good, I will write to them. I do not doubt but to make them help me with my harvest. And as for Hawkins, I perceive the great service that he would do me will come to his own profit. I told him before that if he did by the tithe,[2] he could have none of me, and I pray you, let him have none.

I hope you do not let the Parson have the hay of the little close:[3] I pray you, let me not take no wrong at their hands, for it will anger me more than three times the worth of it. I mean Master Parson shall go further off the next year if he will lie with Hawkins's wife. For I mean not to give him twenty nobles any more years to dwell in my house without they were profitable tenants. Neither shall he have any custom days[4] of mine, for I promised him none. I thought of his own honesty if I had given them him that he would not have had them since he see I needed them myself. But since I see

---

1 We include this letter because of its household concerns. Elizabeth Bourne's many talents are on display from her ability to give directions for care of oxen to reminding her lover (and the holder of all her property and her daughter) that she looks forward to their reunion.
2 Tithe, *v.*2 I. To pay one tenth of one's produce, earnings, etc., and related senses. 2. a. *transitive*. To collect or exact a tithe from (a person); (more generally) to exact a payment from. Also *figurative*. †b. *transitive*. To collect or exact one tenth from (goods, produce, livestock, etc.) by way of tithe. *Obsolete*. †II. To take one tenth of, and related senses. 3. *transitive*. a. To take every tenth thing or person from (the whole number or quantity); to take one tenth of; to divide into tenths. *Obsolete*.
3 Close, *n.*1 2. In many senses more or less specific: as, An enclosed field (now chiefly local, in the English midlands); spec. (with capital initial), at certain schools, the name given to a school playing-field.
4 † Custom-day *n. Irish English Obsolete* (*hist.* after 16th cent.) a day on which a feudal tenant is obliged to render a service (service *n.*1 8b) to his or her lord; *spec.* = *plough day n.* (a) at plough *n.*1 Compounds 2.

his good will, I will provide for him thereafter. I pray you, give him warning to provide him a new dwelling.

I hope my own knight will so provide for me as I shall live in my own house the next year. And of myself without anybody but myself who is and must be all one. I pray you send a team to help with my corn, my [oxen] that if they let them bear in the day in the field as they load, they will do well enough if they sit in the court[5] all night. And give them some hay, which you know I have enough, so as you shall not need to hire any grass for them. Your men that go with the team may board at Bear's, and I will pay for them. I reserved four fleshes of bacon at Sarsden to get in my harvest. Let Bear have them towards their finding. I should have malt there, too, but I know not what is become of it. I would fain have a reckoning. Hawkins wrote to Master Francis that he had some corn of mine. But I know not how much I lost in a chamber with Mistress Hawkins, 18 quarter of malt and seven strike,[6] and all James Coke's wheat unthreshed. I know not what is become of it. My lady hath had some. I know not what. I would fain know what were become of it. I had in the barn by judgement eight quarter of barley. Thus you may see I am half undone. Therefore, you had need to help me. For I am in such a miserable case I cannot speak with any of my folks to take any account of them, nor to write to them to look to anything I have.

So as I cannot tell what to do, but I lay all my trust in you, in whom I only rest contented, to whom only I live to love and rejoice in. For my son Conway, I think anything now you tell me the cause that you would not have him come to me. I feared seeing the worst as I do in all things. But now I am satisfied I see you, which I hope shall be for the year end, or else rid me out of my pain, for I die in thinking the time longer, to see the eyes of my joy and behold the chief of delight. And this commending my with all his longings to you most hardily. I end and ever will remain yours ever,

E. Bourne

This messenger hath gone so long early and late that he is all not dead.

---

5 Court, *n*1. I. An enclosed area, a yard. 1. *a*. A clear space enclosed by walls or surrounded by buildings; a yard, a courtyard; e.g. that surrounding a castle, or that left for the sake of light, etc. in the centre of a large building or mass of buildings; formerly also a farmyard, poultry yard. At Cambridge, the usual name for a college quadrangle.
6 Strike, *n*.1 2. *a*. A bundle or hank of flax, hemp, etc.: = strick *n*. 1 b.? A handful of cornstalks.

46 [Undated], Mistress Elizabeth Bourne to Sir John Conway

(© British Library Board, BL, Add. MS 23212, fol. 169)

To my very good brother Sir John Conway, Knight, these. Pray you, so soon as Androse, my man, comes, take my money and send it me, for I have none.[1]

I must crave pardon for staying your messenger. I have not been so well in health as I could now wish myself because I desire to live to enjoy the thing my heart most delights in, which is you, my joy and life, whom I love and honor. Therefore, I stayed your messenger for the increase of my health and till I was better able to send you these few lines of my many thanks for your comfortable letters. You could not bestow them in a time more need, for I have no comfort but what I receive of them. They be more than welcome to me. Therefore, receive my loving thanks, true heart, and good will as a recompense for all your love and careful travails. It is all I have to give you. And I will never let you want so long as it likes you.

My own, shall I not see you before you go to the term? How shall I live then? Or how can you endure to be so long from me? Oh, what a comfort it is for friends to live together in love. Therefore, let it be so and let never unkindness be more between us. But let us live on to content [one] another in true and perfect love and friendship. And they that first break friendship or offer any discourtesy, I pray God bereave them of his joys in heaven. This is all I can say, hoping by this time you think yourself assured of me. And so I end and ever will remain ever yours. I give you many thanks for my good cheer you send me. It is too good for me without I had a better stomach or better company. I write in so little ease as if the man did not like me well.

To whom I write should be very merry. For besides that I am not well, I have never a place or anything handsome to write on, so as I know not how to do. If you send me anything to write while I am here, I know not how to do.

I pray God bless my two daughters. It grieves me to think how they lost their time, for I wish I had one of them with me to be some comfort to me, but such is my ill hap that I must wish and want not one, but all my delights.

---

1 This significant request is written with the address.

I will not end thus: away grief and welcome my love whose good will and carefulness will salve all my griefs and bring me to all my delights: In joy, whereof, I end.

Yours till death most assured nothing can remove,

E. Bourne

47 [Undated], Mistress Elizabeth Bourne to [Sir John Conway]

(© British Library Board, BL, Add. MS 23212, fols. 153–154)

My own good knight,

    I cannot but awake surprised with great joy to hear you so welcome home. Although weary, yet happily and welcome to me ten thousand times. I am that true friend I should be. I joy in your good fortune and sorrow in your ill esteeming. All chances that happen to you as if they were my own, and, therefore, how glad I am that you have recovered the Lordships' favor and friendship, you may imagine, for I cannot write it. I hoped well when I heard you were gone. So did I not cease to pray for the confining hope ever since you went. And as it comes happily, so it is double welcome, and I thank God greatly for it.

    Now me thinks I feel help coming towards us and some quietness that we may live on to delight one another according to our hearts' desires. Oh, my own, I send you all the delight I can, which is heartful, fraught with love everlasting, constant, and ever lengthening that it lack his delight, which is you, my own sweet self, whom I love and honor more than my own life. I shall long till I hear by what degrees you were made free. Therefore, hold on your determination, and I will thank you more than a great deal and bid you welcome more than that.

    Alas, I am sorry for my poor Moll that has been all this while in so bad a place. Therefore, I pray you let me have her.[1]

    I will write the letter anew, and I like the altering of it well, but you send me not word what I shall say to my son Conway's letters. Therefore, I cannot send it till I hear how I shall send it.[2]

---

1 Bradford writes that Mary Bourne was transferred, after Lady Conway's death, to "John T[r]acey of Ludington," which may be the "bad place" Elizabeth mentions. See Bradford for the violent outcome of Anthony's attempt to remove his child from Tracey (109–113). From Tracey, Mary is taken to Lord Norris (Bradford 113). See also the Acts of the Privy Council, 1589, NA, PC 2/16, fol. 553.

2 We are not sure to what letter Elizabeth Bourne refers unless it is in regard to her daughter, Mary.

I send you a band.[3] Although I show, yet I am sure, and I think I have made your last for you. In as I love [you] which I am sure is long enough, an[d] so I end in hope to see you shortly.

All yours everlasting,
E. Bourne
Alas, shall I live in prison till Christmas?[4]

3 Perhaps, band, *n*.2 4. *spec*. a. The neck-band or collar of a shirt, originally used to make it fit closely round the neck, afterwards expanded ornamentally. Hence, in 16th and 17th century, a collar or ruff worn round the neck by man or woman.
4 This last is written on what might have been an address.

48 15 March 1589, At Greenwich, [Acts of the Privy Council]
(NA, PC 2/16, fol. 553)

Mistress Bourne's daughter released.[1]

Lord Archbishop
Lord Chancellor
Lord Treasurer
Lord Chamberlain
Lord Buckhurst

Master Treasurer
Master Comptroller
Master Vice Chamberlain
Sir John Perrot
Master [John] Fortescue

A letter to the Lord Norris signifying that at the humble suite of Mistress Bourne, wife to Anthony Bourne, esquire, who informed that her daughter Mary Bourne committed to his Lordship's custody by their Lordships' order, being now fourteen years old and therefore not to be committed to the custody of any, either for her education or marriage, notwithstanding the title Sir John Conway did pretend from the said Anthony Bourne, their Lordships thought good, notwithstanding their former order and direction given to [sic] their Lordships for the sequestration of the said Mary Bourne, to pray his Lordship upon receipt of their Lordships' letters to set her at liberty.

---

1 This record from the Acts of the Privy Council shows us that it is Mistress Elizabeth Bourne and neither Anthony Bourne nor John Conway who effect any change in Mary's location.

Places

Adderbury. One of the largest parishes in north Oxfordshire. In 1511, John Bustard leased the demesne of Adderbury manor. In 1534, the lease passed to John's eldest son Anthony Bustard, husband of Jane Horne, Elizabeth Bourne's aunt.

Arrow. A manor house and parish in the county of Warwickshire. The Conway family held the manor from the late 1400s, along with several other estates in the parish including Kingley. In 1591, John Conway purchased Ragley manor, also in Arrow.

Battenhall. A manor in the parish of St. Peter, Worcester. In 1545 Battenhall was granted to John Bourne, which was confirmed by Queen Mary in 1555. The manor passed to Anthony Bourne upon his father's death in 1575. Anthony Bourne sold the manor and copyhold on the property to Thomas Bromley in January 1576/7.

Belne. An obscure name for Brian's Bell, a manor in the parish of Belbroughton, in the County of Worcester owned by John Conway. In 1592, John Conway and his son Edward Conway conveyed the manor to Humphrey Perrott.

Broken Wharf. Located in the Parish of St. Mary of Somerset, across Tames Street from the church in London. Both John Norris and Elizabeth Bourne sign letters from Broken Wharf c. 1586–1587, which suggests that the Norris family might own property in that area.

Calais, France. A major port in northern France. Controlled by England from 1347–1558.

Canon Row. Also called Channel Row, a small street in the City of Westminster between the Thames and King Street (now Parliament Street).

Chipping Norton. A parish and market town on the northeast edge of the Cotswolds, northwest of Oxford in the county Oxfordshire.

Churchill. A parish and manor in the Cotswolds in the County of Oxfordshire. Adjacent to Sarsden, Churchill is located a few miles from the market town of Chipping Norton. It is likely this is the Churchill referenced; however, John Bourne also purchased a portion of the manor at Churchill, a parish in the County of Worcestershire, in 1555.

After John Bourne's death in 1575, Anthony Bourne sold some of the land to his tenants.

Common Hall, New College, Oxford. A general meeting place and dining hall. Officially named St. Mary's College of Winchester in Oxford, the college was referred to as New College to distinguish it from Oriel College, which is formally known as The Provost and Scholars of the House of the Blessed Mary the Virgin in Oxford. New College is located on New College Lane next to All Souls College.

Cornwall. A county in southwestern England bordered by the Celtic Sea and the English Channel.

Court of Wards. Established in 1540, the court oversaw feudal dues and the granting of wardships. William Cecil served as Master of the Court from 1561–1598.

Cumnor. A parish and manor in the county of Berkshire a few miles west of Oxford in what is now the Vale of White Horse district in Oxfordshire. In 1560 at Cumnor Place, Robert Dudley's first wife Amy Robsart was found dead at the bottom of a staircase. In 1574, Robert Dudley sold Cumnor to Henry Norris of Rycote.

Cutteslowe. Located north of Oxford, the manor consisted of two hides of land that was, in succession, an Augustinian Priory, Cardinal College, and Henry VIII's College. An original agreement dated 1 November 1575 noted that John Chamberleyn and his wife Elizabeth had agreed to sell Cutteslowe to Anthony Bourne; however, the sale seems to have been finalized on 2 January 1577. Anthony Bourne sold Cutteslowe to William Lenthall c. 1588.

Flanders. Northern portion of Belgium also referred to as the Low Countries, which included the wealthy port city of Antwerp. During the latter half of the 1500s, Flanders was involved in the Eighty Years' War. English troops fought alongside protestants in the Low Countries against Spain. John Conway was stationed in Flanders during the late 1580s.

Fonthill. A parish and estate in Wiltshire, also known as Fonthill Gifford. In 1566, James Mervyn inherited Fonthill from his father, John. At the time, the estate included the majority of the parish lands, as well as land neighboring parishes.

Greyfriars. Located in the City of London near Newgate, Greyfriars was the home of a Franciscan Friary until the monastery was dissolved in 1538. In 1546, Henry VIII gave the priory and church to the City of London. The church became known as Christ Church. In 1552, Christ Hospital was founded, a school for the education of poor children.

Holt. A parish and manor Worcester. John Bourne purchased a portion of Holt manor from Anselm Guise (son of John Guise) in 1557. In 1559, John Bourne purchased the remaining lease on the manor from Martin Croft (son of John Croft). The estate passed to Anthony Bourne after his father's death in 1575. In 1578, Anthony sold a portion of the estate to Thomas Fortescue and Edmund Hardy. The estate was settled on Elizabeth Fortescue on her marriage to Thomas Bromley. Anthony sold the lease on Holt to Thomas Bromley. Henry Bromley inherited the manor from his father in 1587.

Kidlington. A manor and estate in Oxford. In 1570, the manor house was purchased by Gerard Croker. In 1585, John Croker, son of Gerard Croker (a friend of Anthony Bourne), sold part of Kidlington to John Temple and the other to William Freer.

Kingley. A manor in the parish of Arrow in the County of Warwickshire. In the late 1400s, Kingley passed from the Burdet family to the Conway family through Anne Burdet's marriage to Edward Conway.

Lambeth. A parish in northeastern Surrey. The Thames serves as the northern border of Lambeth, which is located across the river from Westminster.

Luddington. A manor southwest of Stratford-upon-Avon in the County of Warwickshire. In the late 1400s, Luddington passed from the Burdet family to the Conway family through Anne Burdet's marriage to Edward Conway.

Lyneham. A farm in the Cotswolds in the parish of Shipton-under-Wychwood in the County of Oxfordshire. Lyneham is located south of Sarsden and Churchill near the market town of Chipping Norton. In 1542, Henry VIII granted Lyneham to Edmund Horne and his descendants.

Milk Street. Located in Cripplegate Ward in the City of London, Milk Street runs north–south parallel to Wood Street between Cheapside and Lad Lane.

Milton. Unknown, possibly Milton-under-Wychwood, a small parish in the County of Oxfordshire close to Chipping Norton and Lyneham or in reference to the manor houses and parishes of Greater and Little Milton located south-east of Oxford near Rycote.

Newington. Likely the parish of St. Mary, Newington located just south of the Thames.

Ostend. Located on the North Sea, Ostend is a port town in Flanders. John Conway was the Governor of Ostend in 1586. Edward Norris, younger brother of John Norris, was appointed Governor of Ostend in 1590.

Oxford. A city in the county of Oxfordshire. Oxford became a city when the diocese was established in 1542.

Oxfordshire. A county in southern England bordered by the Thames on the south and the Cotswolds to the west.

Paternoster Row. Located to the northwest of St. Paul's Cathedral in the City of London, the road became widely associated with the London book trade.

172   Places

Rycote.   A manor and park in Oxfordshire east of Oxford. Margery, wife of Henry Norris, inherited the manor from her father John Williams, Baron of Thame.

Sandford.   Likely Sandford (now known as Sanford St. Martin's), a manor, estates, and parish about seven miles east of Chipping Norton, in the county of Oxfordshire.

Sarsden.   A manor, lands, and parish in the Cotswolds in the county of Oxfordshire. Sarsden is located a few miles from the market town of Chipping Norton. Elizabeth Bourne inherited Sarsden from her father Edmund Horne. Edmund's mother, Elizabeth de la Ford held jointure of Sarsden during her lifetime based on John Horne's will. In 1542, Henry VIII granted Sarsden to Edmund and his wife Elizabeth Tame and their descendants, along with the advowson of the parish church. After Elizabeth Bourne's death in 1599, Sarsden should have passed to her daughters Amy and Mary, but instead the property was sold to Sir John Walter.

Shoreditch.   A northern suburb of the city of London, north of Morefields and Bethlehem Hospital.

Star Chamber.   A common-law and equity court held in the Palace of Westminster and thought to be named after the gilded stars on the ceiling of the chamber (Stowe 1598). The court was composed of members of the Privy Council and common-law judges.

Stowell.   A small parish in Gloucestershire that was once a part of Northleach, a Glouchester abbey estate that included Stowell and Hampnett. The estate came to Elizabeth Bourne through her father Edmund Horne's first wife, Elizabeth Tame. In 1550, Hampnett was sold to Anthony Bustard. In 1577, Stowell was sold to Robert Atkinson and his wife Joyce.

Taynton.   A parish in the Cotswolds in the county of Gloucestershire primarily known for agriculture.

Tower of London.   Both a royal residence and a prison, the Tower was primarily used to house people of high status who had been imprisoned by the monarch. The Lieutenant of the Tower (Sir Owen Hopton 1573–1590; Sir Michael Blount 1590–1595) saw to the needs of the prisoners, who were generally held for short periods of time.

Upton-upon-Severn.   Upton is a parish on the bank of the Severn in Worcestershire. In 1551, the manor at Upton was granted to John Dudley, Earl of Warwick and his wife Anne. The manor was forfeit to the Crown in 1553. In 1578, Queen Mary granted it to John Bourne. Despite this, Anne Dudley (now remarried to Sir Edward Unton) maintained control of the property until her death in 1588, which complicated Anthony Bourne's attempts to convey the manor to John Conway in 1577 in trust for Anthony Bourne's daughters. The conveyance was confirmed in 1589. Anthony Bourne, Mary Bourne, and her husband

Sir Herbert Croft sold Upton to Henry Bromley and his wife Anne in 1593.

Wales.   Annexed by England in the Laws of Wales Acts of 1535 and 1542, Wales is located to the west of England and is bordered by the Irish Sea to the north and west and the Bristol Channel to the south.

Warwickshire.   A county in the midlands, Warwickshire lies north of Oxfordshire and northwest of Glouchestershire. The Conway family held significant property in Warwick, a county town of Warwickshire.

Westminster.   Previously a parish, historically in the County of Middlesex, west of the City of London. When Henry VIII dissolved the monasteries, Westminster Abbey was briefly made a Cathedral and the area was given the status of a city.

Whetstone.   Tenements owned by Robert Whetstone in Gutter Lane in Westcheap in the City of London. Hugh Morgan, Queen Elizabeth's apothecary and husband of Lucy Morgan, was one of the tenants.

Whitefriars.   An area in the Ward of Farringdon Without (the City of London wall) between Fleet Street and the Thames adjacent to Water Lane.

Wiltshire.   A county in South West England. Oxfordshire and Gloucestershire boarder Wiltshire to the north.

Worcester.   A city in the county of Worcestershire in the West Midlands of England.

People

Admiral, Lord. *See* Edward Clinton.
Alice, Mistress. Unknown.
Androse. Servant and messenger of Elizabeth Bourne.
Anne. Mistress Mark's maid, enticed by Anthony Bourne.
Archbishop, Lord. Either John Whitgift, Archbishop of Canterbury or John Piers, Archbishop of York.
Arrasmythe, Raffe. Anthony Bourne's man in Calais, France.
Atkinson, Robert (d. 1607). Lawyer and Oxford City recorder (1566–1607). Son of Richard Atkinson, five-time mayor of Oxford, and his wife Agnes. Married to Joyce Ashfield. Anthony Bourne and Elizabeth Bourne conveyed the manor at Stowell to Atkinson in 1577.
Audley, Lucia. *See* Lucia Tuchet.
Bate. Unknown.
Bear. Unknown. Possibly a tenant farmer of Elizabeth Bourne's.
Bess. Servant of Mistress Blount.
Blount, Michael (c. 1530–1609). High Sheriff of Buckinghamshire (1576) and Oxfordshire (1586 and 1597). Lieutenant of the Tower of London (1590–1595), succeeding Owen Hopton. Son of Sir Richard Blount and Elizabeth Lyster. Married to Mary Moore. Michael Blount and Elizabeth Bourne were second cousins through their paternal grandmother, Elizabeth de la Ford. Elizabeth de la Ford's first husband was Richard Blount (father of Sir Richard Blount) and her second was John Horne (father of Edmund Horne).
Blount, Mistress. Woman who runs a gambling house.
Blythe. Likely a servant and messenger of John Conway.
Bourne, Amy (c. 1570–November 1647). Eldest daughter of Anthony Bourne and Elizabeth Bourne. Married to Fulke Conway, second son of John Conway and Eleanor Greville. Originally, contracted in marriage to Edward Conway, eldest son of John Conway.
Bourne, Anthony (c. 1545–after 1603). Eldest son of John Bourne and Dorothy Hornyold. Married to Elizabeth Bourne (27 September 1565). Father of Amy and Mary.
Bourne, Dorothy (d. 1576). Daughter of John Hornyold and Kathryn Butler. Married to John Bourne. Mother of Anthony, Charles, Elizabeth

(m. George Winter), Margaret (m. William Clark), Persida (m. Thomas Powell), and Anne.

Bourne, Elizabeth (c. 1549–25 August 1599). Daughter of Edmund Horne and Amy Clarke. Stepdaughter of James Mervyn. Half-sister of Lucia Mervyn. After her father's death, Elizabeth was a ward of Henry Jerningham, a member of Queen Mary's Privy Council and Master of the Horse. Married to Anthony Bourne (27 September 1565). Mother of Amy and Mary.

Bourne, John (c. 1518–1575). Secretary of State to Queen Mary (1553–1558). Member of Parliament for Guildford (1539), Midhurst (1542), Preston (1545), Worcester (1553), and Worcestershire (1554, 1555, 1558). Married to Dorothy Hornyold. Knighted (1553). Father of Anthony, Charles, Elizabeth (m. George Winter), Margaret (m. William Clark), Persida (m. Thomas Powell), and Anne.

Bourne, Mary (1575–1659). Youngest daughter of Anthony Bourne and Elizabeth Horne. Married to Herbert Croft (c. 1591).

Brace, Francis (d. 1599). Son of William Brace and Margery Porter. Bailiff of Droitwich (1566). MP for Droitwich (1571). Lord of Doverdale Manor. Married to Mary Purslow (m. 1562). Cousin and friend of Anthony Bourne. Son Thomas married Frances, daughter of William Freer of Oxford.

Bromfield, Master. Unknown.

Bromley, Thomas (c. 1530–April 1587). Appointed Solicitor-General (1569) and Lord Chancellor (1579–1587). Knighted (1579). Son of George Bromley and Jane Lacon. Married to Elizabeth Fortescue. Anthony Bourne sold Newland, a manor house in Norton Juxta Kempsey, Worcestershire, to Bromley (January 1576/7).

Broughton, Richard (1542–1604). Servant of both Walter Devereux, the Earl of Essex, and later Robert Devereux, the Second Earl of Essex. Son of Robert Broughton and Jane Vychan (or Vaughan). Married to Anna Bagot.

Buckhurst, Lord. *See* Thomas Sackville.

Burghley, Lord. *See* William Cecil.

Bustard, Anne. *See* Anne Green.

Bustard, Anthony (c. 1530–1590). Son of John Bustard and Elizabeth Fox. Uncle to Elizabeth Bourne through his wife, Jane Horne (d. 1568), sister of Edmund Horne, Elizabeth Bourne's father. Edmund Horne sold Hampnett to Anthony Bustard (1550).

Bustard, William. Eldest son of Anthony Bustard (d. 1590) and Jane Horne (d. 1568). Cousin to Elizabeth Bourne through William's mother Jane Horne, sister of Edmund Horne, Elizabeth Bourne's father. William Bustard quitclaimed Hampnett to Robert Atkinson (1587).

Butler, Thomas (c. 1531–1614). 10th Earl of Ormonde, 3rd Earl of Ossory (1546). Treasurer of Ireland (1559–1614). Lord General of

176 *People*

the Forces in Munster (1582–1583). Order of the Garter (1588). Son of James Butler and Joan Fitzgerald. Married to Elizabeth Berkeley, Elizabeth Sheffield (m. 1582), Helena Barry (m. 1601).

Caesar, Julius (c. 1558–1636). Received BA (1575), MA (1578), and DCL (1584) from Oxford. Admitted to Inner Temple (1580). City of London's civil law counsel (1583). Court of Admiralty (1584–1605), Chancery (starting in 1585), and Requests (starting in 1591). Called to the bench at Inner Temple (1591). Knighted (1603). Chancellor of the Exchequer (1606–1614). Privy Council (1607). Master of the Rolls (1614–1636). Son of Cesare Adelmare (d. 1569) and Margery Perient. Married to Dorcas Lusher (1583).

Carey, Henry (1526–1596). MP Buckingham (1547, 1554, 1555). Carver of the Privy Chamber (1553). Gentleman of the Household to Elizabeth (1553). Knighted (1558). Baron Hudson (1559). Order of the Garter (1561). Governor of Berwick (1568). Warden of the East Marches (1571–577). Privy Councilor (1577). Lord Chamberlain (1585–1596). Son of William Carey and Mary Boleyn. Married to Anne Morgan (1545).

Cecil, William (1520/21–1598). Chief Clerk of the Court of Common Pleas (1541). In service of the Duke of Somerset (1547). Secretary of State (1550–1553 and 1558–1572). Knighted (1551). 1st Baron Burghley (1571). Order of the Garter (1572). Lord High Treasurer (1572–1598). Son of Richard Cecil and Jane Heckington. Married to Mary Cheke (1541) and Mildred Cooke (1545).

Chamberlain, Lord. *See* Thomas Radcliffe (1572–1583) and Henry Carey (1585–1596).

Chamberleyn, John. Son of Leonard Chamberleyn (d. 1561). Married to Elizabeth Owen. Sold Cutteslowe to Anthony Bourne (January 1577). Served as one of the arbitrators appointed by the Privy Council to settle the disputes between John Conway, Anthony Bourne, and Elizabeth Bourne (January 1583/4).

Chancellor, Lord. *See* Thomas Bromley (1579–1587) and Christopher Hatton (1587–1591).

Charles, Master. Unknown.

Cholmeley. Unknown. There were several branches of the Cholmeley family (also known as Cholmondeley) during the late 1500s, including Hugh Cholmondeley of Cheshire, Jasper Cholmeley of Highgate, Middlesex, and Roger and Richard Cholmeley of Yorkshire.

Clarke, Amy. *See* Amy Mervyn.

Clarke, Cousin. Unknown. Possibly related to Roland Clarke, Elizabeth Bourne's uncle.

Clarke, Master. Possibly, William Clarke, brother-in-law to Anthony Bourne.

Clarke, Roland (d. c. 1590). Son of Valentine Clark and Elizabeth Bridges. Brother to Amy Mervyn. Uncle to Elizabeth Bourne. Possibly the same

Roland Clarke married to Catherine Strange who was an Extraordinary Lady of the Privy Chamber (1559) at the same time as Amy Mervyn.

Clarke, William.   Married to Margaret Bourne, sister of Anthony Bourne.

Clinton, Edward (1512–1585).   9th Baron Clinton (1517). Knighted (1544). Governor of Boulogne (1547). Lord High Admiral (1550–1553, 1558–1585). 1st Earl of Lincoln (1572). Son of Thomas Clinton and Jane Poynings. Married to Elizabeth Blount, Ursula Stourton, and Elizabeth FitzGerald.

Clinton, Henry (1539–1616).   MP for Lincolnshire (1571). 2nd Earl of Lincoln (1585). Appointed a Knight of the Bath (1553). Son of Edward Lincoln, 1st Earl of Lincoln, and Ursula Stourton. Married to Catherine Hastings (1557) and Elizabeth Morrison (1586).

Coke, James.   Unknown.

Compton, Henry (1544–1589).   1st Baron of Compton (1572). MP for Old Sarum (1563). Knighted (1567). High Sheriff of Warwickshire (1571–1572). Son of Peter Compton and Anne Talbot. Married to Frances Hastings and Anne Spencer.

Comptroller, Master.   *See* James Croft.

Conway, Amy.   *See* Amy Bourne.

Conway, Edward (c. 1564–1631).   Baron Conway (c. 1624). Viscount Conway (1627). Knighted (1596). MP for Penryn (1610). Privy Council (1622). Secretary of State (1623). Eldest son of Sir John Conway and Eleanor Greville. Married to Dorothy Tracy (d. 1613) and Katherine Hueriblock (d. 1639).

Conway, Eleanor (d. Nov 1588).   Daughter of Sir Fulke Greville (d. 1559) and Elizabeth Willoughby, 3rd Baroness Willoughby de Broke (d. 1562). Married to John Conway (d. 1603). Mother to Edward (m. Dorothy Tracy), Fulke (m. Amy Bourne), John, Thomas, Elizabeth, Katherine, Mary, and Frances.

Conway, Elizabeth.   Daughter of John Conway and Eleanor Greville.

Conway, Frances (b. c. 1575).   Daughter of John Conway and Eleanor Greville.

Conway, Fulke (c. 1565–1624).   Second son of Sir John Conway and Eleanor Greville. Married to Amy Bourne. Served in Ulster, Ireland, and remained there after the conflict. James I granted Fulke the lands of Killultagh in County Antrim, Ireland (1611).

Conway, John (d. October 1603).   Governor of Ostend (1586). Knighted (1559). Son of Sir John Conway and Katherine Verney. Married to Eleanor Greville (d. 1588). Father to Edward (m. Dorothy Tracy), Fulke (m. Amy Bourne), John, Thomas, Elizabeth, Katherine, Mary, and Frances.

Cooper, John.   Unknown. Possibly, John Cooper (1552–1610). MP for Whitchurch (1584, 1586). Soldier with close ties to John Norris.

Cressy, James (b. c. 1552.) Purchased the wardship of Richard Wenman, son and heir of Thomas Wenman (d. 1577), from Robert Dudley, the Earl of Leicester. Married to Jane West, widow of Thomas Wenman.

Croft, Herbert (c. 1565–April 1629). Eldest son of Edward Croft and Anne Browne. Grandson and heir to Sir James Croft. Married to Mary Bourne (1591). Knighted (1603).

Croft, James (c. 1518–1590). MP for Herefordshire (1542, 1563, 1571, 1572,1584, 1586 and 1589). Knighted (1547). Gentleman of the Privy Chamber (1551). Lord Deputy of Ireland (1551–1552). Privy Councilor (1570). Comptroller of the Household (1570–1590). Son of Sir Richard Croft and Catherine Herbert. Grandfather to Herbert Croft, who married Mary Bourne. Close friend of Dorothy Bourne and an executor of her will. One of the arbitrators appointed by the Privy Council to settle the disputes between John Conway, Anthony Bourne, and Elizabeth Bourne (January 1583/4).

Croker, Gerard (c. 1525–1577). Knighted (1575). Son of John Croker and Isabell Skynner. Married to Mary Blundell. The Croker family owned property in Sandford and Kidlington.

Curtis. Unknown.

Daffarne. Unknown. Possibly John Daffarne. Graduated Lincoln College Oxford B.A. (February 1559/60), M.A. (1563). He appears as a witness in several documents between 1560–1585.

Danvers, John (1540–1594). MP for Wiltshire (1571) and Malmsebury (1572). J.P. of Wiltshire (c.1573). Sheriff 1574–1576). Knighted (1574). Son of Sylvester Danvers. Married to Elizabeth Nevill.

Drewry, Tom. Unkown.

Duckett, Francis. Rector of Sarsden (1562–1575). While Duckett is no longer the rector of Sarsden during this time, he is still connected to Elizabeth Bourne, Sarsden, and named as Parson Duckett by James Mervyn (NA, SP 15/26, fol. 30–31 14 May 1579).

Dudley, Anne (1548/9–1604). Maid of Honor (1559) and Lady in Waiting to Queen Elizabeth. Daughter of Francis Russell, second earl of Bedford, and Margaret St. John. Married to Ambrose Dudley, Earl of Warwick.

Dudley, Robert (1532/3–1588). Master of the Horse (1558). Privy Councilor (1562). Earl of Leicester (1564). Lord Seward of the Royal Household (1587). Command of the English land forces during the Spanish Armada (1588). Fifth son of John Dudley, Duke of Northumberland (d. 1553) and Jane Guildford (d. 1555). Married to Amy Robsart (m. 1550, d. 1560) Lettice Knollys (m. 1578).

Fortescue, John (1533–1607). Member of Princess Elizabeth's Household (c. 1555). Keeper of the Wardrobe (1559). Chancellor of the Exchequer and Under-Treasurer (1589–1603). Privy Councilor (1589). Knighted (1592). Chancellor of the Duchy of Lancaster (1601–1607). Son of

Adrian Fortescue and Anne Reade. Married to Cecily Ashfield (m. 1556, d. 1570) and Alice Smith.

Forth, Robert (d. 1595).   LL.D Cambridge (1562), incorporation as D.C.L. (1566).

Francis, Master.   Unknown.

Freer, William (d. 1612).   MP for Oxford (1571). Hanaster of Oxford (1571). Member of the Mayor's Council (1583–1603). J.P. of Oxfordshire (c. 1591). Sheriff (1596–1597). Son of Edward Freer and Ann Bustard. Married to Mary Bamfield (m. 1560). Cousin of Anthony Bustard.

Gifford, George (1552–1613).   MP for Morpeth (1584) and Cricklade (1597, 1601). Knighted (1596). Son of John Gifford (d. 1563) and Elizabeth Throckmorton. Married to Elizabeth Bridges.

Goodere, Henry (1534–1595).   Member of Elizabeth's household (1558). MP for Strafford (1563–1566/7). Knighted (1586). High Sheriff of Warwickshire (1591). Son of Francis Goodere and Ursula Rowlett. Married to Frances Lowther. One of the arbitrators appointed by the Privy Council to settle the disputes between John Conway, Anthony Bourne, and Elizabeth Bourne (January 1583/4).

Gostwick, Mistress.   Unknown.

Greene, Anne.   Daughter of Anthony Bustard and Jane Horne. Married to William Green (d. 1622). Cousin to Elizabeth Bourne through Anne's mother Jane, sister of Edmund Horne, Elizabeth Bourne's father.

Greville, Brother.   One of Eleanor Conway's brothers, possibly Robert or Edward. While the Greville family held substantial property in Warwickshire, Elizabeth Bourne's reference to John Conway's Brother Greville suggests that he was her tenant.

Greville, Eleanor.   *See* Eleanor Conway.

Grey, Master.   Unknown. Possibly John Grey (d. 1594). MP of Staffordshire (1563, 1571, 1586). Son of Thomas Grey and Anne Verney, sister of John Conway's mother Katherine. Married to Jane Harcourt.

Hardy, Edmund.   Servant to Thomas Bromley.

Hatton, Christopher (1540–1591).   MP for Higham Ferrers (1571) and Northhamptonshire (1572). Part of Commission that found Mary, Queen of Scots, guilty of treason (1586). Lord Chancellor of England (1587–1591). Son of William Hatton and Alice Saunders.

Hawkins.   Elizabeth Bourne's tenant and caretaker at Sarsden.

Hawkins, Mistress.   Wife of Hawkins, Elizabeth Bourne's tenant and caretaker at Sarsden.

Heneage, Thomas (1532–1595).   Gentleman of the Privy Chamber (1565). Treasurer of the Chamber (1570). Keeper of Records, Tower of London (1575–1595). Knighted (1577). Privy Councilor (1587). Vice Chamberlain (1587–1595). Chancellor, Duchy of Lancaster

(1590–1595). Son of Robert Henage and Lucy Buckton. Married to Anne Poyntz (1555) and Mary Browne (1594).

Hobby, Elizabeth. Daughter of Anthony Bustard and Jane Horne, Elizabeth Bourne's aunt. Cousin to Elizabeth Bourne.

Hobby, Richard. Married to Elizabeth Hobby, cousin to Elizabeth Bourne.

Hopton, Owen (c. 1519–1595). MP for Suffolk (1559, 1571), Middlesex (1572, 1584), and Arundel (1589). Knighted (1561). Lieutenant of the Tower (1570–1590). Son of Arthur Hopton and Anne Owen. Married to Ann Echingham (m. 1542).

Horne, Edmund (c. 1490–1553). Esquire of the Body of King Henry VIII (1537–1538). Son of John Horne (d. 1526), sheriff of Oxfordshire (1490 and 1506), and Elizabeth de la Ford, widow of Richard Blount. Half-brother of Sir Richard Blount. Married to Elizabeth Tame (d. 1548) and Amy Clarke. Brother to Mary and Jane, wife of Anthony Bustard. Father to Elizabeth Bourne.

Horne, Elizabeth. *See* Elizabeth Bourne.

Hornyold, Dorothy. *See* Dorothy Bourne.

Jackson, Jane. An alleged mistress of Anthony Bourne.

Killigrew, John/Jack. Possible reference to either John Killigrew (d. 1584) or his son John Killigrew (d. 1605). Likely, John Killigrew (d. 1584). J.P. Cornwall (c 1559). Captain of Pendennis Castle (1568–1584). MP Lostwithiel (1563), Penryn (1571, 1572). Married to Mary Wolverston, who was accused of piracy. The Privy Council reported that Lady Killigrew aided in Anthony Bourne's escape from the authorities (8 May 1577).

Knollys, Francis (1511/2–1596). Knighted (1547). Master of the Horse to Prince Edward (1547). MP for Oxfordshire (1563, 1571, 1572, 1584, 1586, 1589, 1593). Vice Chamberlain and Privy Councilor (1559). Captain of the Guard (1565). Treasurer of the Chamber (1567–1570). Treasurer of the Household (1570–1596). Order of the Garter (1593). Son of Robert Knollys and Lettice Peniston. Married to Catherine Carey (c. 1540).

Lane, Edward (c. 1552–c. 1596). MP of Mitchel (1572). Son of John Lane and Elizabeth Pakington. Brought suit against John Conway for Anthony Bourne's goods forfeit when Anthony left the realm without license.

Lane, William (c. 1553–1618). MP of Gatton (1593) and Northamptonshire (1601). Brought suit against John Conway for Anthony Bourne's goods forfeit when Anthony left the realm without license.

Leicester, Lord. *See* Robert Dudley.

Lieutenant, Master. *See* Owen Hopton.

Lyttelton, Gilbert (c. 1549–1599). MP for Worcestershire (1570, 1571). High Sheriff of Worcestershire (1584–1585). Eldest son of Sir John Lyttelton and Bridget Packington. Married to Elizabeth Coningsby.

Margaret. A maid under Mistress Mask, in the service of Lord Clinton. An alleged mistress of Anthony Bourne.

Martin, Richard (d. 1617). Liveryman of the Worshipful Company of Goldsmiths (1558). Alderman of Farringdon Within (1578–1598) and Bread Street (1598–1602). Sherriff of London (1581–1582). Master of the Mint (1582–1617). Knighted (1588/9). Lord Mayor of London (1589, 1593–1594). Married to Dorcas Eccleston. Martin's daughter Dorcas was married to Julius Caesar.

Mask, Mistress. Keeps house for Lord Clinton in Canon Row.

Mervyn, Amy (b. c. 1530). Daughter of Valentine Clarke and Elizabeth Bridges. Mother to Elizabeth Bourne and Lucia Tuchet. Widow of Edmund Horne, Elizabeth Bourne's father. Married to James Mervyn. Extraordinary Gentlewoman of the Privy Chamber (1559).

Mervyn, James (1529–1611). Knighted (1574). MP for Wiltshire (1572). Esquire for the Queen's Body. Son of Sir John Mervyn and Jane Baskerville. Married to Amy Clarke Horne. Father to Lucia Tuchet. Stepfather to Elizabeth Bourne. Held substantial property in Wiltshire, including Fonthill Gifford, and a house in London in Farringdon-Without.

Mervyn, Lucia. *See* Lucia Tuchet.

Morgan, Hugh (d. 1613). Apprenticed to William Chick (1543). Member (1552) and Warden (1574) of the Grocer's Company. Apothecary-in-ordinary to Queen Elizabeth (15 July 1583). Son of John Morgan and Joan Copcott. Married to Lucy Sibel (d. 1606).

Morgan, Lucy (d. 1606). Married to Hugh Morgan (d. 1613). Daughter of Nicholas Sibell.

Norris, Cousin. Unknown. A female relative of Elizabeth Bourne through her father's side of the family. *See* Henry Norris.

Norris, Henry (c. 1525–1601). Ward (1536) and subsequently servant (1544) of King Henry VIII. Gentleman of Edward VI's Privy Chamber. MP for Berkshire (1547). He and his wife inherited Rycote from his father-in-law (1559). Knighted (1566). Ambassador to France (1567–1570). MP Oxfordshire (1571). Baron Norris of Rycote (by 1572). Lord Lieutenant of Oxfordshire and Berkshire (1585–1599). Son of Henry Norris and Mary Fiennes. Married to Margery Williams, daughter and co-heir of John Williams, Lord Williams of Thame. Elizabeth Bourne's great-aunt, Anne Horne (sister of John Horne, Elizabeth Bourne's grandfather), was the third wife (m. c. 1478) of William Norris (d. 1507). William Norris's eldest son Edward died in 1487 before William (d. 1507). Edward's eldest son John Norris (c. 1481–1564) inherited the family property. John Norris's younger brother Henry was beheaded (1526) on suspicion of adultery with Anne Boleyn. John Norris cared for Henry Norris and his sister Mary after their father's execution. John Norris died without issue and settled his estates on Henry Norris. Elizabeth Bourne's great-aunt is the third wife of Henry Norris's great-grandfather.

Norris, John (c. 1547–1597). Solider and military commander in France and the Low Countries (1567, 1578–1584, 1586, 1591–1594), Ireland (1573–c.1577, 1595–1596), and Spain (1589). Knighted (1586). Second son of Henry Norris and Margery Williams.

Ormond, Lord. *See* Thomas Butler.

Osbaston, Humfrey. Unknown. An Osbaston family is connected with Oddington, Oxfordshire.

Owen, Master. Likely Richard or William Owen. Sons of George Owen (d. 1558), royal physician. Richard owned Wolvercote Manor and Godstone. Married to Mary Chamberleyn, sister of John Chamberleyn. William was MP for Oxford (1572). Richard and William's sister, Elizabeth, married John Chamberleyn. Referenced in BL, Add. MS 23212, fol. 5–6.

Owen, Master. Likely Thomas Owen (d. 1598). MP for Shrewsbury (1584). Serjeant (1589). Queen's Serjeant (1593). Justice of Common Pleas (1595). Referenced in NA, SP 12/205 fol. 124 and BL, Add. MS 23212, fol. 183.

Pagnam, Mistress. Anthony Bourne's longtime mistress. While there is not a definitive answer as to the identity of Mistress Pagnam, there are references to their affair. Elizabeth Bourne consistently refers to her as Mistress Pagnam. Anthony Bourne in HH, CP 160/117 refers to her as Mistress Pakenham. In another letter he mentions Jane Pyckeman (BL, Add. MS 23212, fol. 47r). The *Calendar of State Papers Foreign: Elizabeth, Volume 11, 1575–1577*, lists her name as Packington (16 April 1577). And the *Acts of the Privy Council of England* records that "one Anthonye Boourne hath very wickedly intysed away the wife of one Robert Packingham" (7 May 1577).

Parry, Blanche (1507/8–1590). Lady-in-waiting to infant Princess Elizabeth (by 1336). Gentlewoman of the Privy Chamber (1558). Chief Gentlewoman (1565). Daughter of Henry Myles and Alice Milborne.

Parson, Master. Unknown. Possibly, Francis Duckett, former rector of Sarsden (1562–1575) who is still connected to Sarsden and Elizabeth Bourne. It could also be William Berd, rector of Sarsden (1575–1592).

Peckham, George (d. 1608). Knighted (1570). Sheriff of Buckinghamshire (1572). Son of Edmund Peckham and Anne Cheyne. Married to Susan Webbe.

Peniston, Cousin. Unknown. Possibly, Thomas or Elizabeth Peniston. Elizabeth Peniston was a cousin of John Conway through his father's sister Anne, who was Elizabeth Peniston's mother.

Perrot, John (1528–1592). MP for Sandwich (1553, 1555), Wareham (1559), Pembrokeshire (1563), and Haverfordwest (1589). Knighted (1549). President of Munster (1570–1573). Privy Councilor (1589). Son of Thomas Perrot and Mary Berkeley. Rumored to be the illegitimate son of Henry VIII. Married to Anne Cheyne and Jane Prust.
Perry, James. Unknown.
Piers, John (1522/3–1594). Archbishop of York (1589–1594). Magdalen College B.A. (1545), M.A. (1549), B.D. (1558), and D.D. (1555–1556). Fellow of Magdalen College (1546). Holy orders (1558). Master of Balliol College (1570). Bishop of Rochester (1576). Bishop of Salisbury (1577). Lord High Almoner (1576).
Powell, Thomas. Son of Thomas Powell and Elizabeth Probart. Married to Persida Bourne. Anthony Bourne's brother-in-law.
Prestall, Meg. Unknown.
Radcliffe, Frances (1531–1589). Lady of the Bedchamber to Queen Elizabeth. Daughter of Sir William Sidney and Anne Packenham. Married to Thomas Radcliffe, Viscount FitzWalter, and the Earl of Sussex (m. 1555).
Radcliffe, Thomas (c. 1525–1583). Viscount Fitzwalter (1542). Lord Deputy of Ireland (1556). 3rd Earl of Sussex (1557). Lord President of the North (1568). Privy Councilor (1570). Lord Chamberlain (1572–1583). Son of Henry Radcliffe, 2nd Earl of Sussex, and Elizabeth Howard. Married to Elizabeth Wriothesley (m. c. 1545, d. 1555) and Frances Sidney (m. 1555).
Reynolds, John. Unknown.
Sackville, Thomas (c. 1536–1608). MP Westmoreland (1558), East Grinstead (1559), and Aylesbury (1563–1566). Knighted and created Baron Buckhurst (1567). Order of the Garter (1588). Chancellor of Oxford (1591). Lord High Treasurer (1599–1608). Son of Richard Sackville and Winifred Bridges. Married to Cicely Baker.
Sale. Unknown.
Sparks. Unknown.
Stafford, Francis. Unknown. Possibly, Francis Stafford (d. 1609). Knighted (1599). Captain of the Queen's forces in Ulster, Ireland.
Sussex, Lady. *See* Frances Radcliffe.
Tacey. Unknown. Possibly a servant of Elizabeth Bourne's.
Talbot, John. Possibly, John Talbot (1545–1611). Son of John Talbot and Frances Giffard. Married to Katherine Petre (1561). A staunch Catholic.
Tandy. A shoemaker.
Thayer, Thomas. Unknown.
Tomlinson. Amy Mervyn's man.
Treasurer, Lord. *See* William Cecil.
Treasurer, Master. *See* Francis Knollys.

184   *People*

Tuchet, Lucia (c. 1560–1609/10).   Daughter of James Mervyn and Amy Clark. Half-sister of Elizabeth Bourne. Married to George Tuchet, Earl of Castlehaven, Baron Audley, and Baron Tuchet.

Unton, Anne (1538–1588).   Daughter of Edward Seymour, Duke of Somerset and Ann Stanhope. Married to John Dudley, Earl of Warwick (d. 1554), and Sir Edward Unton (d. 1583). Anne was still referred to as the Countess of Warwick after John Dudley's death, despite her remarrying and the title passing to Ambrose Dudley's wife, Anne Dudley (née Russell). The manor at Upton was granted to John Dudley, Early of Warwick and his wife Anne in 1551. Two years later, it was forfeit to the crown. In 1578, Queen Mary granted Upton to John Bourne. Despite this, Anne Dudley (now remarried to Sir Edward Unton) maintained control of the property until her death in 1588.

Unton, Edward (1534–1582).   Appointed a Knight of the Bath (1559). MP for Malmesbury (1554), Oxfordshire (1563), and Berkshire (1572). High Sheriff of Berkshire (1567). Son of Alexander Unton and Cecily Bulstrode. Married to Anne Seymour (m. 1555), widow of John Dudley, Earl of Warwick.

Unton, Henry.   One of the arbitrators appointed by the Privy Council to settle the disputes between John Conway, Anthony Bourne, and Elizabeth Bourne (January 1583/4). Son of Edward Unton and Anne Seymour.

Vaughan, Anne.   Unknown. An alleged mistress of Anthony Bourne.

Vaughan, Thomas.   Unknown.

Vice Chamberlain, Master.   *See* Thomas Heneage.

Walsingham, Francis (c. 1532–1590).   King's College, Cambridge (1548). Grey's Inn (1552). MP for Bossiney (1559), Lyme Regis (1563), Surrey (1572, 1584, 1586, 1589). Ambassador to France (1570–1573). Privy Councilor (1573). Principal Secretary to Elizabeth I (1573–1590). Knighted (1577). Chancellor of the Garter (1578–1587). Son of William Walsingham and Joyce Denny. Married to Ann Barne (m. 1562, d. 1564) and Ursula St. Barbe (1566).

Warwick, Countess of.   *See* Ann Unton.

Warwick, Lady.   *See* Anne Dudley.

Waste, Master.   Unknown. Anthony Bourne enticed Master Waste's wife.

Wenman, Thomas (c. 1548–July 1577).   MP for Buckingham (1571). Son of Sir Richard Wenman and Isabel Williams, sister of Henry Norris's wife Margery Williams. Married to Jane West (1572).

West, Thomas (c. 1550–1601/2).   Knighted (1587). MP for Yarmouth, Isle of Wight (1586) and Aylesbury (1593). Chamberlain of the Exchequer (1590). Baron of Delaware (1595). Son of William West and Elizabeth Strange. Married to Anne Knollys (1571).

Whitgift, John (c. 1530–1604).   Archbishop of Canterbury (1583–1604). Queen's College Cambridge (1549). Pembroke Hall Cambridge (1550).

Fellow of Peterhouse (1555). Holy orders (1560). Lady Margaret's Professor of Divinity Cambridge (1563). Bishop of Worcester (1577). Son of Henry Whitgift.

Whitney, Uncle. Unknown. Possibly Will Whitney.

Whitney, Will. Unknown. Receiver for Staffordshire.

Wilson, Anthony. Servant of Elizabeth Bourne.

Wilson, Jane. An alleged mistress of Anthony Bourne.

Winnington. Unknown. Anthony Bourne enticed a woman from Winnington.

Wood, Besse. Unknown. An alleged mistress of Anthony Bourne.

Index

Alfar, Cristina León 1, 12
Amussen, Susan Dwyer 3, 7
Arrow 32, 57, 131, 152, 153, 169,171
Atkinson, Robert 29n5, 172, 174, 175
Audley, Lucia *see* Tuchet, Lucia

Battenhall 2, 12, 29–30, 36n5, 38n9, 50n2, 108, 169
Beam, Sara 86n48
Blount, Michael 83, 84, 110, 174; *see* Tower of London 172
Bodden, Mary-Catherine 8n34
Bourne, Amy 1, 15–16, 17, 19–22, 31–32, 106–107, 109, 111–112, 116, 118, 123, 136n4, 140n5, 141n2, 144n5, 174–175; *see* Sarsden, 172, and Greville, Fulke 177
Bourne, Mary 1, 17, 19–22, 24, 53n4, 65n1, 65n2, 106–107, 109, 111–112, 116, 117, 118, 123, 134, 135, 136, 140, 145, 159, 160–161, 166n1, 166n2, 168, 174, 175; as "Moll" 53, 166; *see* Sarsden 172; *see* Upton-upon-Severn 172; *see* Herbert Croft 178; *see* Henry Norris 166n1, 168
Brace, Francis 83, 175
Bradford, Charles Angell 1n2, 2n4, 13, 166n1
Bromely, Thomas 20, 29n1, 30, 35–36, 38n9, 50–51, 83n38, 99n7, 147n5, 175; *see* Battenhall 169; *see* Holt 170–171
Broughton, Richard 45, 50–51, 175
Butler, Sara 3n12, 8n38, 12–13n50, 14–15, 18n64, 19–20

Caesar, Julius xv, 3, 4, 5, 10, 20, 24–25, 55n1, 67–69, 92–96, 98, 105, 151n5, 176; *see* Martin, Richard 181
Calais 20, 40, 72, 79, 80n30, 169

Carey, Henry 158, 168, 176
Cecil, William 35, 37–41, 48n2, 76n13, 176; *see* Court of Wards 170; *see* Burghley, Lord 42n1, 175
Chamberleyn, John 29n4, 30, 50, 62, 83–84, 108–120, 121, 127, 176, 182; *see* Cutteslowe 170
Chipping Norton 62, 72, 80, 90, 97, 120, 122, 169; *see* Churchill 169; *see* Lyneham 171; *see* Milton 171; *see* Sandeford 172; *see* Sarsden 172
Clarke, Amy: *see* Mervyn, Amy
Clarke, Roland 134, 176–177
Clarke, William 62, 109, 111, 112, 114, 115, 116, 159, 176
Coke, James 52–53, 163, 177
Compton, Henry 37, 41, 46, 47, 61, 111, 177
Conway, Edward xiii, 5, 15–16, 20, 22, 31–32, 69, 98n3, 105, 123, 127, 136n4, 140n5, 144n5, 151n7, 174, 177; *see* Belne 169; *see* Kingley and Ludington 171
Conway, Eleanor xv, 14, 16, 21, 24, 57, 61, 65n1, 65n2, 131, 132–133, 134n1, 135n1, 136n4, 141–142, 152n1, 155n1, 166n1, 174, 177; *see* Greville, Brother 179
Conway, Frances 31, 177
Croft, James 2, 117, 119, 121, 124, 127, 178
Cutteslowe 29, 111, 115, 118–119, 123–125, 130, 132, 170; *see* Chamberleyn, John 176

Daybell, James 1, 5n23, 23
divorce 1–10, 12–13n50, 18n64, 24, 68, 69, 75n6, 98n1, 107, 126–127n12; and Elizabeth Bourne's petition 85–91; and Julius Caesar's

response 92–96; and *a mensa et thoro* 2, 3; and *a vinculo matrimonii* 2
Dolan, Frances 4n19, 8
Drake, William Richard 2n3
Duckett, Francis 52, 178; *see* Parson, Master 182
Dudley, Anne 57n4, 178
Dudley, Robert 132–133; *see* Cumnor 170; *see* Cressy, James 178

Erickson, Amy Louise 20n69, 20n72

femme sole 4, 12, 14, 15n56, 18n65, 21, 126–127n12; *see* sole life and separation 126

Goodere, Henry 108–120, 121, 127, 179
Gowing, Laura 3, 3n13, 4n14, 5n20, 8n36, 9, 10

Hardy, Edmund 50, 179
Harris, Jonathan Gill 81n32
Hawkins 17, 61, 150, 153, 162–163, 179
Hawkins, Mistress 162, 163, 179
Hill, Lamar M 3n10, 3n12, 13
Hobby, Elizabeth 62, 81, 180
Hobby, Richard 53, 62, 81, 134, 180
Holt 12, 30, 50n2, 73n1, 108, 170
Hopton, Owen 41, 76n14, 180; *see* Tower of London 172; *see* Blount, Michael 174
Horne, Edmund xvn1; 2, 17, 179; *see* Lyneham 171; *see* Sarsden and Stowell 172; *see* Blount, Michael 174; *see* Bourne, Elizabeth 175; *see* Bustard, Anthony 175; *see* Mervyn, Amy 181

indenture of award 4n18, 12, 16–22, 25, 31–32, 106–107, 112–119, 121–127, 141–142n3, 158n5, 159

Kennedy, Gwynne 16
Killigrew, John/Jack 39, 180
Kingdon, Robert 86n48
Knollys, Francis 180; *see* Master Treasurer 168

Lane, Edward 126, 180
Lane, William 126, 180
legal rights: in separation agreements 19–21

Lyneham 29–30, 171
Lyttelton, Gilbert 51, 181

marriage: separation 2–4, 7–8, 10, 12, 68, 87, 89; and Julius Caesar 92–96; and limits of 14–16, 24; and legal acknowledgement of 18, 126; and property rights 17–20; of Bourne daughters 13–14, 15–16, 21–22, 31–32, 99, 107, 108, 111, 112, 118, 123, 135n1, 138–140, 143n1, 146n3, 146n4, 158, 168
Mervyn, Amy 2, 11–12, 55, 56–57, 58–59, 181; *see* Clarke, Amy 2, 176; *see* Horne, Edmund 180; *see* Mervyn, James 181
Mervyn, James xvn1, 2, 9, 11n45, 22, 29, 37, 43, 51, 52, 55, 56, 72, 79, 80, 82, 90, 109–110, 111–112, 114–116, 123, 126, 136n6, 139, 148, 159, 181; *see* Fonthill 2, 128, 170
Mervyn, Lucia: *see* Tuchet, Lucia
Middleton, Thomas and Thomas Dekker 67n3, 80n29
Morgan, Hugh 49, 180; *see* Whetstone 173
Morgan Lucy 25, 48–49, 180; *see* Whetstone 173
Mukherji, Subha 4n15, 8n35, 20n72

Norris, Henry 24, 135, 166n1, 168, 180; *see* Cumnor 170; *see* Rycote 137, 172
Norris, John 135, 182

Ostend 140, 143, 146, 171; *see* Conway, John 177

Pagnam, Master 38, 42n1
Pagnam, Mistress 1, 9, 12–13, 20, 22, 33, 34n5, 37–38, 42n1, 44n1, 46n9, 47n2, 67, 68, 69, 71, 75–79, 81–82, 83, 87–89, 100–103, 104n17, 117, 182
Parry, Blanche 48, 182
Pollock, Linda A. 16
Powell, Thomas 37, 42n1, 43, 71, 82–83, 183
privy council xv, xvi, 1–2, 3n10, 4n18, 14, 20–22, 24, 33n1, 58n1, 64n1, 65n2, 70n1, 71, 72n16, 73, 75n10, 76n13, 78n22, 92, 97, 108, 109, 117, 121, 126, 127, 132, 134n1,

135n1, 138, 141, 146n1, 157, 159n6, 160n1, 166n1, 168

Radcliffe, Frances 57, 183
Radcliffe, Thomas 42, 43, 183
Richards, Jennifer 1n1

Sackville, Thomas (Lord Buckhurst) 147, 168, 183
Sarsden xii, 17, 29n2, 38n11, 52–53, 57, 61, 62–63, 72, 74n4, 111, 115, 129n3, 130, 134, 163, 171, 172, 178
Schwarz, Kathryn 5
Smith, Daniel Starza 13
Star Chamber 38, 172
Stowell 29, 172; *see* Atkinson, Robert 174
Stretton, Tim 3n9, 3n10, 4n15, 4n16, 4n19
Strype, John 1–2n3

Thorne, Alison 1n1
Tower of London 13, 20, 41, 44, 55n1, 72, 76, 77, 78, 80, 83, 110, 172

Tuchet, Lucia 11–12n45, 25, 57n6, 128–130, 184; as Lucia Mervyn 2
Tudor, Elizabeth, Queen of England 1, 2, 11, 13–14, 17, 20, 22, 31, 40n17, 48, 56, 79n24, 99, 101, 109–110, 114, 119, 121, 122, 123; and Anthony Bourne's debt to 111–114, 132

Unton, Anne (Countess of Warwick) 57n5, 116, 184; *see* Upton-Upon-Severn 172
Unton, Edward 61, 116, 184
Unton, Henry 117, 119, 121, 124, 127, 184

Vaughan, Anne 75, 184
Vaughan, Thomas 37, 184

Wales 15, 39, 77, 78, 102, 173
Walsingham, Francis 3n11, 11, 20, 40, 58–59, 68, 83, 99, 110, 184
Wenman, Thomas 35, 184
West, Thomas 109, 184